MILLENNIUM III, CENTURY XXI

MILLENNIUM III, CENTURY XXI

A Retrospective on the Future

Peter N. Stearns

Routledge
Taylor & Francis Group
New York London

First published 1998 by Westview Press
First published in hardcover by Westview Press in 1996

Published 2019 by Routledge
52 Vanderbilt Avenue, New York, NY 10017
2 Park Square, Milton Park, Abingdon, Oxon OX14 4RN

First issued in hardback 2019

Routledge is an imprint of the Taylor & Francis Group, an informa business

Copyright © 1998 Taylor & Francis

Library of Congress Cataloging-in-Publication Data
Stearns, Peter N.
    Millennium III, century XXI : a retrospective on the future /
Peter N. Stearns.
        p.   cm.
    Includes bibliographical references and index.
    ISBN 0-8133-2870-5 (hardcover) — ISBN 0-8133-3457-8 (pbk.)
    1. Twenty-first century—Forecasts.   2. Millennium.   I. Title.
CB161.S725   1996
303.49′09′05—dc20   96-12807
                                                                                                        CIP

ISBN 13: 978-0-367-31686-0 (hbk)
ISBN 13: 978-0-8133-3457-8 (pbk)

CONTENTS

PREFACE TO
THE PAPERBACK EDITION

This book is introduced in the Preface to the First Edition, which follows these few remarks. I indicate there that I wrote the book (a few years ago now) out of a real interest in anticipating the kinds of information people would find useful as discussions and invocations of the millennium and turn of the century accelerated during the last years of the 1990s. I've been gratified by response to the original edition—including its use without credit in a number of television discussions. Clearly, the coming calendar changes encourage us to think about various aspects of history and their uses, and that's what this book highlights.

In revising the book for the paperback edition, I've made modest alterations in various sections, eliminating a couple of errors and expanding on a few developments that are clearer now than they were three years ago. I've also added a final section on what's been happening very recently, by way of relating the book's content—which mostly, in my judgment, remains valid and useful—to recent millennial news. I use this new section also to admit that I made a few wrong guesses when I wrote the original version, not in content, but in what I anticipated in terms of popular emphases. But since part of my argument involves some cautionary notes about predicting, I don't feel abashed by the result, though I do think the adjustments are interesting. It's also obvious that various questionable uses of the millennium are proceeding despite the fact that the book clearly warns against them—but that I did predict. This is a work designed to encourage those who like a slight remove from media frenzies. Responses to date have more than convinced me that this goal is served.

PREFACE TO
THE FIRST EDITION

When I was in grade school in the 1940s, I became aware that it was quite possible that I would live into the 21st century. The idea was oddly exciting. Somehow (perhaps because I had a historian for a father) this kind of marker seemed personally meaningful. I remember spending some of the downtime in class calculating life expectancy and realizing that, statistically, I was likely to make it past the year 2000. I did not know at the time about the issue of whether 2000 or 2001 would really constitute the beginning of the new century—we'll touch on this matter again later, but for the moment I should posit that 2001 makes much more sense, since there never was a year zero. On the other hand, my estimate of average male longevity erred on the conservative side.

I haven't made it to the 21st century yet, but at the risk of tempting fate I can mention that statistics are even more on my side now. I begin on this personal note only to confess my own complicity in the kind of thinking that makes turns-of-the-century meaningful. This book focuses on exploring what kinds of meaning are involved.

I don't know when I realized that the year 2001 would also mark the start of a new millennium. Certainly by the time I was in college, I had begun to absorb information about the significance of millennial thinking in the Western tradition (although I did not learn until much later how erroneous much of this information was). Over the past decade, as the new millennium draws closer and a few books and articles have begun to take advantage of that fact, often very misleadingly, I have been thinking about trying to provide some of the data and perspectives that can help us approach this quite artificial and quite exciting marker with understanding.

We live in a confusing age (most ages are confusing) in which sorting out the significance of a new century and a new millennium would be challenging in the best of circumstances. We inherit a culture that has surprisingly recently established centuries and probably millennia as significant measurements of time, which ensures that we can't avoid the challenge of figuring out some semblance of meaning. We also live in a media-drenched age in which any event or nonevent can be the occasion for massive outpourings of hyperbole and half-truths that can stimulate, mislead, and distract. We live, furthermore, in a highly commercial time, when hosts of people selling products and services seek to take advantage of any attention-getter to push their own wares. We already have a car model called Millennium (Mazda), and there is a growing crescendo of references to this or that being exactly what we need for the 21st century. The first barrage of millennium books appeared almost a decade ago, between 1986 and 1990, attempting to set an anticipatory mood. A *New Republic* article wonders, tongue in cheek, if the noticeable American weight gain since 1980 is due to jubilant appetites anticipating the celebration and fear of a new era—and how many behaviors will be explained by the imminent millennium over the next few years? This is surely just the tip of a coming iceberg. We live, finally, in a culture addicted to predictions, without much concern for their basis in truth (more on this later).

Party planning is well advanced, so that we know we can anticipate a celebratory climate. Some groups organized to begin reserving festive sites in the mid-1980s. The Millennium Society of Washington, D.C., plans standing-room-only vigils, with suitable feast fare, at places like the Acropolis, the Eiffel Tower, and the Taj Mahal. Top dining spots in the United States and Western Europe have long since been sold out for December 31, 1999; such is the foresight of committed hedonists. Apparently, the preference is to see in the new numbers rather than the real first year of the new century and millennium.

These points add up to the following: We can expect more and more attention over the next few years to the advent of the 21st century and of the third millennium A.D. or C.E. (A.D., of course, is the abbreviation for the Christian calendar term Anno Domini, in the year of the Lord. History writers are increasingly turning to the more neutral, politically correct designation Common Era, abbreviated C.E., but the dates are the same.) We can expect much of this attention to be self-serving (to promote newspaper sales or commercial goods) and wildly excited, given our addiction to hyperbole (how many crimes of the century do we have every twenty years?), our uncertainty about our own age, and our penchant for sweeping predictions of future change. We can also expect a good bit of millennial coverage to be inaccurate, because drama is best served by false renditions of millennia past. This, by the way, is no idle forecast; most of the anticipatory books of the late 1980s used a distorted view of the last millennium's advent to sensationalize a historical account and to give it a veneer of present relevance. Millennial calendars and prophecies are already on sale for those in the know.

This book is intended as a survivor's guide to turn-of-the-century and millennial furor. It offers data about similar events and relevant cultural traditions in the past, but it also offers a framework within which to consider how we will interpret the waning age and how we can sensibly look ahead. The book is not written to spoil the upcoming party as we greet a new time, however artificially defined. My own irrational interest in the imminent new century and millennium has persisted since childhood. I can't claim that it really caused my choice of a career as a historian, but it has clearly continued to fascinate me. The root of the fascination is more than personal: The turn of time must force us to think about relating our history to our prospects, which is the essence of what historians are good for. At the same time, I have developed a certain amount of dread of the repetitious and misleading media celebrations that may lie in store for the next few years. This book represents my own attempt, before the height of the frenzy, to provide some information and a vantage point that can help make sense of what may be one of the great sobering moments (although also quite possibly one of the great celebrations) of recent times.

My method is simple. A sketch of how we came to calculate time as we do, amid many alternatives, gets things started. Information about past celebrations of millennia and centuries then gives a baseline for assessing what we are about to experience and for determining the truth claims of some of the seers and sellers who will be trying to grab our attention. Discussion of how we give historical meaning to past periods, and most particularly the second millennium and the 20th century, while more subjective, can also help orient our reception of other accounts. And debate over how we predict the future and how we can evaluate prediction, while even more subjective, rounds out the intellectual arsenal that should be available before we are swept along by media pundits. The web connecting all these tasks is a sense of history, offered, however, not in conventional descriptive fashion but as needed for surviving and also profiting from the millennium blitz. There is no way to assess our own turn-of-the-century plans without looking at what was done before, and there is certainly no way to get a fix on where we stand in relation to past and future—a common need as a new chunk of time looms up—without various historical perspectives.

One last personal note: I've been plotting this handbook for some time, thinking about meaning and forecasting. Getting these ruminations down on paper is a real pleasure, one fruit of what is now a long career (though one that I still hope will stretch into the next century) in teaching and thinking about history. Coming closer to the book's execution, I also learned a number of new facets of the millennium and the century as subjects. Simply asking why we define and celebrate such units and when our culture began to do so launches the process of gaining perspective on what we're about to experience. The fact is that Western society has been greeting centuries for a while now (although elaborately only once before, around 1900), but we've never yet actually celebrated a millennium. Here is the first target to explore.

Human beings inevitably think about time; it's one of our burdens and opportunities as a species. We are aware of the passage of time in our own lives, and our societies gain awareness of the passage of time in their existence as well. Aware of time and also eager to find meaning, most cultures try to think about how to demarcate time, not just over weeks and years but also over longer spans. And some cultures think about such demarcations in the future—about how time will be organized in years yet to come.

This granted, however, the first point to insist on in talking about the upcoming new millennium is this: The idea of setting up centuries and millennia is highly unusual, clearly artificial. This doesn't mean it's silly or wrong, but it does mean that there is nothing inevitable or inherently sacred about our fascination with these units. To be sure, a number of cultures besides our own have talked about the end of time, and we'll hear a lot about this as part of the doomsday side of millennial discussions. But even this approach isn't inevitable.

It's hard to escape the compelling qualities of man-made dates. To be sure, although the millennium stirs notice, few groups pretend to anticipate the whole span—for reasons we will address. Centuries are a different matter. Democrats and Republicans vie in purporting to prepare the United States for the 21st century. The American Historical Association discusses, quite interestingly, how history will be done in the 21st century. Objectively, planning of this sort is not necessarily much different from, say, planning for 1993 back in 1988. But it seems different because of the magic of numerical labels. And there's nothing wrong with using artificial markers to stimulate our vision, so long as we don't take ourselves too seriously.

Perspective here is vital. Achieving this perspective requires, first, a brief cross-cultural excursion, to illustrate how unusual Western thinking about millennia is. And then it demands a highlighted history of how Western thinking itself developed to the point that centuries and millennia drew attention in the first place. Both these topics are essential for accuracy in approaching our coming celebration, but the second is particularly important because an erroneous alternative is readily available.

After handling the perspective issues, we can turn to other approaches to the millennium, including what the past millennium may mean, if anything, and whether we can sensibly forecast much about the millennium to come. The key issue here, beyond the complexity of Christian thinking about the millennium, involves how the first millennial experience, in the year 1000, was greeted. But we must also comment on ongoing millennialism and what it portends for the next few years, before the dust settles after 2001.

Centuries, less dramatic, occupy the second section of the book. The hailing of a new century raises issues that will help us understand our own upcoming celebration, and we can get a more precise historical fix than is possible looking only at the millennium. One hundred years ago at this time, for example, reviews and previews of the waning and coming century were rampant. A mood called "fin de siècle" enveloped groups in Western Europe. Do these patterns provide analogies that help us understand our own probable reactions to a century's end and another's beginning? Where is fin de siècle this time around? Looking at past approaches to time and examining meaning and forecasting provide both information and orientations that will help us sort out how the year 2000 or 2001 is presented to us and what kind of reflective celebration we wish to have. After a look at the past and at forecasting generally, I will briefly discuss what our century has meant and how we may forecast the next. There's still time to order the champagne.

However briefly and artificially, the turn of the century/millennium will create a mirror in which we may be able to see where we've been coming from and where we are heading and wish to head. That's what the last turn of a century offered, with complex and instructive results. It's odd, in fact, that we have debated our own upcoming turn so little to date—this is one of the issues I will discuss in a later chapter—for a hundred years ago the analogous discussion was much farther along. Certainly, it is time now to set some wheels in motion, beyond the largely abortive millennial warnings of the late 1980s. Aware of what we will engage in, we have a chance to do a creditable job in setting the mirror up and evaluating our own image. We need to avoid too much entanglement in intellectual nonsense—hence the importance of getting some facts straight, particularly about past millennial analogies. But we also need to begin debate about the trends of our age and about how we can project the age to come and how much is in our grasp. We're sure to want a good party, around late December 1999, and maybe, to be strictly accurate about the calendar, again in late 2000 as well. We can also insist on making the whole transition interesting, and for this we need not wait for party time.

*   *   *

A number of friends and colleagues have helped me with this book. Steve Beaudoin provided invaluable research assistance. Eryq Dorfman, Dwayne and Christina Seppi, Gregor Dallas, Abraham Marcus, Richard Enos, Andrew Barnes, Karen Callas, Baruch Fischhoff, and Donald Sutton pointed me to a variety of materials about how time is calculated in different cultures and about current millennial interests. John Modell provided a constructive sounding board. Peter Kracht, of Westview Press, provided useful suggestions as well as encouragement. My sincere thanks.

Peter N. Stearns

PART ONE

THE MILLENNIUM
AND THINKING ABOUT TIME

Figure 1   The Dragon and the Beast. The Pierpont Morgan Library, New York. M. 524, f10v.

one

THE MILLENNIUM
IN PERSPECTIVE

MOST SUNDAYS, AT VARIOUS TIMES OF THE DAY, on many television stations in the United States, Dr. Jack Van Impe and his wife, Rexella, hold forth on the imminent end of the world (which they anticipate between 1999 and 2003). The show reviews a host of markers that Van Impe has uncovered, based on the Book of Revelation, about the end of the world: Ten members of the Common Market are thus precursors to the ten horns of the Beast of the Apocalypse (Van Impe recognizes that there have been more than ten members for some time but predicts that the surplus will soon fall away; I am unaware of his reaction to the additional memberships of Finland, Sweden, and Austria). The number 666, used on many computer forms and bar codes, is a numerological sign of the end of time. Van Impe's fascination with the collapse of the world goes back to the creation of the state of Israel, for changes in the Holy Land (and ultimately the destruction of the Jewish state) are common elements of apocalyptic visions. The Van Impes also offer a number of videos dramatizing the seven years of tribulation ruled by Satan (which presumably must already have begun) that are to be followed by the thousand-year reign of Christ.

The December 26, 1994, issue of *Newsweek*, eager to capitalize on the approach of the millennium, offered a series of predictions in a special section, introduced by the irrefutable comment that "the start of a new millennium doesn't roll around every day." The fact that this platitude came six years early foreshadows the frequency with which the millennial theme will be sounded over the next half-decade. *Newsweek*'s response, however, differed greatly from that of the Van Impes. Noting how hard it is to think about a whole millennium, or even a full new century, the special section embraced a rather scattered series of forecasts about probable developments over the next ten to forty years.

These two poles of anticipation, the one zealously predicting catastrophic change followed by redemption, the other acknowledging a special marker but returning quickly to prediction-as-usual, suggest the range of responses that we will be encountering until the millennium in fact arrives. Some of us will harbor both responses to a degree—a corner of fascination with blinding visions juxtaposed to a larger prosaic expectation that nothing very special is about to happen. Attention to the millennium will mount. Not only writers of science fiction but also philosophical novelists like John Crowley already refer to the new era routinely as part of thinking about life and the phenomenon of change. The second act of the popular Broadway show *Angels in America* is entitled "The Millennium Approaches"; it presents the millennium, a bit vaguely, as a point at which earthlings must choose whether to continue their profligate ways or settle down and take care of things. But even as we think about the term and as we encounter it with growing frequency, our reactions will be mixed, which is one important facet of the phenomenon that we must explore simply to grasp what is going on around us and why different groups react to the millennium in such dramatically different ways.

The insistence that the upcoming millennium designates an artificial, human-constructed span of time is an essential starting point, lest we somehow see our attention to a new era as the pinnacle of world cultural achievement. There is nothing magical about the unit, even in terms of the traditions of the Christian calendar, except to the extent that one thousand may seem like a nice round number, and there is certainly nothing inherently special about the unit in terms of the calendars of other cultures, which start at very different points. A year is a year, determined by the seasonal cycle, although it may start at quite different points and may vary slightly in length depending on the culture. Units beyond a year, if any, are human inventions.

The fact that thinking in terms of thousand-year units is unusual will not prevent some from seeing the hand of God or fate in the arrival of Christianity's third millennium. Indeed, Christianity is supposed to be unique in its possession of truth. Even for skeptics, there is no need to attack special celebrations of the millennium's advent; merely because it is an artifact does not mean we need to deny ourselves a good party or forgo some more solemn thinking about time past and time to come. Excessive mystification, however, is unnecessary. In a shrinking world, it is even useful to know that some people will have little sense of what all our shouting is about.

The Biblical Base

What seems to be the initial statement of the idea of a millennium does have an august pedigree: It occurs in several New Testament passages that can be taken cumulatively. Jesus forecast a future time of suffering for the faithful in Mark

13:24–26: "But in those days, after that tribulation, the sun shall be darkened, and the moon shall not give her light, and the stars of heaven shall fall and the powers that are in heaven shall be shaken. And then shall they see the Son of man coming in the clouds with great power and glory." Later, however, in Acts 1:7, he warned against trying to set dates for the world's end.

After early Christian hopes for Christ's quick return to usher in the Day of Judgment were dashed by reality—the Messiah did not appear—religious leaders understandably turned to a more elaborate, though temporally vaguer, forecast of the final reckoning. Probably written around A.D. 95, the Book of Revelation, the last book in the New Testament, trumpeted the triumph of God in the Second Coming: "And I saw an angel come down from heaven. . . . And he laid hold of the dragon, that old serpent, which is the Devil, and Satan, and bound him a thousand years. . . . And I saw thrones, and they sat upon them . . . and I saw the souls of them that were beheaded for the witness of Jesus . . . ; and they lived and reigned with Christ a thousand years" (Rev. 20:1–2, 4). The First Resurrection, lasting a thousand years, assured Christian martyrs of their eternal salvation. It would be followed, however, by Satan's return and a period of awesome trial, filled with fire and brimstone and a second death for other mortals, followed by the final damnation of many but the equally final resurrection (the Second Resurrection) of those slated to be saved.

This millennial vision of biblical Christianity helped establish the association of massive change, of hope and terror, with the thousand-year unit. It may well have absorbed the widespread use of units of a hundred in Greco-Roman culture, for in other Mediterranean cultures measurements by sixty were more common. Romans grouped troops by centuries, under centurions, and they also counted property qualifications of voters by units of one hundred (although they did not apply similar thinking to measurements of length, weight, or volume; this idea would have to wait for the French Revolution). So thinking in terms of hundreds and, by extension, thousands may have seemed particularly logical. It is important to note, however, that this first millennial statement was not attached to any particular calendar (and, indeed, the Christian dating system had yet to be established). There was no prediction as to when the First Resurrection would occur, only that it would last a thousand years once it did arrive. The notion of attaching divine meaning and anticipation of cataclysmic change to a thousand years is millennial thinking—but in this case without a precise millennium. Unsurprisingly, as we will see, millennial thinking was not picked up in Christian calendar celebrations for a long time—literally, for over a millennium—because there was no particular reason to do so. Revelation undeniably established some basis for millennial awe, however, and participants in the upcoming millennium may find real meaning in its predictions. It will be interesting to see how often and how accurately the Revelation precedent is cited by those who approach the millennium from a religious standpoint.

The Comparative Perspective

For all its vagueness in terms of pinpointing a specific time, the millennial vision of Revelation has been very powerful. The thousand-year unit gives precision to an impulse present in many cultures, to see this world as a finite experience, due to end at some point. The words of Revelation invite thinking about what the end will be like and when it will come. To be sure, the first Christian precedent for millennial reverence opens a host of debates, depending on one's own religious views and on how important the link between the calendar and the Day of Judgment is held to be. The second vantage point on the millennium is more clear-cut: The idea that there is any particular meaning attached to a literal millennium is very unusual in the panoply of human cultures worldwide. What's in a thousand years? Most peoples, most times, would answer: nothing much, even if the thousand years were predicated in terms of their own calendars rather than of the Christian one.

The broader comparative vantage point has, in turn, two parts. First, it is worthwhile recalling that many large and successful cultures do not look to celebrate the advent of a future time much at all, at least beyond the level of revelry for a single new year. Second, it is important to note that many cultures do anticipate dramatic breaks in the future without, however, relating them to calendar time.

A few writers, beginning to drum up enthusiasm for the upcoming millennium, have written in terms of some inevitable or at least sweeping human impulse to look for radical change—often divinely inspired change—at some point in the future. Although this kind of thinking is not necessarily phrased in terms of measurement in units like a thousand years, its existence can be taken as preparation for statements of impending great events as our own millennium looms. The association between great events and the calendar is not logical, to be sure, but millennial thinking has never made huge claims to calm reasoning. Hillel Schwartz, for example, in an often intriguing book, starts with his assertion of the human need to anticipate shocks, then offers a truly scholarly consideration of how slowly Christian thinking about the millennium emerged, only to conclude, in a long section, with speculations about the mystical meanings of the year 2000 or 2001. A hasty reader, jumping from introduction to conclusion, might well think that Schwartz had proved that humans must seek out an awesome turning point to come and that (thanks to the Christian calendar) we are about to encounter one, with signs and portents at every hand.

Chronological Thinking in China and the Mediterranean

The first sobering point to surface when we consider fact instead of fancy is that several major cultures are completely devoid of any millennial thinking, whether calendrical or not. All cultures (as far as I know) do consider the problem of time as they think about origins and about what happened up to the present. All cultures that have writing also need an extensive calendar, allowing precise references both to past and to future years over a long time span. But they do not necessarily think about organizing past or future time into numerically tidy chunks.

The chief evidence here must be China. The Chinese calendar used until this century dated back to the mythical founding of the empire. It was easy to refer to a year in the past. The future, however, was a different matter. Many Chinese thinkers had a general idea that time moves in cycles, but they did not formalize a cyclical future beyond a recurring series of animals dominant in a given year (the year of the dog, the pig, and so on). Although celebrations marked the beginning of a new year and other religious festivals marked annual birthdays of the gods, there was very little effort to anticipate longer units of time. Priests in some Daoist temples made offerings to gods over three-year or even ten-year cycles, but there was no pattern outside individual temples. In individual lives, birthdays were and are marked on the first day of the year, with a special celebration for a man's sixtieth birthday (and some notation of each adult decade that Confucius had singled out). Organizing time into sixty-year cycles combined several strands of Chinese thought, including astrology, but aside from the impact on men's birthdays, it had little celebratory significance. And, understandably enough, irregular and unpredictable events, like comets or supernovas, were viewed with misgivings about the future.

The Chinese experience was, of course, affected by Buddhism, which, in some of its branches, generated expectations of a future time of salvation or a radical purge of earthly corruption—a form of millennial thinking not tied to a specific unit of time. Within the Confucian tradition, Meng-tzu (Mencius), writing in the later Zhou dynasty and optimistically predicting a better future, said that every five hundred years a true king would arise. And much more recently, Mao Zedong spoke of cultural revolutions coming once every twenty years, a prediction happily unrealized. These are interesting qualifications to mainstream Chinese culture, as individuals or groups thought about future change or progress in distinctive ways. The fact is, however, that most Chinese intellectuals considered time mainly in terms of past rather than future, as organized by irregular dynasties and reigns of emperors. A cyclical quality attached to this thinking, too, reflecting the rise and fall of dynasties, but the units involved were of very different lengths and were both unpredictable and impossible to celebrate in advance. With some fairly isolated exceptions, this great culture did not mark regular chunks of past or future in a way that would lend itself to identifying centuries, millennia, or any systematic units of this sort. Only under Western influence, in the past century, have the Chinese taken to celebrating anniversaries, like the fifty-year anniversary of the May 4th movement, as they impose a new kind of numerical regularity on some of their thinking about time.

Another case of irregular (by our standards) thinking about organizing time and the future occurs culturally closer to home. Neither Greek nor Roman society gave rise to much millennial thinking. During much of the Greco-Roman ascendancy, calendars varied widely around the Mediterranean, with quite different dates for the New Year. In Athens, months were known by the names of festivals that occurred in them, but they did not suggest more systematic celebrations of time. There seems to have been no regular system for noting time, either past or future, beyond yearly designations, though the Greeks had a vague idea of past "metal" ages—of gold, silver, bronze, and then iron. For a long time, Roman calendars were equally irregular, the original one consisting, in fact, only of ten months and conveniently bypassing part of the winter. March was for many centuries the first of the year. The Romans did have a means of calculating from the imagined foundation of the city, such that the year 153 B.C. was the year 601 by Roman reckoning. But there was no agglomeration of years to note special points of ceremony, meditation, or anticipation—nothing like centuries, nothing like the idea of a thousand years of first resurrection that John introduced in Revelation. Romans and Greeks, of course, worried about the future, and they patronized astrologers, oracles, entrail readers, and others for signs of what was to come. But they did not think of the future in terms of uniform units of time, and so they saved their revelries for other kinds of occasions, including the beginnings of both a ten-month and a twelve-month new year. From the Etruscans, the Romans did pick up the concept of *saeculum*. The first *saeculum* usually meant, in any town, the lifespan of the inhabitant with the greatest longevity from the town's founding. It was followed (the next *saeculum*) by the longest lifespan from the day the first *saeculum* ended. Counting the years this way provided the basis for local, irregular calculations, but nothing more. For civil purposes, the Etruscans and Romans also saw a *saeculum* as 110 lunar years, and a period that did call for some celebrations by priests. Only during the Roman Empire, from the middle of the second century A.D. onward, did some emperors use the *saeculum* as a means of celebrating their triumphs into the future. Imperial calculations of *saecula* did not, however, produce a clear overall calendar or durable centennial movements, and, indeed, the *saeculum* still did not usually mean one hundred years. Here was a basis for later regularization, but it was only one element among many of a very diffuse Roman calendar. Even the *saeculum,* as we have seen, was judged differently by different people. Thus, secular games, supposed to be held once a *saeculum,* actually occurred every forty to sixty years, although the last one, in 248 C.E., was supposed to coincide with the thousand-year (mythical) anniversary of the city of Rome.

Point one, then, in our brief effort to expand on the fact that human thinking about time has rarely agreed on phenomena such as the century or millennium: Several mighty cultures, including one regarded as fundamental to the West, did not structure past or future very precisely and so lacked fixed moments of celebration beyond the advent of a new year. Several major cultures also lacked any idea of the end of time, while others, like the Greek culture, toyed with the notion without bringing it into prominence.

The Religious Element: Judaism and Islam

To move closer to what we usually associate with millennial thinking, an additional ingredient is needed: some idea of a future goal for humanity or some portion of humanity, a change in situation that will make the future (sometime) look very different from the present or the past. Many cultures, including most of those associated with the so-called world religions, have this idea, which is why millennial thinking crops up in a host of times and places. Since Christian culture shared in this kind of millennial potential—this is the initial source of the interest we still devote to centuries and millennia—it will help to understand our own thinking if we look briefly at what religious millennialism consisted of.

One caveat, however: Very few cultures, including Christianity until fairly recently, attached their fears and expectations about some great change in the future to a regular calendar or fixed units of time. "Millennialism" (whose root is the Latin *mille,* or thousand) is in this sense a misleading term, in that it rarely applied to a thousand years or to celebration of any set intervals. In Christianity, Judaism, and Islam, in fact, "messianism," or the expectation of a Messiah who would transform the world at some unspecified point in the future, would be a better term than "millennialism," the latter deriving simply from the Revelation-based association of such a second coming with a subsequent period of a thousand years.

Thus, Jewish expectations of a coming Messiah, which organized a great deal of hope for the future, were never associated with calendar units. The expectations did fuel prophecy, and Christian millennialists often refer to Old Testament books like Daniel and Ezekiel as well as to Revelation. But the Jewish calendar, although heavily focused on celebrations of each new year, was not subdivided into centuries, much less millennia, even though it stretched over several thousand years. The current Lubavitcher sect, anticipating a Messiah soon, nevertheless acknowledges earlier Jewish tradition that held that a savior would come "when God decides"—and God was not pinned to anything so petty as a regular calendar. Buddhist millennialism, as it cropped up periodically in eastern Asia, was similarly free from time specificity.

Millennialism in Islam shows the power of belief in an apocalyptic future without precise time linkage. The Islamic calendar begins, of course, with the prophet Muhammad and his migration from Mecca to Medina (the Hegira, in A.D. 622), making it the most recent time span of any major calculation system used in the world. Muslims did not, however, celebrate the one millennium they have experienced since their age began. Recently, to be sure, the turn of the fifteenth Muslim century (in 1979–1980) was given a major celebration by the Conference of Islamic Countries, but this was probably a response to the power of Western anniversary celebrations; it did not have Islamic precedent. There is no evidence that the millennium, which fell in 1591 by our calendar, occasioned much fuss.

Most important, Islam did not connect its vision of a drastic change to come with any particular unit of time. There was no analog to Revelation in suggesting special power in a thousand-year span. Muslims anticipated a drastic future, however, with at least as much fervor as did Christians. References to the Last Day, the Day of Doom, and the Day of Resurrection abound in the Koran and the Hadith, and Muslims were enjoined to believe in this awesome future just as they were enjoined to believe in Allah. Frequent references associated "belief in God and the Last Day." But discussions of this apocalyptic day focused on the nature of paradise and punishment, not on its timing. To be sure, a length was assigned to the day itself: 50,000 years, "till the judgment among men is finished." It was as if Muhammad upped the ante on Revelation by so greatly extending the period in which God would sort out human affairs. But the reference led to no Muslim impulse to count subordinate units of time in reference to the ultimate span: "The ancients, and the later folk shall be gathered to the appointed time of a known day. Then you erring ones, you that cried lies, you shall eat of a tree called Zakkoum, and you shall fill there with your bellies and drink on top of that boiling water lapping it down like thirsty camels. This shall be their hospitality on the Day of Doom." But what relationship this dread day had to any calendar was never specified.

Islamic theologians elaborated on the concept of the apocalyptic end, building on the stipulations in the Koran that the sun will dim, the stars will fall, the heavens will split, the seas will boil, and the earth will be crushed. The dead will be rejoined with their buried bodies. All people, living and dead, will be judged in

God's tribunal and held accountable for their deeds, the righteous receiving salvation in paradise and the sinner damnation in hell. With this prominent doctrine, a host of Islamic movements had a clear millenarian or messianic quality. Shiite Islam developed the belief in the hidden Imam, who would return as the Mahdi, or savior, to restore justice in the world. Many Shiite sects periodically backed leaders regarded as saviors and helped bring them to power. Sunni Muslims condemned the idea of the Mahdi as unorthodox, but Mahdist revolts occurred periodically in mainstream Islam as well, for example, in the late 19th century in Sudan. In the 14th century (Christian calendar) a popular strain of Islam held that a descendant of the Prophet would appear as Mahdi at the end of time to bring justice and to rule over the Muslim community. Drastic changes in the natural order would accompany all this—the floods, earthquakes, and so on that were frequently held to signal the realization of the end of time. Muslim messianism could focus on the restoration of justice in this world, short of the full apocalyptic vision, or it could go the whole route. Clearly, a framework existed for Muslims at all social levels to think about a dramatic intervention in future time and, ultimately, the end of the earthly order. Equally clearly, neither the religious leaders nor subsequent popular movements specified timing, for Islamic messianism provided no basis for celebrating abstract units of time as particular moments for reflection or forecasting.

Islam did, to be sure, develop a tradition of centenary celebrations. These were not associated with the ultimate apocalypse and did not focus particular attention on a millennium, but they did go beyond many religions in linking some large spans of time with religious meaning. A common feature of Islam involved religious reformers who appeared around the turn of a century and claimed to be the mujaddids, or renewers of Islam for the century. The tradition of a renewer of the faith went back to Islam's first century, with the caliph Umar II, who came to power in the Muslim year 99 and was particularly revered for his piety, in contrast to his predecessors. He was viewed as a renewer of the faith in an age of increasingly profane rule, and later mujaddids and their movements in various parts of the Islamic world followed his precedent. Islam, then, sets the framework for using hundred-year periods (although on a calendrical basis quite different from the Christian: Not only do Muslims and Christians consider different centuries to be the "first" century, but the first year of a Muslim century differs from the first Christian century year, and greater Muslim reliance on lunar months complicates the relationship still futher) as a time for particular religious contemplation and orientation toward the future.

Still, the basic point should be clear. Although all cultures consider time and most have some interest in prophecy, there is no inherent need to stipulate long units of future time. A large number of cultures, however, do postulate some idea of the world's end, usually associated with divine intervention and often judgmental. This idea is not tied to particular units of time, so it does not lend itself to anxious concentration on, or celebration of, some particular passage of years as part of an inexorable progression toward the final cataclysm. Messianic or millenarian impulses may cause great fear or hope and may prompt people to anxiously take stock of an eclipse or a comet as a portent, but they are by the same token linked to random events rather than to some calendar-based concentration. Most of the great messianic forecasts of the world's end, including the recent Lubavitcher movement in Judaism or the American Millerites, who went to their hilltop to await the end of the world in 1843, did not, in fact, use tidy units of time for their expectations. Things were supposed to happen soon, and most prophets are loath to wait till a convenient end of century, much less millennium, to see how things work out. End-of-world beliefs, in sum, provide a powerful reason to think about the future, but they are not usually conducive to clear organization of intermediate future time. The Islamic interest in centennials, although not directly tied to its millenarian strain, was to this extent unusual.

Other Ends of Time

There are other variants on these main themes. Norse mythology included the idea of the end of the world at some point, but it does not seem to have been emphasized. The Etruscans developed their concept of "centuries," based, however, not on one hundred years but on the death of the oldest surviving member of a generation; we have seen that the Romans picked up this idea, along with its irregularities. Each Etruscan generation was, thus, a "century," and its passing was the occasion for divinations (the reading of entrails, the search for atmospheric signs) about the future. And the Etruscans, preoccupied with death and its rituals, had an idea of the end of time for themselves, after which their race would be no more. No people could survive more than eight to twelve *saeculae,* and the Etruscans did indeed fade away in their ninth.

Most interesting, and most relevant to our own upcoming revelries, were the ways that forecasts of a major transformation were joined to the unusually detailed Mayan astronomical calculations. Mayans stipulated a calendar based on a 5,125-year cycle. The cycle began August 6, 3113 B.C., and will end (or rather, a cycle will begin anew) December 21, 2012, when another transformative vision will occur. Mayan culture did not survive long enough to pick up on this message, and beyond the calculation there is little known of the thinking behind the forecast. But the precision was unusual, its proximity to our own upcoming year 2000 is beguiling (What's a twelve-year error among friends?), and the ignorance and mystery that shroud our approach to the Mayans add spice to the whole brew. In 1987, a Mexican writer, José Argüelles, in *The Mayan Factor,* revived the Mayan prediction that focused on the year 2012, adding that the Mayans were, in fact, an extragalactic people who would come back in the waning years of the 20th century to prepare the New Age. Their presence would show in inner lights or as "feathered serpent rainbow wheels turning in the air." Their effect would enliven deadened 20th-century man "like an awakening from a cultural trance." Argüelles and other New Age adepts argued that humanity must cleanse itself and its environment in preparation for the new galactic harmony. A first gathering on mountaintops in 1987, for healing, sought 144,000 sun dancers (the number was based on combining various numerologies, including Etruscan and Mayan). The argument ran that the Mayan gods were reappearing and that the serpent god of peace, Quetzalcoatl, would come for a brief reign, revitalizing humanity as he did before on the Yucatan peninsula, before departing in—you guessed it—1999, when a goddess of destruction would take over for humanity's last act.

Clearly, as the New Age usage suggests, enough cultures have generated enough apocalyptic visions and enough numerology for all sorts of imaginative combinations to be made. Some have predicted an even greater surge of precedent-amalgamation in anticipation of the upcoming millennium, though the barely noted New Age surge in 1987 has not, in fact, spawned a significant progeny thus far. The cross-cultural historical data are more sober. Although the impulse to predict dire futures is widespread (though not universal), the idea of tying such predictions to any particular date, much less to a new century or millennium, is actually rather unusual. Messianism in mainstream religions has usually been prudent, avoiding the kind of precise chronology that can so easily be disproved by the passage of prosaic time. Minority movements have been readier to hail the end of the world as we know it but are usually far too impatient to wait for the artificial units of anyone's calendar (beyond, perhaps, the end of a year). Given not only the diversity of cultural approaches but also the rarity of literal centenary or millennial thinking, a bit of humility may be in order before we try to make too much of our upcoming, man-made marker.

Yet diverse cultural evidence may be beside the point. The new century and the new millennium are Christian calendar events (however spiced by Mayan or other associations). The excitement of these events within our own cultural context, as they channel our own impulses to organize time, to reflect, and to forecast, may easily override the understanding of the artificiality of millennial units and the lack of wide precedent for literal millennial demarcations. It's important to know how unusual Christian millennial beliefs may be, lest we fall into the trap of seeing our own enthusiasms as some natural expression of universal human tendencies or of too easily accepting hodgepodge combinations of selected numerologies as the best approach to the future that other cultures have to offer (extragalactic interventions aside). But it's our calendar. We've converted much of the world to it—witness Japanese New Year zeal every January, or the 1995 effort of Muslim fundamentalists to limit revelry on January 1, which has no meaning in the Muslim reckoning. So we are not even clearly selfish in hailing our calendar's high points, even if we must be careful in claiming cosmic significance. It's time to look at our own precedents for imbuing time with meaning.

THE STRUGGLE FOR
A CHRISTIAN CALENDAR

When I contemplated writing this book, I expected to do a certain amount of debunking, of the sort that some cultural relativism provides. It seemed clearly important to establish that a fixation with centuries and millennia was of human invention, not inherent in the species (and not necessarily divinely inspired). But I also thought it would be useful and important to sum up the traumatic and fascinating Christian experience with the millennium as a means of providing accurate historical data on a subject that will surely be often evoked as we approach the second millennial transition defined by the Christian calendar. The basic purpose was sound, but I was amazed to learn how complex even the Christian precedent is and how much misleading mythology surrounds it. The goal of providing accurate historical data stands, but let the reader beware: The millennium that many of us thought happened a thousand years ago just isn't there. It, too, was largely invented.

The Church Fathers and the Apocalypse

We can begin innocuously enough by noting that early Christian thought, despite the Book of Revelation, clearly fell into the second, messianic approach to time that we described in Chapter 1 for Judaism and Islam. That is, Christian thinkers had a clear idea that there was an end to time, an apocalyptic change to come, but they did not associate it with precise units of time and did not celebrate centuries or anticipate millennia as bearing any particular meaning. Saint Augustine and other church fathers were at pains to insist that Christ's Second Coming, while definite, was not imminent and should not be associated with any precise anticipated date. Like any mainstream church, Christianity saw the need to avoid a forecasting trap by the time of the later Roman Empire. Nor did Christians quickly incorporate the idea of centuries into their calendrical scheme, despite some Roman precedent and the parallel movement soon to develop in Islam. Christianity, per se, does not lie at the origins of celebrations of anticipated time, despite the importance of the thousand-year reference in Revelation.

To be sure, one of the first real Christian histories, by a Roman named Sextus Julius Africanus, laid out an extremely tidy pattern using the Book of Revelation but also Etruscan ideas that to him (he distorted somewhat) implied the end of the world in six thousand years. Sextus posited five thousand years from creation to the Babylonian Captivity of the Hebrews, and another five hundred to prepare for Christ. This left a final five hundred years from his birth to the Second Coming when the millennial anticipations of Revelation would take over. This scheme was modified several times, with a final calculation of the world's end in A.D. 800 rather than A.D. 500. But Augustine attacked this notion of an imminent millennium, arguing that what Revelation was talking about was purely symbolic. Augustine also struggled against the implication in Revelation that the Second Resurrection would lead to one thousand years of a perfected kingdom on this earth. This idea was too materialistic for the great church fathers, and it also risked running afoul of the Roman Empire, which had by now embraced the new religion but might look askance at the idea that its earthly kingdom so needed improvement. Again, the idea of a millennium was diluted, its symbolism emphasized over any precision. Augustine's *City of God* argued that the resurrection of souls had been occurring since Christ's own resurrection, so there would be not a precise period of salvation but, rather, an ongoing process; nor would there be any earthly progress at all until the Last Judgment ended worldly life. Everything of significance that was to happen in human history had occurred up to the point of Christianity's acceptance in Rome.

So Revelation 20, which was itself not really focused on a calendar millennium in any event, was no longer read literally by major theologians all through the ensuing Middle Ages. Ideas of historical change or progress, correspondingly, dropped away. The bleak political and economic conditions of Western Europe after Rome's collapse undoubtedly further inhibited thinking about some process of positive change or a clear organization of historical time. Only in Eastern Christianity did a version of millennialism survive, in its looser, non-calendrical sense, with a few works arguing that some hero would come to inaugurate a wondrous time before the reign of the Antichrist and the end of the world. These works were not, however, known in Western Europe, although one 10th-century monk did transform the hero idea into a claim that a great Frankish king would preside over the last days before the Antichrist. Nor did much millennial anticipation develop in 10th-century Eastern Europe, much of which was only recently converted to Christianity in any event. (Russian Orthodoxy celebrated its thousand-year anniversary two decades ago, but this has nothing to do with millenni-

alism.) Overall, millennial thinking, millennial movements, and precise organization of the calendar were absent from most Christian culture between the fall of
Rome and the 12th century.

Although we must come back to the point in Chapter 3, it seems fairly clear
that Christians were not thinking millennial thoughts and did not have a clear
calendar schedule telling when the first millennium after Christ ended and the
second began. This truth is inconvenient for those many modern writers who
would like to see all sorts of religious agonizing associated with the first millennial
celebration, but inconvenience cannot rewrite the record. We will return to the
largely nonstory of the year 1000 soon, but first we must explain how and why
Western calendrical thinking developed so slowly. Before real millennial calculations could develop—which happened only well after the year 1000—scholars
and ordinary people alike had to become much more interested in dates.

Working on the Christian Calendar

Actual calculations of time in early Christianity were quite varied, which followed
from the Greco-Roman habits of diversity and looseness. Many Western Christians
still counted from the date assigned for the founding of Rome and would slot
Christian events, such as the Crucifixion, into this sequence. Byzantine Christianity continued this approach for a long time. They sometimes counted from each
Olympiad, from the first one presumably held in 776 B.C.* Many cities counted
differently. Some based the first year of their calendar on the Diocletian era or on
Egyptian dates. The Byzantines did develop a notion of the lunar year and of solar
cycles of 28 years, and these were compounded into larger cycles, of 532 years, to
fix the dates of Easter. The same cycles allowed calculation of eras from Creation.
Thus, in one such calculation, Christ's Incarnation occurred in the year 5500 or
5501. But there were disputes, and although the Byzantines sacralized their calendar, sacralization did not improve its regularity. Chroniclers always had to reconcile and combine overlapping systems. Only in the 8th century was a standard system adopted, citing creation as 5,508 years prior to Christ's Incarnation.

Western Christians struggled in similar ways, hampered after Rome's fall by a
lower level of intellectual activity overall. It was important to find an agreed-upon
date for the calculation of Easter because this was determined by lunar phase
rather than a set date. In the early 6th century, the pope commissioned Dionysius

---

* Although it is increasingly desirable to use B.C.E. (Before the Common Era) and C.E. instead of the
Christian-specific B.C. and A.D., the new initials would be distracting in a treatment focused on Christian calendrical ideas.

Exiguus, a monk, to work on the problem. Western Christianity had previously relied on counting from the reign of Diocletian, somewhat ironically given his nastiness to Christians, but now the papal charge was to base a calendar on "the number of years from the Incarnation of Our Lord Jesus Christ." Dionysius Exiguus attempted to figure out the date of Christ's birth from the old Roman city founding calendar, and his decision stuck; from this point onward it was possible to note time before Christ and then begin a new tally after his birth. Dionysius Exiguus's figures were disputed—the great medieval English historian the venerable Bede warned against them. And indeed they were wrong; Jesus was born at least four years before the official year 1, a disparity that we're still stuck with, as Dionysius Exiguus had tried to figure the date out from the end of Herod's reign. Bede, although critical, certainly found the new system useful and noted dates A.D. in the margins of his detailed chronicle of English history. The English church officially adopted the new reckoning in 663.

Here, then, was a basis on which centuries and millennia could have been predicated. But they weren't. Most educated people in Western Europe actually used a different system, particularly in the royal courts. Time here was reckoned in fifteen-year cycles, the cycles having started with the accession of the Emperor Constantine in the year 312. A particular year was positioned in the cycle, and then the cycle's number was noted. This system continued into the 11th century and beyond, until it was rapidly dropped in the 13th century when, as we will see, a more standardized system finally began to gain ground. Notaries used the system until the 16th century.

A few other calendars gained fleeting popularity. The Spanish had one based on their own history. Another calendar started the modern year 1 at the first Easter, thirty-three years after Christ's birth; this calendar had a brief vogue, particularly in France, in the 11th century when, indeed, thoughts about the millennium of Easter were better developed than thoughts about the millennium per se.

Western calendar history reflected the random and disparate traditions of the classical Mediterranean. There was no particular need to do better so long as arguments over Easter's date could be settled. Few people needed to think in long spans of time—hence, the fifteen-year cycle worked well for most purposes. Almost everyone who thought about the matter assumed that the world wasn't very old; even in the 18th century some Christians, such as Bishop Ussher, were pushing the notion that Creation had occurred in the year 4004 B.C. History wasn't very elaborate anyway, and most chronicles simply moved dryly from one year to the next, talking in terms of the fifth year of Henry's, Otto's, or Valdimir's reign.

Something had to happen before a more systematic calendar sense could develop, and this something only began to take shape in the 12th century. We have deliberately moved beyond the first millennial celebration, in 1000, because in terms of the history of the calendar it occurred at an awkward time—by the way most people still calculated, in the Constantine-based cycles, it might not have been noticed at all. But now we must deal with the first millennial turn before coming back to the more modern, and recognizable, development of the Western calendar in Chapter 4.

THE YEAR 1000: REAL AND IMAGINED PRECEDENTS

WHAT HAPPENED THE LAST (AND ONLY PREVIOUS) time a millennium transition occurred in the Christian calendar tradition? We will certainly hear a lot about our one precedent as our own new millennium gets closer. Whether this precedent suggests much about our own mood may be open to question—we have a much different context and culture, a thousand years later. But as part of the let's-get-mystified school of millennial studies, there will be people eager to tell us to expect some of the same anxieties that they describe as afflicting our ancestors. More immediately, there will be dispute about what the precedent is, for there is a wide gap between what many people believe about the last millennium and what actually seems to have taken place. We deal here with an intriguing, pervasive case of historical myth. Because most Christians had no regular calendrical basis for even noting a millennium, our own widespread belief that something spectacular happened is suspect on its face.

I begin this chapter with the dramatic error—much more fun than the truth, it must be confessed, but seriously misleading. Then I turn to the real record of the year 1000, which is actually fairly clear, a few debatable details aside, if sedulously ignored even by sober reporters in the present. Millennialism seems to encourage nonsense, either because it really does provoke disconcerting fear or because it is now taken as a kind of joke where normal rules about reporting the truth can be suspended or both. I turn finally, in this chapter, to the ongoing uses and abuses of the great myth.

Invented Terrors

Beware accounts like the following, from the famous French historian Jules Michelet, beguiling as they are:

The world of the Middle Ages had not the outward regularity of the antique city; it was very difficult to discern its intrinsic and profound order. That world saw in itself but chaos; it aspired to order, and fixed its hope of it on death . . . the world's end was at once hope and terror. . . .

Recent years had seen the fulfillment of an unusually complete list of apocalyptic signs, prophecies, and calculations: in 987, the last Carolingian ruling dynasty had fallen, thereby fulfilling Adso's interpretation of the fall of Rome; in 989, shortly after the council of Charroux, Halley's comet made a striking appearance; in 991, the bishop of Laon betrayed the last Carolingian pretender, much as Judas had done to Jesus; in 992, the Annunciation and the Crucifixion coincided, a moment, according to current lore, when the End would occur; and, of course, the approach of the millennium of the Incarnation loomed ever more ominously on the horizon.

It seems as if the order of the seasons were inverted, and that the elements followed new laws. A terrible pestilence desolated Aquitaine, the flesh of the patients seemed scorched with fire, and rotted from their bones. The unfortunate sufferers thronged the roads to the places of pilgrimage, and besieged churches, particularly that of St. Martin at Limoges; they thronged 'round the gates in stifling multitudes, nor could the stench that surrounded the church repel them. Most of the bishops of the south repaired thither, carrying with them the relics of their own churches. The throng augmented, and so did the infection; the sufferers died upon the relics of the saints.

It was still worse some years afterwards. [The author didn't hesitate to include events that occurred well into the 11th century, as follows.] Famine ravaged the whole world from the East, overspreading Greece, Italy, France, and England. . . . The rich wasted away and grew pale; the poor devoured the roots of the forests; horrible to relate, men even devoured human flesh. The strong seized upon the weak on the highways, tore them in pieces, roasted and ate them. Some offered children an egg or fruit, and enticed them aside to devour them. This delirium, this rabid frenzy, rose to such a pitch, that the brute was safer than man. As if it had thenceforth become an established custom to eat human flesh, there was one who even dared to expose it for sale in the market of Tournus. He did not deny the fact, and he was burnt. Another went by night, dug up that same flesh, ate it, and was burned likewise. "In the forest of Macon, near the church of St. Jean de Castanedo, a miscreant had built a hut, in which he cut the throats by night of those who demanded hospitality of him. One man, who perceived bones in the hut, contrived to escape. There were found in it forty-eight heads of men, women, and children. The torment of hunger was so frightful, that many persons, digging chalk out of the ground, mixed it with flour. Another calamity supervened. The wolves, attracted by the multitude of unburied corpses, began to attack men. Thereupon, the people who feared God dug pits, whither the son dragged the father, the brother his brother, the mother her son, when they saw their strength failing; and the survivor himself, despairing of life, often threw himself into it after them. Meanwhile, the prelates of the cities of Gaul having assembled in council to devise a remedy for such evils, resolved, that since it was impossible to feed all the famishing, those of them who seemed the most robust, should

be supported as well as could be done, lest the land should remain uncultivated."
[This is in quotations but not attributed to anyone.]

These excessive miseries broke the stubborn hearts of men, and gave them some touch of gentleness and pity. They sheathed the sword, themselves trembling under the sword of God. It was no longer worthwhile to fight, or to war for that accursed earth which men were about to leave. Vengeance was a thing no longer wanted; every man saw clearly, that his foe, as well as himself, had but a short while to live. Upon the occasion of the pestilence of Limoges, they threw themselves at the feet of the bishops, and pledged themselves heartily and sincerely to remain peaceable thenceforth; to respect the churches; no longer to infest the high roads; and, at least, not to molest those who traveled under the safeguard of the priests or the monks. All warfare was prohibited during the sacred days of each week, from Wednesday evening to Monday morning. This is what was called the peace, afterwards the truce of God.

In this general dismay, the majority found a little repose only under the shadow of the churches; they thronged to them, and deposited upon the altar donations of lands, house, and serfs. All these deeds bear the impress of one common belief. "The evening of the world is at hand," they say, "every day accumulated fresh ruins; I, count or baron, have given to such a church, for the weal of my soul . . ." or, again, "Considering that serfdom is contrary to Christian liberty, I enfranchise such a one, my serf, himself, his children, and his heirs."

But in most cases, all this was not enough to reassure them; they aspired to quiet the sword and baldric, and all the signs of mundane warfare. They took refuge among the monks, and under their guard, asking them for a very small place in their convents, wherein to hide themselves. The only trouble the secular clergy now had, was to prevent the great ones of the earth, the dukes and kings, from becoming monks or lay brothers.

The image is clear: In a culture imbued with religion, terrified by natural and man-made catastrophes, the year 1000 loomed as the end of the world. People rich and poor raced to prepare themselves for the final judgment, perhaps encouraged by a credulous or greedy clergy. As another historian put it: "A general consternation seized mankind; many relinquished their possessions, and abandoning their friends and families, hurried with precipitation to the Holy Land, where they imagined that Christ would quickly reappear to judge the world." And another:

In the year 999, the number of pilgrims proceeding eastward, to await the coming of the Lord in that city, was so great that they were compared to a desolating army. . . . Buildings of every sort were suffered to fall into ruins. It was thought useless to repair them, when the end of the world was so near. . . . Knights, citizens, and serfs traveled eastwards in company, taking with them their wives and children, singing psalms as they went, and looking with fearful eyes upon the sky, which they expected each minute to open, to let the Son of God descend in his glory.

A fearful society thus widely believed in the millennial prophecies of Revelation and applied them, as the Bible had not, to the specific Christian calendar. As one historian put it: "It was universally believed, in the Middle Ages, that the world was to end with the year thousand of the Incarnation." Natural calamities, which may have increased in any event in the later 10th century according to this line of historical argument, seemed to herald the world's end. Another historian of the retrospective apocalypse school: "Comets always frightened people in the Middle Ages, who were not even too sure that the moon might not fall and crush them." A credulous populace virtually abandoned its earthly pursuits in a frantic effort to cope with the world to come.

Finally, having unexpectedly survived the dread day, seeing the world still extant around them, a grateful Christian people rejoiced at their reprieve by a host of celebrations and good works. Hillel Schwartz puts it this way:

> When nothing remarkable happened, when the world entered intact upon the year 1000, Sylvester II [the pope] at his special midnight mass in Rome turned to the astonished congregation, who lifted up their voices to the Lord in the Te Deum and hallelujah choruses while clocktowers chimed the second Christian millennium and bells rang out from all the steeples. Grand sighs of relief became even grander breaths of fresh air as people turned to the rebuilding of dilapidated chapels, the foundation of monasteries, the creation of Romanesque cathedrals, until the landscape was cloaked in a "white mantle" of churches.

The Uses of Myth

Most of the contemporary writers who have retold this story of the year 1000 seek both to call attention to the coming millennium and to introduce some of the same fear into a modern populace—if not wholesale, then at least through some kindled sparks. Richard Erdoes, in a book called *A.D. 1000: Living on the Brink of Apocalypse* (which is mostly the biography of an interesting pope, Sylvester II, Gerbert of Aurillac, with the apocalyptic theme only briefly evoked as a somewhat misleading come-on), retells the old story. At the year 1000, Christians knelt "trembling in church," "waiting for the last trumpet to sound." Many "died from fright" after spending much of the 10th century in tremendous anxiety. A host of symbols and revelations about the end of the world accumulated. And why ought we to know this? We too have before us meteors and portents aplenty. We too have reason to use the coming millennium to take stock, to wonder if the end of the world is upon us. We too dread the coming millennium, says Mr. Erdoes (reminding us also that the Mayan cycle, with its culminating goddess of destruction, is about up): "Doomsday is in."

Russell Chandler's passage in his book *Doomsday*, widely and completely uncritically quoted in wire service stories about apocalyptic thinking in the mid-1990s, uses similar devices to grab the reader's attention. The familiar myths return: On New Year's Eve 999, "St. Peter's was packed with pilgrims. Priests were hearing all sorts of confessions. Merchants had given away their produce. Prisoners had been let out of jail. Debts had been forgiven. People were really expecting that when the bells chimed at the big cathedral this was going to be the final countdown for the end of the world." Only later did prisoners have to be recaptured and debts revived. (For the record: There were no real jails in 999, in the sense of places that served as sites for long-term, formal punishment, so the account wavers on this factual point as well.) Again, drama substitutes for facts; we can believe anything we want about our medieval ancestors because they're not around to complain.

French observers, who, as we will see, have a special reason to comment on the history of the year 1000, often take a similar tack. A sober, very useful history of accounts of the earlier millennium can't resist a final apocalyptic punch, even though this has nothing to do with the material covered in the book: After referring to the "nuclear Apocalypse" as a sword of Damocles constantly suspended above us, the author refers to "other menaces, no less terrifying—the ravages of AIDS, ecological catastrophes and the ascendancy of religious fanaticism among others" that incite collective anguish. He foresees that later historians, at subsequent millennia (note the comforting assumption that our species will make it that far) will also ask if their ancestors were really afraid of the year 2000. France again: A 1990 television show was based on the question "Must we be afraid of the year 2000?" And earlier, in 1947, an eminent French medievalist noted at the end of a sober study of the year 1000 that, thanks to the bomb, "Humanity lives and will live under the sign of terror."

It may be very salutary for Americans and others around the world to use the symbolic date of 2000 (or, more properly, 2001: Medieval people and medievalists alike seem unconcerned with chronological niceties) as a time for some anguished soul-searching. This is an issue worth discussing more fully on its own. There is no question that histories of the year 1000 will be revived—and have already been revived, in the several books issued between 1987 and 1990, in a first attempt to rouse the millennial spirit—to push people toward soul-searching. The effect may be rather like a good Halloween story. If told with relish, even an audience that doesn't believe in ghosts may wonder a bit about some coming fright; a few will buy into the full terror package. In the process, books or magazine articles will be sold, the public will have another kind of sensation to distract them, and maybe some useful chastening of modern pride and superficiality will occur.

The problem is that the history being used in this way is largely untrue. Whether or not we want or need a good scare, as we approach the year 2000 we should at least get the facts about the past right and be properly suspicious of those who try to dish up demonstrable nonsense.

Inventing the Myth

The apocalyptic history of the year 1000 turns out to be one of the most successful, large-scale frauds in modern treatments of the past. Sometimes the fraud has been unwitting, due to sloppy exaggeration or repetition with no real research, but sometimes it has been quite calculated. Despite frequent disproof, the fraud persists because it provides such a good yarn; perhaps because it appeals to some vestigial superstition in our own nature, which we handle best by casting back to the Middle Ages; and because, quite simply, the story was so often repeated in the 19th century. Textbooks and many professional historians (although not those expert on the Middle Ages) continue to repeat the old assumptions.

The idea of sweeping fear confronting the year 1000 was created by Enlightenment historians of the 18th century and was then furthered by anti-Catholic Romantic historians, particularly in France, during the 19th century. The great accounts of popular terror, cited earlier, come from William Robertson, a Scottish historian of the 18th century, and above all from the great French Romantic and radical, Jules Michelet. This is why most of the details come from France rather than from other parts of Christendom. Michelet and his ilk, good nationalists if lousy medievalists, readily equated their nation with the whole of Christian history. Others of this vintage joined in (and there had been a few 17th-century Catholic histories that had talked about the burst of creativity that followed the frights of the millennium). Enlightenment historians in several countries used accounts of the year 1000 to attack the superstition and corruption of the medieval church. Sometimes sharing a belief that the New Testament had pointed to a precise millennium, these historians readily highlighted the abysmal conditions of medieval people. It was historians of the Enlightenment, after all, who coined the term "Middle Ages" to denote a low point between two historical highs: Medieval fearfulness and crude reactions made such a pleasant contrast with the knowledge gains of the Century of Light.

Romantic writers were in principle more sympathetic to the Middle Ages because they were less wedded to science and rationalism. But in France, many of them hated the church and so played up its manipulation of medieval fears. An anti-Catholic Parisian play in 1837, entitled *The Year 1000*, featured a monk who took advantage of an eclipse that occurred (so the play pretended) on January 1 to persuade several rich men to give him their goods lest they be condemned to eternal damnation. The widely read novelist Eugène Sue devoted his last book to the same topic, spurring the dissemination of this version of history in the process. According to Sue, priests galore managed to take over huge amounts of property—"land, houses, castles, serfs, flocks, splendid furnishings, sumptuous clothes"—from the wealthy by terrifying them with the millennial vision. The priests blasted their dupes as incredulous fools, for they knew that the only end of the world involved was "the end of the world for the stupid people," "while a splendid new world opens before us, priests of the Lord."

This use of the millennium recurred in France in the 1880s as republicans fought conservative Catholics. A classic republican history by Charles Delon emphasized how priests and monks deliberately played upon fear to gain wealth: "The Year 1000 passed, and the trumpet did not sound, and the end of the world did not come: the land remained in the hands of the monks. More than one of the barons, I think, regretted their action . . . but it was too late." In 1900, in the aftermath of the Dreyfus affair, new battles in France over the separation of church and state provoked yet another round of Middle Ages bashing: Medieval people were tragically afraid because of Catholic superstition, and the church deliberately used this to become "immensely rich."

How much of this use of the year 1000 by modern historians was deliberately political and how much mirrored widespread assumptions, particularly about medieval backwardness, is hard to say and not really relevant to our purposes in any event. It is clear that, building on a misleading reading of Revelation, historians for almost two centuries took a real delight in using an elaborate story of the millennium to advance their own religious, philosophical, and political views. They simply invented facts. They had such success (despite some counterattacks by Catholic writers) and the story was so interesting that even later accounts without the same political and religious agenda (except perhaps for an abiding belief in medieval backwardness) have repeated the same yarns. The most recent repetitions do not seem to be particularly anti-Catholic, and they are certainly not pro-modern. They are simply historically sensationalist or bent on using the myth of the millennium to venture a bit of random fear-mongering about our own upcoming event.

What Happened: A Nonevent

Expert medievalists began to work seriously on the actuality of the year 1000 early in the 20th century. Some of the best minds in the business dealt with the millennium myth, particularly from the 1920s to the 1950s—after which (save in the conceptions of the general public and its exploiters), the case seemed closed. The subject was important because of the light it might shed on medieval attitudes, including fears, and on the causes of developments (such as the crusades) during the 11th century and beyond. Not surprisingly, some of the top guns in this inquiry, which peaked in the years after World War II, were French. And their conclusions were uniform and clear: the millennial terror had not happened. It is not comforting to have to admit that all this professional firepower did not manage to squelch the legend; there are situations in which the power of a story lives long past the discovery of the truth. As we approach our own millennium, however, and cope with some renewed myth wielding, it's important to try again to set the record straight.

The original accounts of medieval anxiety before the year 1000 were based on little or no evidence. This is what medieval historians began discovering when they actually started to look at the record early in the 20th century. The accounts were not complete invention. Church art often featured the Last Judgment, although it was not tied to the millennium. Some medieval charters and wills did offer prologues or epilogues referring to the last age of the world—although this pattern long preceded the late 10th century and continued after it, in accordance within the actual biblical approach to the apocalypse. A French medievalist has shown that most such references occurred well before A.D. 985 and that the rest of them occurred after 1000; none was found between 985 and 1000, when one would most expect them to cluster if millennial fears were rampant; there were not very many references in any event. A few scattered writings in the 10th century did discuss the Antichrist, and two may have prophesied an impending judgment. One of these, in turn, was chronologically quite vague; the other more specifically referred to the coming of the Antichrist in the year 1000. A comet caused fears in 975; other observers were concerned about the fact that Annunciation Day fell on Good Friday in 992.

This, however, is pretty skimpy evidence. Most of it has nothing to do with the year 1000. Comets caused some fright whenever they occurred, for example, and the fact that one was sighted twenty-five years before the millennium was sheer coincidence. The main 10th-century treatment of the Antichrist did not argue that he was at hand, and, indeed, its author argued that as long as the kings of France continued to reign the event would not occur. A contemporary account refers to one preacher in Paris who spoke of the end of the world in the year 1000, but the same account notes that other preachers quickly refuted him from Scripture. The incident was unusual and occurred several decades prior to the millennium. Furthermore, the refutations were brief and matter-of-fact—not what one would expect if fears were really widespread.

We also know that Catholic theologians had worked hard to combat literal millennialism and that the Bible does not point to a particular calendar unless it is considerably misread. Measurements of time remained imprecise before 1000, and although ordinary people might well have ignored formal theology—as they did on other religious topics—they did not have calendars and did not generate much behavioral evidence of millennial concern. Even the elite, as discussed in Chapter 2, did not base their calendars mainly on Christ's birth and so had no reason to notice the year 1000 particularly. Most of the claims of the retrospective apocalyptics are outright inventions. There were no panicked rushes to churches, no pilgrimages to the Holy Land, no widespread new donations to clergy greedy or otherwise, no massive cannibalism, no systematic neglect of buildings or other worldly concerns. This kind of specificity resulted from Romantic license, in a period before rules of historical evidence were as clearly established as they later became, indiscriminate political zeal, or both.

Given beliefs and conditions at the time, there is no reason to expect that unusual attention was paid to the advent of a new millennium in the 10th century. On the basis of almost all the available evidence, there is no reason to expect that anything special occurred—no special fears, in an age that felt fear recurrently but had no reason to pin it to an abstract date; no special ceremonies; no special assessments or projections. Claims to the contrary are sloppy or self-serving and by the later 20th century inexcusable.

The vital evidence (from an age for which evidence is admittedly meager) is this: Various monks in France and elsewhere kept regular historical chronicles. They recorded the doings of kings and nobles, monstrous births, and famines in an often undifferentiated mixture. The striking fact is that almost none of these repetitious, dutiful chronicles mentioned the year 1000 as special in any way, and those that did note the arrival of a millennial year did so simply in passing. There are no accounts of terror or of terror-inspired reactions such as crime or flight or special religious acts. One chronicle, the *Annales of St.-Benoit-sur-Loire,* does mention floods and the birth of a monster in the year 1003, but this was the stuff of the age, nothing unusual, and it was reported with no millennial reference whatsoever. The millennium passed virtually unnoticed. The myth is a myth. I hope that one of the points we can assimilate before we actually celebrate our own millennium—although, as we will see, the auguries are not good—is that we have been victims and often remain victims of outrageous historical exaggeration designed simply to titillate, to scare, or to make us feel superior by contrast.

History is rarely totally clear-cut, to be sure. There is no reason to revisit the debunking of the millennial myth, but it is important to admit one area of uncertainty. One interesting but limited bit of qualifying evidence from the age itself must be introduced, and then a modest and still-debated revision of the professionally accepted debunking of medieval millennial hysteria must be noted. Lest all this historical honesty confuse: There remains no basis for positing widespread terror. What is at issue is a more modest aftermath, suggesting that there might have been some religious concern.

The 11th Century: Signs of Relief?

In 1044 a Burgundian monk, Radulphus Glaber, completed his *Five Books of Histories*. Glaber wrote after the fact, of course, but he indicated that he did find both the millennium of Christ's birth and that of the Passion (1033) significant. Glaber believed that a considerable amount of church building occurred after 1000; the millennium was enough noticed to inspire some new enthusiasm. He found a host of problems, including a terrible famine, afflicting France before 1033, followed by a great recovery thereafter. Nowhere, however, did he express any fear or expectation that the world would end, and on the whole, Glaber devoted more attention to the anniversary of the Crucifixion than to the millennium per se. Glaber demonstrates that some sense of the millennium existed, despite the vagueness of the calendar, and his work provides a bit of the evidence (which he may have invented; there were even fewer standards of accuracy back then), particularly concerning church building, that was later used in otherwise falsified histories of the year 1000.

Glaber, like other Christian leaders, was accustomed to looking for signs and portents both as indications of God's will for the world and also as evidence of the secondary but powerful acts of the devil. (Glaber himself believed that he had suffered direct encounters with Satan.) Glaber's accounts mentioned a comet in 1014 and assumptions that something terrible might be about to happen in its wake. An eclipse in 1033 caused widespread fear. Many of the warnings he offered, however, had nothing directly to do with the millennium. For example, his account of a late–10th-century epidemic around Limoges noted popular anxieties, but the crowds quickly turned to the local church, which produced its saints' relics, thus contenting the crowd and in Glaber's judgment eliminating the plague as well. Worry could be cured; it did not revolve around a sense that the world was about to end. Glaber was also convinced, admittedly, that around 1033, at the millennium of the Crucifixion, Christian belief was beginning to decay. There was more heresy, more corruption in the church. In Glaber's mind, these developments were associated with the apocalypse, which he was sure would ultimately occur, only in that they provided warnings to good Christians that one could never be sure when the end would come. It was vital to mend one's ways now, before it was too late. Glaber, in sum, was worried, and he urged worry as a Christian motivation in rousing the faithful from sloth. But he did not really argue that the end was nigh.

Glaber's contentions about a recovery, finally, were designed to show that repentance paid off. Christians had learned to attack heresy more vigorously, to give alms more abundantly, to take more religious pilgrimages—all of which Glaber cited with glee. Here was a sign, clearly, that the apocalyptic references, while real for Glaber, had also been rather tentative. Until God disposed otherwise, the world could rediscover a Christian path. Glaber, in sum, is evidence of the possibility that various Christians grew a bit more concerned about the status of the faith in light of the millennium of Christ's death (not his birth), but his own reactions indicate a balanced approach rather than a belief in some imminent transformation.

Glaber, long forgotten, was rediscovered by a Catholic historian, Cardinal Cesare Baronius, in the 16th century. Baronius cited Glaber in his discussion of the year 1000 as part of a more favorable discussion of the church than that emanating from Protestant sources, and he did seize on the year as a demarcation point (as Glaber had not himself done). But this was long after the event, at a point when, as we will discuss in Chapter 4, thinking in terms of centuries was beginning to take real hold. Baronius's work was a way-station toward the distortions of the 19th century, but it did identify what evidence was available to provide a slender empirical basis for elaborate fancifying. But the actual legend of the year 1000 would take shape only around 1800. One historian has found only eight texts written before 1800, including Baronius's, that make any reference to the year 1000 at all. After 1800 the barriers dropped, primarily because of the usefulness of the legend in attacking the church but also because modern people became more accustomed to the idea of a decisive, chronologically convenient break—between past and present and between present and future.

The only aspect of Glaber's account that has attracted any historical credence, aside from its evidence of the views of one Christian commentator who was aware of the apocalypse but hardly consumed by it, is the notion of heightened Christian activity during the 11th century. It seems probable that there was an increase in church building, in pilgrimages, in commitments to monasticism, and possibly in alms giving. During the century as a whole, there were new monastic reform movements and, at the very end, the first crusade was launched. Glaber used the earliest of these developments to urge Christian repentance, and he implied that they were a response to the growing religious anxiety of the first third of the century. Given limited evidence, it is impossible to disprove this motivation. No terror here, but some concern about personal salvation may have been heightened by awareness of the millennium. On the other hand, historians have also pointed out the many other causes for these developments: The European economy was reviving, which provided funds for churches and alms but also some anxieties about change and the growth of commerce that could spur the same developments. Nobody at the time said explicitly that economic trends plus some political consolidation helped spur new religious acts, but almost nobody said that millennial anxieties did so, either. The medievalists who carefully worked over the millennium myth during the middle of the 20th century tended to conclude that millennial concerns may have played a slight role in new religious behaviors but that other, more familiar causes

easily predominated. Glaber's efforts to spur Christian repentance are quite understandable, but they form a fairly isolated expression; other factors, including standard (not millennial) medieval piety may be taken as sufficient.

Renewed Debate—and Its Limits

Over the past ten years, a number of medievalists have argued that the antimillen-
nium fervor has gone too far among practicing historians. Scholars like Richard
Landes insist that the year 1000 did indeed have some significance, although he admits that the full legend is probably false. Landes finds evidence that some groups
were moved by millennial fears during the 990s and points to other developments—
crop disease, the arrival of Halley's comet in 989, the fall of the Carolingian royal
house in 987 (which one observer seemed to judge the final fall of Rome, thus a herald of the reign of the Antichrist)—and a coincidence of the dates of Annunciation
and Crucifixion in 992 (taken as another sign the world might be about to end).

Landes believes particularly that the Peace of God movement in France, com-
bating widespread private violence, gained momentum from a concern that the
world might be about to be punished amid these various portents and the imminence of a new millennium. He focuses on a meeting in Limoges, in 994, which he
thinks, despite a lack of detailed evidence, illustrates the impact of millennial
thinking. He also argues that what he calls the "millennial generation" introduced
long-lasting changes into European religion, including a more emotional approach to Christ. Landes finds a few churchmen displaying some relief when the
year 1000 passed without incident; thus Adam of Bremen wrote, "Meanwhile the
thousandth year since the Incarnation was completed happily." And Landes highlights the fact that some pilgrims did head to Jerusalem in the year 1033—the
millennium of the resurrection.

Landes and several colleagues, provoked by lack of attention to their findings
and perhaps spurred by the chance of gaining notice for medieval history provided
by our own imminent calendar event, are pushing their case vigorously. Landes
himself refers to the "tired and repetitious argumentations of the antiterrors
school." He admits that evidence of massive interest is absent, but he attributes the
lack of records to general preliteracy and to the efforts by leading churchmen to
keep potentially ungovernable apocalyptic thinking under wraps. He urges imagination and speculation, and he belabors the debunkers.

Historians love to debate, and when the historical record is murky, the debates
must be inconclusive. Here is the current scholarly situation. The old myth about
massive terrors and altered behaviors cannot be proved, and no serious historian argues for it. Some aspects of the myth are hard to explain—the motivations of Bario-
nius in instigating the exaggerations are not clear—but there is general agreement

that the myth solidified in attacks on the church. The debunking may have gone a bit too far. It is clear that some church writers were aware that the year 1000 had arrived. Perhaps some people more generally were stirred, though there is no European-wide evidence for this (which one would expect, if there was a mass movement). Signs of attention to the millennium of Christ's death are more extensive than those for the year 1000, but even they are not abundant. A group of medievalists is trying to renew discussion; they have materials that need to be taken seriously plus some impassioned arguments about why there are not more data. (Would widespread popular excitement have been suppressed so systematically in surviving evidence?) Most medievalists, in what is still a vibrant historical field, are more interested in working on other topics. There is a range of argument, interesting and in fact revealing about how historians operate when evidence is limited, but it does not extend to reinstalling the claims about paralyzing fears.

The Historical Record and Contemporary License

This is where the record now stands. The most widely publicized view of the first millennium is a myth. If we want to be afraid of the year 2000 or 2001—Richard Erdoes describes his book as "a history of the Tenth Century for those who hope to see the year 2000"—fine, but let's not pretend that it's because of a clear medieval precedent. If we choose to be scared, fine, but let's recognize that our medieval ancestors were not. If, as is more probable, we want to discuss the next millennium in terms of some besetting modern problems, including environmental degradation and the weapons of war, even finer, but there's no need to pretend some connection to a false history in order to do so. No definite precedent exists for the fear-mongering approach to a specific millennial date, which raises real questions about the motives of popularizers who pretend otherwise. A few interesting developments may have occurred around the year 1000. Scattered people were clearly aware of the millennial date, linking it to the older apocalyptic idea. More may have found the anniversary aspect inspiring, although it is difficult to pin causation down. Here, there might be more genuine relevance for us. Perhaps the surge of hope that may have accompanied the anniversary of Christ's work in the world could be somehow revived in our less-Christian age. Admitting some room for debate over a period in medieval history that is not abundantly documented, the best guess is that most medieval people either ignored the year 1000 or accepted it quite sensibly. Some of them may have noted it, and it may have caused some of them to rethink some established habits and to wonder if better arrangements might not be possible.

Medieval people did not, however, establish very clear precedents for signaling the millennium. It is we moderns, with our different beliefs about chronological markers and the progress of time, who must figure out what we want to do about our next chance to celebrate. There is no need to be distracted by legend and invention, also largely modern.

It is true, of course, that our ongoing fascination with the medieval apocalyptic myth is itself a datum of importance. Although infuriating to knowledgeable historians, the repetition of the dramatic legend of people cowering in fear in 999 may signal more than careless journalism, more even than a desire to reassure us that we moderns have become much saner. The repetition may suggest a certain lurking anxiety that we, too, should be afraid, and in the anxiety may be the basis for wider expressions of terror or anticipation as the actual millennial date looms.

Certainly newspaper accounts, if evidence to date is any indication, delight in repeating half-truths about the millennial tradition with scant concern for accuracy—it is the myth that will not die. In the wake of a tragic mass suicide involving a Swiss apocalyptic sect in 1994, the press shamelessly echoed the myths about the year 999 ("outbreaks of indolence, mass panic, and lawlessness"), while noting glibly that these symptoms had not yet occurred in the modern world. The press reports tried to add fuel through distortions of the biblical tradition of the apocalypse itself. Finally, reporters, while displaying their modern, skeptical credentials by highlighting some of the sillier aspects of the millennial prophecies, also hedged their bets. As one reporter put it: "Perhaps, post–Cuban missile crisis, there is a small part of us which recognizes that any prophecy of doom which names a specific day just could be right, if only by accident." This reportage may accurately echo a widespread sentiment, suggesting that there is just enough of the subcurrent of anxiety in many of us to help keep the myth alive.

Journalists often echo the myths of the year 1000 out of ignorance or because the story is such fanciful fun—sort of like the Disney version of the Pocahontas story but with gloomy exaggeration instead of sugary uplift. I'm a professional historian and hate demonstrable untruth, all the more since, until recently, I blithely shared the popular misconception, not being a medieval specialist. It is important also to acknowledge the renewed discussion about the 11th century, which may improve our understanding of what reactions actually occurred. Certainly, the new millennium's advent will catch the eye of medievalists and give them the chance to venture a more nuanced picture. But the medieval freak show will not be revived, save among careless or self-interested popularizers.

Many readers may care less about historical accuracy, though no one should like to be needlessly duped. What does matter—the importance of truth aside—is how millennialism developed after the year 1000 as part of a new notion of time. Quite ironically, stories of medieval fear invented by rationalistic Frenchmen now help support an ongoing apocalyptic tradition, making its Christian roots seem far deeper than they are. It's time to turn to the next chapter of the Western struggle with time and the apocalypse.

REFINING THE
CALENDAR: VISIONS
AND CENTURIES, 1200–1850

ABOUT TWO CENTURIES AFTER THE NONEVENTS OF 1000, Western intellectuals began to develop a more precise sense of calendar time. Changes were gradual; some literate groups continued well past 1300 to use the fifteen-year cycles that dated from Constantine. But a number of factors prompted interest in a longer sense of time, both backward and forward, for which other measurements were essential. This chapter deals with the solidification of the Western calendar from the late Middle Ages into the 19th century.

In the process, I deal with two quite different results of the new attention to dates. The first result, particularly prominent in the 13th and 14th centuries, was to give a great new boost to millennial concepts and apocalyptic forecasts. This current, and many of the arithmetical calculations as well as the biblical assumptions that it embodied, has continued to the present, with a strong presence in North America from the 17th century onward.

The second result of the new calendrical precision was the emergence of the concept of centuries. This concept first surfaced clearly in 1300 and became even more prominent in the 16th century. By 1700 it was firmly established, and the regular celebration of century turns had begun. This tradition of marking centuries, initially Catholic but soon more secular, gradually helped drive the apocalyptic approach underground, where it maintains a lively but only sporadically noticed existence to this day. Whereas apocalyptics use a firm Christian calendar to establish millennial dates, they play with numbers and calculate irregular intervals to invoke fearsome futures. By contrast, centuries are counted from the same initial date but do not require divine intervention or special episodes as they potentially run smoothly into the future. The thinking is different.

Both the results of the late-medieval attention to the calendar warrant attention. I will turn to the uses of the century concept in Part II, beginning with the great fuss made over the advent of the 20th century. The apocalyptic calendar, far more relevant to the upcoming millennium, requires some contemporary assessment as well, which will be the subject of Chapter 5. For now, I will focus on how both kinds of calculations began to move forward.

Causes of the Systemizing of Calendars

The 13th century provided a turning point in Western chronological thinking. Against a background of millennial ideas that were already available in the religion and of some late-Roman precedent for thinking about units like centuries, the pace of change was picking up in Western Europe. This ever more rapid change created more consciousness of the meaning of time, both on the part of those uneasy about the new more urban, more commercial world and among those who began to think, very haltingly, that some progress was occurring and might continue in the future. This dual sense of historical time constituted a key ingredient that, again very slowly, began to pull Christian thinking about time and its celebration into something like the framework we have today, although it must be emphasized that (in this aspect of culture as in others) an essentially modern view of time was not complete until the late 17th century. During this long transition, lasting from the 12th century to the 17th century, the Christian time sense began to move out of the more conventional type of millennialism, in which some dramatic development is anticipated but without specification in time, to a new sense that time is regular and spiced by special points, notably the advent of a new century, that call for reflection and anticipation.

A key element in this transition was the heightened interest in mathematics and statistical precision, which, along with imitation of the sophistication of the ancient Greeks and contemporary Arabs, was part of the surge of learning in the High Middle Ages. Alexander Murray, in *Reason and Science in the Middle Ages*, has noted how the new numerical sense began to pop up. An astronomer recorded the duration of an eclipse in 1239 as the "time taken to walk 250 paces." A few chroniclers began carefully to list the number of people in armies, while Italian cities, beginning with Milan, began to take statistical inventories. Dante carefully set his *Divine Comedy* in a precise year, the papal jubilee year of 1300. The new sense of arithmetic, in its various but lively manifestations, easily led to impatience with the sloppy and multiple calendars. In conjunction with religious fervor, it also produced a new delight in playing with biblical numbers, and particularly the numbers in Revelation, in ever more elaborate permutations. The basis was set, in other words, both for a new round of apocalyptic thinking, using the calendar to predict the later ages of Christianity, and for a more regularized sense of time, based on uniform centuries. Not surprisingly, given the religious fervor of the time and the fact that the leading mathematicians were priests, the apocalyptic strand came first—ironically, well after the first millennium.

The crusades, which began just before 1100, may have encouraged interest in a conquering hero who would win the world for Christianity. Publicists for various kings aspiring to the role, like Louis VII of France, began to tout their monarchs as religious heroes who would acquire huge territories and inaugurate a marvelous period of peace. Millennial prophecies of this sort were associated with various German rulers named Frederick and French kings named Charles in the 13th and 14th centuries. A number of theologians in the 12th century began to write about and speculate about the length of the reign of the Antichrist, which was supposed to occur after the triumphs of a glorious conqueror. This set the context for the more prophetic work of Joachim of Fiore (born about A.D. 1130), a monk who developed a new theory of historical ages that was based on the steady unfolding of the Trinity and in which each age would be better than its predecessor. Joachim argued that the period of the Old Testament had been dominated by the Father; it was followed by the second age, of the Son; and the thousand-year reign foretold in Revelation would occur after the time of the Antichrist and would be dominated by the Holy Spirit. This millennial age (though Joachim carefully disavowed any precise calendar for the millennium) would be peaceful and unbelievers would be converted. Joachim in essence used the clear division between before Christ and after in the increasingly accepted Christian calendar and added a third age. His rough calculations set forty generations for each age; thus, he anticipated some new developments soon.

What was happening, in sum, was a revival of the biblical attention to the religious future and a growing addiction to prophecy. There were a host of competing theories about the length of the period of religious perfection and about the kind of hero (king or "angelic pope") who might usher it in. Many prophets were spurred by an ardent hope for clerical reform in an increasingly commercial age. This kind of millennial thinking could also inform some movements of popular protest, although most millennial writers called on the poor not to rise up to right wrongs but, rather, to wait for the leadership of supernatural powers. Millennial prophecies—that is, anticipations of a great spiritual cleansing to come in the future—were also spurred by comets or other portents or by calamities such as the Mongol invasion or the collapse of the Christian state in the Holy Land; such portents and calamities were often taken as signs of God's wrath, which might precede a great religious transformation.

Most of this thinking about historical stages and futures was chronologically vague. Joachim of Fiore tried to tie his forecasts down by setting each age at forty generations, arguing that the Bible predicted the Antichrist's triumph sometime between 1200 and 1260 and probably between 1256 and 1260. Needless to say, this attempt at precision lost credibility when nothing had happened by 1260. Joachim's doctrines were condemned by the church, despite their ongoing influence on those awaiting the millennium.

The Emergence of the Century

The revival of Christian millennialism was one factor in another development: the first celebration of the end of a Christian century in A.D. 1300. On February 22, 1300, Pope Boniface VIII issued the bull *Antiquorum,* granting Christians indulgences if they visited the main Roman basilicas during the year in commemoration of the century past and in celebration of the new age to come. The pope claimed backing from tradition: He cited Roman precedents for celebrating centuries and also claimed that pilgrims told him their forefathers had experienced a similar centennial in 1200. Whatever the precedents, Boniface's move was new, both in fixing the importance of the century as a unit and in associating this unit with the expectation of momentous new spiritual opportunities. Boniface intended his move to bolster the papal position, at a time when it faced competition from rising secular rulers in Western Europe, and to combat subversive millenarianism. He hoped to regularize spiritual hopes and fears by associating them with a precise calendar under papal control, rather than leaving the way open for random numerical prophecies. It is not clear that his innovation was widely noted. Communications were slow, and most people kept no calendars. Several thousand pilgrims did reach Rome—one historian claimed 200,000 arrived during the year. And the pope's proclamation was noteworthy as a sign that ideas were beginning to coalesce, linking a more regular calendar to recurrent Christian impulses to think about a dramatic religious future. The pilgrims themselves believed that indulgences were available for anyone visiting Rome during the first year of the new century, and they knew that this marked a special anniversary of the birth of Jesus. This first step was halting, however; subsequent popes proclaimed jubilees frequently, with no linkage to new centuries; by 1475, a jubilee every twenty-five years had become an established custom. The prospect of making money from pilgrims outweighed any respect for the century. Indeed, many Christian centers established jubilees for a time, at widely scattered intervals; Canterbury hosted a series, for example. Still, the idea was set of a regular calendar that would include centennial jubilees in Rome; between 1475 and 1775, papal jubilees occurred every quarter century.

The next steps in linking the calendar to prophecy occurred in the 16th century. Again, we are not chronicling a great rush to the modern sense of solemnity about passing and coming centuries. A group of German and Polish Protestant writers gathered in Magdeburg to write a thirteen-volume history of Christianity; it was issued between 1559 and 1574. This was the first work to separate history into centuries: Each volume covered a hundred-year period between Christ's birth and the 13th century (the group dispersed before later volumes could be written). The series itself became known as the "Magdeburg Centuries." The over- all purpose of the volumes was to provide direct linkage between Christ and the Reformation and to chronicle the intermediate deviation of the Catholic church. Exactly why the authors organized the volumes around centuries is not entirely clear, but they did establish the term "century" as a unit of time rather than, as had been previously the case, a unit of one hundred of anything. Surely, the recent papal tradition of highlighting each new century played a role. Protestantism it- self ushered in a new period of great anxiety about time and history because for the first time, Western Christianity was suffering a long-term division. The fur- ther gains of capitalism created a growing class of people who thought in terms of more precise time in planning economic ventures and calculating profits; al- though they were not concerned with time at the century level, such thinking could well contribute to a desire for more orderly units in historical treatments. Earlier thinking about stages of God—the sort of stages that Joachim of Fiore had invented and popularized—may have encouraged a greater desire for regularities in the presentation of history and in schematizing the calendar of past and future. These factors probably combined to produce the first clear precedent for century- based history—the sort of history that is still with us in textbooks and many monographs.

Nostradamus and the Spur to Millennialism

Nevertheless, it took several more generations for the notion of the century to be- come important enough to be regularly celebrated. But the 16th century also pro- duced another semireligious prophet in the late-medieval millennial vein. Nos- tradamus was not a calendar addict. Indeed, he used the word "century" simply to mean "one hundred," without reference to years. But he did tie his prophecy to time, and because the time he cited is about to expire, we need to introduce his vi- sion into the story.

Amid voluminous writings, Nostradamus offered a quatrain, which (translated from the French) reads:

> *The year 1999, seven months,*
> *From the sky will come a great King of terror*
> *To resuscitate the great King of Angoulmois*
> *Before, after, Mars will reign by good luck.*

This poem is certainly intriguing, and perhaps ominous, for those of us anticipating the millennial unknown. We will doubtless see the poem (and other quotes from Nostradamus) many times as part of millennial mumbo jumbo. It's always a bit intimidating when someone pins a precise year to vague and menacing forecasts, and one from so long ago (Nostradamus was born in 1503) may take on particularly significant proportions. The prophecy cannot be fully interpreted; who the king was is anybody's guess, although Mars is a bit clearer. The verse does fit as a late addition to the series of anticipations of catastrophe or revivals to come that had dotted the previous three centuries.

Nostradamus himself is a genuine, if odd, historical figure. Born Michel de Nostradame into a grain-dealing family in southern France, he later attended school in Avignon, where he studied grammar, rhetoric, logic, arithmetic—the classic liberal arts. He then went to the University of Montpellier to study medicine, graduating at the relatively early age of twenty-two. His first publication was a mixture of remedies and predictions entitled *Excellent and Most Useful Tract of Everything Needed, for Those Who Wish to Become Familiar with Many Choice Recipes.* The book did well, and he continued a publishing career as he was establishing more exciting personal credentials. He (or perhaps other family members a bit earlier) began to claim descent from the tribe of Issachar (one of the ten lost tribes of Israel), a family that was said to have "understanding of the times." With this fraudulent base, he began to publish almanacs (it should be remembered that this was still the springtime of printing, and that audiences were beginning to expand). The first almanac emerged in 1550. In 1555, Nostradamus issued his initial book of prophecy, *Centuries*—the title simply designating one hundred forecasts. The last volume of this series, in which the quatrain about 1999 appeared, saw the light in 1568. By this time (after a brief brush with the Inquisition), Nostradamus had caught the attention of the royal court of Catherine de Médicis, where his reputation as a doctor successfully treating the plague as well as his widely discussed status as a seer qualified him as physician to the king. He died of congestive heart failure a year later. The forecast in Nostradamus's quatrain; whatever one makes of its applicability to the end of our own century, clearly fit a pattern of self-dramatization and publicity seeking within a context already open to recurrent apocalyptic prophecies.

A number of recent works, trying to build a millennial sense today, have understandably promoted Nostradamus while trying to apply his forecasts more precisely to the conditions of our time. Characteristically, they have accepted as fact much of his own biographical romance, which may make their other findings suspect. Thus, for example, Hillel Schwartz makes him the son of a Jewish notary and the grandson of a royal astrologer, both incorrect claims. John Hogue, in his 1987 book *Nostradamus and the Millennium*, also makes him the son and grandson of doctors and endows him with a happy childhood and a boyhood nickname, "the little astrologer," from his schoolmates—again, arrant nonsense, for no evidence exists for such claims.

It is important to give Nostradamus his due, for there is no question that he had a fascinating mind. The prophet foresaw a host of new leaders, kings and others, and an array of coming disasters. John Hogue has the seer predicting the civil wars in late–16th-century France, including several specific royal murders ("The great man of Blois will murder his friend, The kingdom is placed in evil and double doubt"), which is plausible to a point because religious and political divisions were widening well before Nostradamus wrote, but Hogue also has Nostradamus predicting the advent of a later French leader named de Gaulle. Nostradamus can be read to predict the British Empire, Oliver Cromwell, the 1666 Great Fire of London (and its exact year). Hogue has him predicting Hitler (under the name of Aries, the god of war) and his attack on Poland. If a line about the "elder sister of the British Isles" accurately refers to the American colonies (which I find implausible; why "elder"?), then Nostradamus may have forecast American independence, and he predicted another birth fifteen years later (her brother) that Hogue wants to make the First Republic of France. Rousing apocalyptic lines about people stirred up against their king and Paris in trouble, although evoking some familiar apocalyptic fare about earthly chaos, could foreshadow the turmoil of the French Revolution. Vaguer quatrains might refer to World War II: "a great roaring storm will be raised by land and sea, The naval battles will be greater than ever; Fires, creatures which shoot making more tumult." Hogue (and others) go on to have Nostradamus foresee Mao Ze-dong, the *Challenger* disaster ("Nine will be set apart from the human flock"), and the assassination of John F. Kennedy ("The great man will be struck down in the day by a thunderbolt . . . of young age"; but if this prediction sounds pretty accurate, note that the same verse foretells conflict in Reims and London and pestilence in Tuscany, which don't seem to have happened unless one wants to count student riots in Paris in 1968—Reims is not too far away—and a flood in Tuscany in 1966).

Clearly, there's meat here for a host of speculations and gullibilities and some real sense of wonder, in whatever mixture a reader might prefer. It is also important to note that Nostradamus's final book largely focuses on coming disasters for the church. He predicts, however, that the church will be rescued by a great leader—another set of verses that can be stretched to apply to 20th-century papacies but that more clearly extended the millenarian prophetic tradition that anticipated the chaos preceding resurrection and the Antichrist. (The indefatigable Hogue suggested a number of candidates for Nostradamus's Antichrist references, including Muslim leaders such as the Ayatollah Ruholla Khomeini, Muammar Gadhafi, and Abu Nidal, which began to seem a bit silly just a few years later as these leaders died or faded from prominence without having overturned the world. Hogue, unlike his mentor, tried to be too precise.) Did Nostradamus's most famous verse, referring to 1999, form part of a prediction of a quarter century of war ending our millennium, along with new plagues and famines? (And should we ignore the fact that this war, clearly World War III, should have started twenty years ago?) Then we can also anticipate terrible winds, spring flooding in England, a great earthquake that may split east Africa into three pieces by the mid-1990s—which we've already passed—a 1997 nuclear attack on New York (if "new city" indeed means the Big Apple and "a huge scattered flame" means a nuclear device).

The game of applying ominous verses to contemporary history and geography (aided by some liberties in translation) is great sport, and surely, given recurring disasters, the verses are potentially relevant some of the time with only a little mental stretch; we'll have to see. And Nostradamus also foresaw, in good millennial fashion, a subsequent thousand-year peace, which should take effect toward the middle of the next century. We can certainly predict that the seer will often be mentioned as our own millennium nears. Perhaps, along with hyperbole, his intriguing verses will spark some new flights of imagination.

Nostradamus was, however, nearly the last of his breed in early modern Europe. With growing attention to science, dramatic millennial forecasts were actually declining by the 16th century. An obscure trickle of millennial calculators has persisted well into our own time, as we will discuss in Chapter 5, and important apocalyptic predictions not tied to a thousand-year date—like that of the Millerites, who awaited the end of the world in 1843—have surfaced recurrently. But mainstream millennial forecasts did die down by the 16th century as part of a change in religious thinking and of new approaches to time that began to privilege centuries as units of chronological organization.

The Triumph of the Century

It was the growing use of century designations that constituted the most important development in conceptions of time and its markers in early modern Europe. Prior to this point, not even new years had been explicitly noted; instead, an abundant festival tradition observed the long, twelve-day Christmas celebrations and other religious markers. Indeed, earlier Roman celebrations of new years were downplayed as pagan, and although some popular ceremonies may have survived, a shift in religious climate was required to permit more notation of secular calendar events, much less to expand on the advent of centuries.

Some references in the 1590s discussed the coming end of the century. During the 1600s, British writers began to refer to centuries routinely; thus Mede, for example, wrote of "every one of the last three centuries." The term was becoming standard for writers and readers of history. The first mention of a century's termination being publicly referred to as the end of an age seems to have occurred in 1701. On January 2, 1701, the *Post Boy*, a British newspaper, included the following: "This Year, which closes the Age, and which we may now count among those Elaps'd, will be remarkable in History, not only by the great Events, but also by Singularities very surprising and extraordinary, which excited more than ever the attention of Spirits." It was also around this time that people first started debating whether 1700 or 1701 should properly be taken as the 18th century's first year. A number of treatises in England, France, and Germany heatedly discussed the topic. Many people exchanged new-century greetings by letter; Samuel Pepys wrote his nephew in January 1700 wishing him a prosperous new century. Samuel Sewall, a Massachusetts judge, paid four trumpeters to signal the dawn of the new century by a blast on the Boston Common on January 1, 1701; Sewall also wrote "Verses upon a New Century," which he had the town crier read. A number of popular almanacs appeared, covering the whole new century. During the 1700s, writers often referred to their belonging to this particular century. Pierre Beaumarchais wrote: "I am unaware of any century in which I would rather have been born." Another Frenchman wrote about the uniqueness and unpredictability of his century (in 1759, by the way, well before the century's most interesting developments had in fact occurred): "Ages may repeat themselves, but can this century ever have a twin?"

These themes were extended between 1799 and 1801, in a period of rapid change and uncertainty thanks to the French Revolution and Napoleon. A host of newspaper retrospectives covered the departing 18th century. "The good Old Lady known by the name of the EIGHTEENTH CENTURY, who resigned all sublunary cares on Wednesday night last, was quietly buried in the family vault of Eternity," noted the *London Chronicle* in its first issue of 1801. A Massachusetts paper found that "in reviewing the events of the last hundred years, the mind is warped in astonishment. The most important scenes of the old world require an encyclopedia to record them." Forecasts also abounded, for thinking in terms of centuries involved not only identifying the century past but anticipating the one to come, with a sense that it would have a special flavor. And there were celebrations galore. German intellectuals in Weimar attended a fancy dress ball on New Year's Eve, 1800. Many people of varying ranks enjoyed the centennial festivities, writing friends such sentiments as "Now we find ourselves in the remarkable 19th century! O it deserves the loveliest garland of roses—may it bring us Peace and Good

Fortune!" (this last from a German woman, Johann Gottfried Herder's wife, in a period when renewed war between Germany and France might have been easy to predict).

Of course, celebration and rueful contemplation of a century passing and another one aborning were more widespread still during the 1890s—a point to which I shall return, for this celebration forms the most immediate backdrop to what we might expect as we greet our own new age over the next few years.

What had happened, by 1700, to create the modern interest in marking centuries (and, potentially, millennia) as meaningful units of time, occasions for particular reflection? I have noted a number of developments that finally combined to produce the outlook that many Westerners have shared now for three hundred years (assuming that the centennial celebratory spirit will fully surface by 2001). The combination emerged haltingly; there was no dramatic single transformation.

The first ingredient was widely shared: Almost all human cultures measure time and often think about past ages, whether stages of a divine plan or simple royal dynasties. This fact provides some perspective on the present, however oblique.

Second, many cultures also look toward some point in the future, however undefined, as a time of tremendous change. This millennial vision seems particularly associated with major religions that postulate a finite time for human history. It lends itself, recurrently, to fearsome forecasts of upheavals to come. All the major Mediterranean religions generated this prophetic streak, which helps explain why many people of Jewish, Muslim, or Christian heritage are open to the impulse to look to the future with a mixture of dread and anticipation.

Third, more prosaically, by the 1500s Western intellectuals and leaders had clearly begun to think in terms of centuries and had sometimes used their advent as occasions for celebration. The Western calendar was firmly established. With printing and spreading literacy, popular access to calendars and almanacs began to increase, although this was even more clearly the case by 1700. A sense of secular change,* of departures from past precedent, had spread from the Middle Ages onward, triggering a renewal of millennial prophecies but also helping to establish a need to fix on definite units of historical and future time.

And fourth, by 1700 a sense not simply of change but of progress was developing, associated with the new knowledge brought by the scientific revolution and by commercial advances. This sense seized on centuries as units of time to help

---

* The word "secular" came from the Latin term for a generation or age, which, as we have seen, had roots in the Etruscan *saeculum*. It began to be widely used to mean "this-worldly" in the 13th century as attention to change and awareness of social shifts spread. In French the word for century, *siècle*, comes from the same root.

establish how different one's own age was from the age just past and to speculate on how different the age still to come would be. Historians, becoming a bit more numerous, both grasped this impulse and extended it, frequently talking of centuries as if they had definite characteristics. It was in the 1780s that the evocative German word *Zeitgeist,* or "spirit of the age," entered the language, for example. This sense of progress was not millennial in that it did not look to distant futures or the coming of an Antichrist. But the millennial spirit had helped prepare the idea that centuries should be celebrated and anticipated, and far-reaching claims could still accompany the new culture of time. Hitler, after all, would hail a thousand-year Reich, recalling the millennial unit even if missing the mark by about 988 years. Turns of the century were more common and their significance a bit more modest, yielding fewer sweeping prophecies but reflecting a shared understanding that the present was different from the past and was moving toward a future that was also different; the admittedly artificial idea of hundred-year spans could help to capture this process. The modern, Western sense of historical time was set, and with it a pervasive desire to celebrate a new century's arrival.

Apocalypse Again and Its Immigration to America

Along with the modern sense of time, marked by recognition of secular change (usually with some sense of progress) and focused on centuries as convenient units of assessment, the old apocalyptic tradition continued. Many Protestant reformers, including Martin Luther, were convinced of an apocalypse to come, and some of the radical sects hoped to bring it about imminently. The Anabaptists believed that they were locked in a struggle with the Antichrist and that Christ's return was imminent. Prophecies and accusations of being the Antichrist returned with a vengeance during the English civil wars of the mid-17th century. But then apocalyptic prophecies toned down, as peace returned to England and ideas of science and natural regularities, plus religious tolerance, gained firmer hold. After the 17th century, the apocalyptic vision was for the most part an undercurrent in Europe, not a culturally dominant expression.

A strain of popular Christian fascination with the apocalypse migrated to the European colonies in North America. Indeed, given the frequency of 17th-century apocalyptic imagery in English Protestantism, which associated the pope with the Antichrist, it was no wonder that American Protestantism imported a considerable dose. Various New England ministers wrote about forthcoming days of doom. Another strain translated millennial visions into praise for American society as the center of the forthcoming utopia, in which the prophecies of peace and plenty would be realized.

This was not simply a random migration. Because millennialists often faced religious persecution in Europe, they could see the American scene as a chance for a premillennial purification. Although most immigrants were not millennialists, a disproportionate current of millennialism continued. It was in the 1790s, for example, that the founder of the Shakers, Mother Ann Lee, came to the United States from England, where the now sedate Quakers looked down on her excited religious views and her expectation of an imminent Second Coming. "I knew that God had a chosen people in America," she wrote. "I saw them in a vision, and when I met with them in America, I knew them." Migrations of this sort, continuing with the more secular utopians of the 19th century, helped fill the United States with greater religious excitement and expectation than was common in modern Western culture. The same push helped the process of trying to link a new national definition with dramatic hopes for the future.

Indeed, New England Puritans tried to associate closely their justifications for the New Land with a millenarian vision, which may have implanted this strain more firmly in the American Protestant psyche than it was by this point in the European psyche, even though Americans also participated strongly in science and rationalism. The Mathers and others in Boston often argued that America might be the model for the New Jerusalem after the apocalypse, the "seat of the Divine Metropolis" during the millennium. Prophecies abounded, and so did nervous reactions to disasters such as the bloodshed of King Philip's war, which, it was argued, had been foretold as the "red Horse" (Indians) of the apocalypse. A Boston earthquake in 1755 convinced many that the Day of Judgment had arrived and led to a spate of published predictions about wars, the rise of the Antichrist in 1761, and the end of all in 1763. This combination of triumphant God-aided Americanism and anxieties about vulnerability to evil has continued to define the apocalyptic strain in the United States well into the 1990s.

While apocalyptic prophecies faded a bit in the mid–18th century, the Great Awakening revived them. Indeed, the recurrence of strong, fundamental Protestant belief in the United States has also included a millennial element, and because this strain is much stronger than the religions of modern Europe, it marks the United States as a particular home for the apocalyptic strand. Jonathan Edwards, for example, believed the millennium was approaching, and he played with biblical numbers to show that the Reformation had been the fifth Vial of Revelation and that the world was now in the sixth, the last before the end. While he backed away from a precise date, he argued that the "glorious work of God" was dawning and that "many things . . . make it probable that this work will begin in America." Not surprisingly, the American Revolution benefited from the strength of apocalyptic thinking. King George was often portrayed as the Antichrist; one revolutionary even calculated that in both Greek and Hebrew the words "Royal Supremacy in Great Britain" totaled 666, an ominous combination in numerology. Religious interpretations of the Revolution's ultimate success renewed the vision of the United States as the seat of God's millennial renewal.

As mainstream U.S. Protestantism toned down in the 19th century, the millennial current was pushed more to the underground, although it entered strongly into popular revivalism. The chief manifestation of the current was the Millerite excitement of the 1830s and early 1840s, which was based on elaborate biblical study and the enthusiasm of as many as 50,000 followers. William Miller focused closely on apocalyptic visions in the books of Daniel and Revelation, and he portrayed the government as a wild beast "with two horns like a lamb" (the second Beast of the Apocalypse) that "spoke like a dragon." Many apocalyptics, indeed, began to use their visions to draw their flocks away from governments and all worldly matters.

The prophetic strain continued even after Miller's bitter disappointment that the world did not end in 1843 (his followers adjusted, becoming the Seventh-Day Adventists). A strain of apocalyptic rhetoric entered campaigns against slavery— the Antichrist wasn't too hard to find here—feminism, and American utopianism. It was not just an impulse of the lower classes or of outcasts. A series of prophets maintained an apocalyptic vision in the final decades of the century, particularly among evangelical Protestants. John Darby, for example, wrote in the 1850s and 1860s of a Tribulation, when the Antichrist would rule for seven years, preceded by a Rapture in which all believers would rise to meet Christ in the air, later to return to defeat evil and usher in Christ's thousand-year rule on earth. James Brooks, in the 1880s, gained widespread publicity in New York in preaching about a period of unprecedented wickedness followed by Christ's return. Late–19th-century evangelists like Dwight Moody preached the imminence of Christ's Second Coming. World War I and the Russian Revolution provoked a new rush of apocalyptic forecasts among American fundamentalists.

Conclusion: The Two Strands

Christian calendrical and millennial history after 1200 became complicated. New calculations about time got the process going: The calendar firmed up. This made possible the explosion of interest in prophecies, with Nostradamus the chief manifestation. New religious excitement, from Joachim and other monks through the Reformation to the ardent Protestantism of North America, fed and was fed by this unprecedented apocalyptic surge. But the passion for calculating time also served governments and leaders (including popes) and capitalists and individuals who saw advantages in a calm, regular calendar in which centuries would be the chief markers, with regular celebrations quite different from—sometimes deliberately different from—the frenzies of the apocalyptic movements. On the whole, the advocates of the century won out in the Western world. Most people came to refer to centuries routinely and to celebrate their coming and going. By the 18th century, with the rise of science and growing prosperity, the apocalyptic sense of time, though still both lively and vivid, became a minority strand. Only in the United States does the apocalyptic current seem to have found a new lease on life, although even here it was not dominant. More groups in the United States periodically rallied to apocalyptic prophecies, including their hostility to institutions of government, and more ordinary people might slip into an apocalyptic mode in reaction to natural disaster or great political stress. The sense of justifying the new land in terms of some special blessing from God helped sustain this current. So did the sheer strength of religion in a new, geographically mobile society in which other ties, including the ties of traditional communities, were rather weak.

This is why, before returning to the century as the unit of choice, we must deal further with the millennium, this odd measure that did not mean much when it first occurred but could, thanks to apocalyptic surges, matter a bit more this time around. The persistence and even periodic intensification of the millennial tradition are undeniably impressive.

Yet this persistence, although important, must not be allowed to mask the essential decline of millennial language and the rise of new attitudes toward time that were more characteristically expressed in terms of centuries. Even the arrival of a new century could provoke a throwback to apocalyptic language, but this was not the common approach. For its part, the apocalyptic current was not usually linked to any precise calendar markers. This is not to suggest that the actual imminence of a millennium will not rekindle flames of apocalyptic rhetoric, particularly since the convenient Cold War targets have not been fully replaced. Apocalyptics are eagerly casting about for new outlets. But although our society is divided in its thinking about time, the use of biblical imagery, itself complex in its implications for any particular calendar, has unquestionably declined. Apocalyptic references, like an inactive virus, were largely ignored, most of them literally unknown to the American majority, even at the height of the Cold War.

This means, of course, that the attitudes most of us probably bring to the upcoming revelries for another new century and a new millennium are relatively modern, perhaps surprisingly so. Although a vague millennial tradition stretches back considerably farther and is relevant to what we will be asked to recall by 2001, our basic sense of how time is organized and of why we should note these particular units of time is only a few hundred years old. Because the idea of some millennium is older and often surrounded by obscure or ominous evocations, we will often be told that our impulse to celebrate a coming New Age is much hoarier than it actually is. We may be attracted to the idea of associating ourselves with mysterious prophets of the past; largely mythical claims may still have impact. But we will understand our own ceremonies better if we see their modern cultural content as well.

The fact that many aspects of our thinking about an age past and a New Age opening up were only fairly recently established does not mean that they are trivial or inaccurate. Three past precedents for hailing a new century and reflecting on the century that just expired are ample bases for extending the tradition in anticipation of 2001. We may wish that the occasion joined us to even more remote ancestors and more mysterious thoughts, but there's plenty to chew on as it is. Artificial, fairly recently constructed, our sense of centuries does help us establish meaning. And for the first time, we will join this modern sense of units of time to a calendar millennium. It will be interesting to see what we make of this.

Five

APOCALYPSE NOW?

COMPLEX HISTORICAL PRECEDENTS for millennial thinking lead to an interesting question about the near future: As we prepare for the celebration of a millennium, how much apocalyptic fervor will enter in? We have seen that calculations about the world's end and predictions about the year 2000 attracted much attention in the past, particularly from the 13th century onward, and they will surely intensify as the year 2000 draws nigh. We have also seen that apocalyptic thinking about time was never universally accepted, even in Christianity, and that on the whole, it has faded with the secularization of Western culture, which included the habits of thinking in terms of centuries and celebrating them in almost entirely secular terms. I would guess that we will hear more about the apocalypse as the year 2000 approaches but that literally apocalyptic visions will remain peripheral for most of us.

This prediction seems to be a safe bet for Western Europe (not to mention most of the rest of the world, where Christianity doesn't reign in any form; it will be interesting, though, to see what fundamentalist gains in Eastern Europe and particularly Latin America produce by way of millennial comment). An apocalyptic strain remains in Europe in small groups; I will give some examples in this chapter. But short of some appalling disaster, prompting everyone to rethink assumptions or retreat in unprecedented religious fear, it is hard to imagine most Europeans, who are firmly, prosaically secular, viewing apocalyptic manifestations as much more than a sideshow.

The case is different in the United States. The apocalyptic tradition is stronger, even though it is a minority current. There are more people directly interested in apocalyptic rhetoric, even in churches that officially disavow any precise effort to pin the millennium to a particular date. There is more tradition, also, of groups that are not normally drawn to apocalyptic thinking pulling in when the going gets tough or when there is a particular reason for religious excitement. Furthermore, in the United States we're in an odd period of political transition at home and an adjustment of our thinking about our place in the world. Our standard of living has been stagnating for two decades, in a society that depends on progress for self-confidence. We've just shifted our national leadership to a group eager to attack government. This is confusing to some people, who have counted on a fairly stable set of government functions since the New Deal. And it is encouraging to others, including some of the millennial sort, who view government as evil. Finally, we are no longer engaged in the Cold War. This is a good thing, but it deprives us of a standard framework for thinking about ourselves in the world. We no longer have a clear enemy to measure our own virtue against. As we will see, this is confusing to the apocalyptics, who need an Antichrist, but it may bother the rest of us too, forcing us to wonder a bit more about our own virtues in a society that is not noticeably virtuous.

Given an unusual history in which millennial thinking still has surprising force and some real, widely shared contemporary concerns about our own identity, we can certainly expect varied rhetoric around the millennium. How much will how many of us believe? We can speculate that a large number of Americans harbor millennial concepts somewhere in the back of their minds, although they may normally concentrate on more prosaic calendars and forecasts. The imminence of a symbolic date may bring this subconscious strand into greater prominence, particularly if events (whether coincidental or divinely planned) make humdrum regularities seem less assured. Certainly, given active minority support, ready media hyperbole, and a wider strand of subterranean nervousness, as The Date approaches, many Americans are likely to be a bit jumpier when they encounter what they might otherwise judge standard disasters in the news. Maybe, just maybe, something might be a Sign.

We are only a few years from the new millennium, yet even in the millennially prone United States, it is difficult to predict what the overall balance will be between skepticism and routine, on the one hand, and apocalyptic excitement on the other. The Christian Right is rising, yet some millennial books directed at a mainstream audience have fared badly. Outright apocalyptic groups are numerous but small; the signals are mixed.

Two points are certain: First, the dominant approaches to time in recent decades have not favored millennialism. Most of us think in terms of years and centuries, following the recent history of calendrical divisions. Second, however, the millennial currents that flowed through the 19th century have survived, finding new, specific handholds in the process. We can explore the contemporary context for the apocalyptics, even if we cannot be sure how much ground they will gain on the eve of what must be, to them, a great event.

The unexpected power of apocalyptic references showed up in the public's reaction to Orson Welles's famous "War of the Worlds" broadcast in 1938—a sign of how close to the surface the apocalyptic imagery is for many Americans, quite apart from adherence to small formal movements. Welles's portrayal of an invasion from outer space convinced one woman that God was punishing mankind through Armageddon, which in turn evoked stereotypes that prompted her to add details on her own. She claimed to have been particularly impressed with the description of a giant sheet of flame that engulfed the entire nation—good Revelation stuff, but no such image had been mentioned in the broadcast.

U.S. involvement in an ever tenser world after 1945 gave still more life to the apocalyptic strand. The atomic bomb easily lent itself to the idea that there would be a final conflagration, and for a moment, in the late 1940s, many Americans seemed to share this fearful vision. Mainstream U.S. culture quickly cast off these fears, with a progress-as-usual optimism, but the undercurrent persisted. The Soviet Union was readily identified as the Antichrist that would usher in the millennium—an image Ronald Reagan would later suggest with his reference to the "evil empire." Tensions in the Middle East also gave new ammunition to revivals of real or imagined biblical prophecies of the destruction of God's chosen people. None of this constituted a tidal wave; the millennial current was still a trickle. But it did generate a steady stream of sermons and books, a few of which, like Hal Lindsey's tracts in the 1970s about the imminence of the earth's end, broke through to bestseller status. In the 1970s, fundamentalist ministers, such as David Welles of the popular Southwest Radio Church, and other prophets like Hal Lindsey were still warning of doom: "If God permits men to use atomic warfare, it will be to accomplish His purpose and to glorify His name." "Our world is in a death-dive. We have peaked and now we're plunging rapidly to the end." "Although Armageddon will be an awesome and terrifying experience for the world, it should be welcomed by the child of God as the day of vindication of our holy and sovereign Creator. . . . What then should be the believer's attitude to the destruction of the world by fire? First of all, he should welcome it and pray for its nearness."

Although the nuclear-war scenario predominated, apocalyptic prophecies increasingly incorporated themes of environmental catastrophe, which positioned them to survive even the end of the Cold War in the 1980s. It was true, however, that most millennial preachers in the United States railed against the Cold War's decline, continuing to cast Russia as the archenemy. A characteristic book painted Mikhail Gorbachev as the Antichrist, arguing that his appealing facade was just what the Beast would convey in the early stages of the apocalypse. And again, although the apocalyptic current was largely subterranean from the standpoint of mainstream American urban culture, it drew loyal audiences even as events seemed to complicate the vision. There were even outright prophecies in the style of Nostradamus. Edgar Cayce, the prophet whose visions occurred largely in his sleep, thus "saw" the destruction of New York City in 1999, confirming one reading of Nostradamus. His Virginia Beach Institute promoted this kind of apocalyptic imagery more widely.

While Cold War visions and their aftermath most clearly focused the millennial strains in the United States in the later 20th century, there were other themes as well. Sheer internal decay and indulgence predictably called forth prophecies of destruction. So, interestingly, did computerization, with some arguing that the Antichrist would turn out to be a computer. Clearly, virtually any major development affecting the United States could be interpreted as a sign of impending doom or a cause of God's wrath. Equally obviously, the apocalyptic fervor was far too great to be confined to any specific chronology during most of the postwar decades. Whatever apocalyptics emphasize in the 1990s, when they may finally feel that the calendar, too, is on their side, it is useful to remember that their kin in the 1970s and 1980s were already convinced that the world would end long before the arrival of a new millennium. This mixture of threat and fear is no respecter of dates or arithmetical niceties.

The millennial strand has become something like a largely dormant virus in the wider culture of the West, particularly in the United States. It does not pervade the body of the culture, but it unshakably persists, vital for small groups, available for others hovering nearer the borderline of mainstream beliefs, and obviously capable of wider impact in time of fear or some special disaster. Sorting out where millennial currents ripple—among the welter of fervent but small prophetic groups, in the incompletely articulated thoughts of a larger number of Christian believers, in the fascinations of some (but not all) youthful New Age adepts—is one of the most challenging tasks of any millennial observer. The balance between fierce enthusiasms and routine-mindedness is hard to calculate and open to sudden change.

The abundant signs of religious revival in the United States may certainly create more fertile soil for apocalyptic views. Sales of religious books have risen 65 percent in the 1990s, fed, publishers believe, by anxieties encountered by aging baby boomers. Male religious groups like the Promise Keepers and the fervor of the 1995 Million Man March are other symptoms of a return to religion; men's concerns might be particularly important given the fact that, historically, men have normally taken the lead in apocalyptic prophecies and movements, in contrast to women's greater role in other kinds of religious ecstasies.

Religious enthusiasm does not necessarily yield millennialism, but it can, particularly as the date approaches and especially when tied to other interests. A group of conservative Christians, many of them retired engineers fascinated with numbers, has produced a series of predictions of the world's end in recent years. In 1988 a former aerospace engineer, Edgar Whisenant, sold 4 million copies of a book explaining why the apocalypse might occur in that year. He later revised the calculations to place the apocalypse in 1989, but he won few new sales. In 1994 another engineer, Harold Camping, calculated that Christ would return and the world would end in late September of that year. He was obviously wrong. Even as he wrote, another retired engineer disputed Camping's predictions, claiming they were off by six years (he also forecast that the nation of Israel would be destroyed in June 1994). Camping, a Christian broadcaster on the West Coast, sold several thousand copies of his book, although he had been turned down by most major Christian publishing houses and had to issue the book at his own expense (after all, there wasn't much time to lose if any readers were to be found alive). Camping's numerical calculations were meticulous, as has been often true of this genre: Using biblical dates, he began with the creation of Adam in 11,013 B.C. and then picked up other Old Testament numbers (not necessarily dealing with dates) to represent symbolic anticipations. A passage on priests walking two thousand cubits ahead of the Israelites (Josh. 3:3–4) is thus interpreted to mean that there will be about two thousand years between Christ's birth and his Second Coming.

In 1994, the mass murder/suicide of forty-eight members of a religious cult in Switzerland reminded the world that the persistence of apocalyptic predictions was not a matter of books and arithmetical calculations alone. Under the leadership of Luc Jouret, a sect called the Order of the Solar Temple had gathered under the banner of an imminent apocalypse. Accounts differed as to whether or not the Order had actively held to the Christian apocalyptic tradition. Jouret, in calling forth an imagery of fire, catastrophe, and ruin, had certainly updated his message by associating the apocalypse with environmental degradation, a link we can expect to hear more about as environmental forecasts become enmeshed with the dark side of the millennium. At the same time, of course, the Jouret cult was obscure and small, and it was not unlike other suicidal cults in the 20th century that did not, in fact, directly focus on the advent of a new millennium. Religious group suicides—and the Order generated another round of suicide or murder late in 1995—are far more common than other overt millennial acts, for they do not depend on a particular calendar; therefore, they do not prove an increase in millennialism save as a convenient rationalization.

The apocalyptic virus was not confined to one sect, however. Beneath the secular surface of U.S. culture, predictions of violent divine punishment for corruption lived on. The Millennium Watch Institute, dedicated to tracking obscure prophecies, claimed that more than a thousand small organizations and private individuals were writing about coming "global transformations, with an increasingly ominous tone." Bumper stickers stated, "If you hear a trumpet, grab the wheel," and New Age adepts could purchase wrist watches inscribed "One hour nearer the Lord's return." Millennial portfolios were on sale that included calendars and dire prophecies. With the prospect of total war diminishing, apocalyptic attention shifted increasingly toward the theme of environmental disaster linked to the millennium's end.

Although the United States was commonly seen as the center of millennial visions, reports of millennial concerns elsewhere have increased as the due date nears. The topic became a staple of Hyde Park Corner lectures during the 1990s in London. Paco Rabanne, a New Age guru best known for the invention of the metal miniskirt, regaled his soapbox audiences with warnings: "Hold on tight. You're going to get it full in the face." He predicted a cataclysmic war within five years, followed by the "vacuum-cleaning" of the planet. There would be massacres and desolation everywhere. Also in London, Sister Marie Gabriel anticipated a comet that would wipe out the earth, although she said that the worst effects of the comet could be averted if governments would end immorality by preventing lewd displays and drug abuse. Her warning was initially associated with the comet that hit Jupiter in 1994, and she rescheduled the catastrophe several times as she continued to predict that the comet was imminent and particularly to argue that the United States, for "poisoning the world with evil films," could be its prime target. Many of these prophets reported having had religious visions since childhood—Rabanne glimpsed the apocalyptic beasts when he was a boy. Another British prophet, a medium, was regularly visited by White Arrow, the celestial incarnation of the son of Sitting Bull, who claimed that irrefutable signs of the world's end would emerge, perhaps from Egypt, "in a month or two." Intense personal conviction characteristically combined with despair at the wanton ways of the modern world in the apocalyptic formulas. The prophets not only spoke on street corners but also wrote the inevitable books, usually combining their own prophecies with calculations that they claimed were based on the Bible. And, of course, they gave interviews, when reporters periodically decided that this sort of thing was news. Although Western Christianity anchored most of the prophets (especially in Protestant areas; Catholics were more resistant), Korean Christians got into the act with one forecast that the world would end in 1992; this particular prophet issued bonds on the strength of his vision, with due dates a few months after the world's end, when money would, of course, be worthless (on the basis of which he cleared a tidy $345,000). Neither African nor Latin American Christians have generated much millennialism, and the millennial strain was absent from the non-Christian majority in the world.

Within the Western context, quite clearly, the millennial subcurrent remains hardy if largely subterranean. Shorn of a conventional target with the end of the Cold War, it may seize all the more eagerly on the coming calendar marker as an outlet for intensely felt fears. Largely ignored by most people in the West, the current will be reported in the press—as it should be, because it is unquestionably interesting. These reports, we can also safely anticipate, may convey a sense that the current runs stronger than it actually does. Reporters are not eager to dampen their own stories by statistical assessments. ("Lifestyle" news is notoriously impressionistic.) It is also true that it is hard to establish a full sense of how widespread the public openness to apocalyptic visions is. A few polls have claimed that upwards of 40 percent of all Americans believe the end of the world is imminent, but these polls are as shy about producing evidence as they are bold in seeking publicity. Scientific method is not an apocalyptic staple.

The apocalyptic vision lives on not only because it has precedent (a more complex precedent than its advocates acknowledge). It has proved immune to repeated failures in predictions. It provides people with an alternative to the rigid, rationalistic scientific framework that dominates our culture; it is a shout that this framework is too narrow and may be missing the most essential, ominous developments that surround us. Of course, in the recent past there have been other enthusiasms that break out of the rationalistic mold—witness the long UFO furor—but now millennialism is trendiest. It attracts unreconstructed Christians, ordinary folks who feel unrepresented by standard discourse, and even scientists, like some of the leading doomsday calculators, who apply intricate numerology to unscientific data. Millennialism can capture at least a piece of many minds.

Over the next few years, we can count on more and more prophecies and visions, and we can anticipate that reports of these prophecies and visions will be designed to titillate us and perhaps fill us with a bit of dread, as reporters try to sell copy and balance skepticism with enough credulity to be able to say, if anyone is around after Doomsday to listen, "I told you so." Playing with the idea of the end is simply too much fun, and the idea is too close to modern anxiety to ignore. Finally, we can be sure that these same reports will compound the deeply ingrained mythology about the first Christian millennium and other aspects of the apocalyptic tradition—although, if we are lucky, we might also see more commitment to accuracy, as one way of greeting either doom or (as I think much more likely) the prosaic first years of the next millennium with greater self-respect.

Recent political developments in the United States, highlighted by the conservative landslide in the congressional elections in 1994, have caused some to speculate that millennial fervor is about to take off again. Christian extremes are on the march, and despite their good reasons to hesitate, they may certainly trumpet the most extreme Christian message about the apocalypse. After all, Reagan's secretary of the interior James Watt, himself highly conservative and a leading member of the Assembly of God, was once reported as saying that there was no need to worry about environmental protection because the world would end well before much further damage could be done. But even our odd current political mood has two sides. Christians, even conservatives, do not necessarily predict a specific time for the apocalypse—majority Christians never have, and for good reason. And eager Republicans, with a whole host of reforms that they want to pass immediately, may well discourage millennial thinking lest it lead their followers to a sense that political programs don't matter much anyway with only a few years of human history left. Why bother attacking welfare cheats if the Day of Judgment is at hand? Forecasting how much millennialism we'll be treated to, beyond the rhetoric of a stubborn minority and the reportage of a sensationalist press, is not easy, even though the millennium is imminent.

Another uncertainty involves terrorism and more general religious clash. Religious tensions have risen at the end of the century, given resurgent movements in Islam and Hinduism as well as some Christian revival; some argue that religious disputes may replace social clashes, and certainly millennial sentiments could be spurred by belligerent religious rhetoric and specific new conflicts in places like the Holy Land. Terrorism is less novel, but some terrorists may be inspired by millennialism to new acts of violence—an element in recent outbreaks in Japan and in the Branch Davidian movement in the United States. In turn, revived terrorism, from whatever source, could spur apocalyptic nervousness among other citizens, particularly if U.S. vulnerability to these acts increases.

It is important not to exaggerate. The millennial virus is small. Reports of its incidence, though rightly suggesting that Westerners in the mainstream culture too often ignore ripples beneath the surface, invariably have a *National Enquirer* tone about them precisely because, as news, the prophets of the apocalypse have trouble rising above the status of a freak show. Barring the unforeseen catastrophe, most Americans will probably continue moving toward the millennium with barely a thought that there might be some radical change in direction—much as most people seem to have done a thousand years ago. It's revealing not only that most millennial products have not sold widely to date but also that many publishers, ever timid, shy away from the subject on the grounds that its market is too small.

Even with the spread of conservative Christianity, for example, most religious leaders avoid the apocalyptic mode, which of course is not firmly anchored in the Christian tradition in any event. While forecasts from 1988 to 1990 won attention, repetition since that time has possibly dulled their impact and reduced the potential audience—although any striking statement can get a moment of newscasters' attention in the contemporary era.

The small but interesting series of efforts to revive the millennial myth beyond the ranks of the faithful minority actually may have trailed off after their brief surge of the late 1980s. Of course, the efforts may revive again. The myth is simply too widespread for us not to anticipate some repetition as the popular media take up the millennial pursuit. But we may not be subjected to as many deliberate attempts to distort history to sow cultish anxiety as the pseudohistories of authors like Erdoes seemed to portend a few years back. The fact that the myth of the year 1000 was revived, for different purposes than its Enlightenment and anticlerical creators had intended, was very interesting. Along with other New Age efforts, such as the anticipatory celebrations of the Mayan cycle, these revivals seemed to indicate a major push to set the millennium up as a countercultural monument. The interruption of this same movement is equally interesting: Despite the dangers of the nuclear age and other undeniable threats, we may not be as vulnerable to a mystifying presentation of millennial precedent as might have been expected.

To be sure, Hillel Schwartz, in his mixture of admirable history and sensationalism, claims that there are parallels between the late 20th century and the late 10th, that both point to a momentous and awestruck greeting of the millennium. In his account, untroubled by precise references, UFO sightings and cases of schizophrenia—the modern equivalents of comets and apocalyptic anxiety—are already increasing. (There is no evidence for either claim.) The year 2000, Schwartz asserts, will be "nervous," just as he claims its millennial ancestor was.

But very recent history has not been entirely kind to the pseudoreligious, pseudoscientific seers. AIDS, a genuine problem, has not yet turned into a massive epidemic (outside parts of East Africa). Environmental issues, at least as genuine, remain a bit unfocused; there is no premillennial crisis yet. Above all, the great events of the end of this millennium seem to have occurred, inconveniently, in 1989–1991, and they reduced fears of nuclear war while also breaking up the West's most convenient Antichrist, the "evil empire" of the Soviet Union. Even environmental concern has dropped off, as evidenced by declining support for groups like the Sierra Club. Despite the conversion of apocalyptics to environmental scenarios, most Americans, rightly or wrongly, judge that we are making progress on this issue. Perhaps we would not have sustained a substantial countercultural millennial movement in any event. Perhaps (heretical thought) historical accuracy would have cut through the misleading statements about the year 1000 as one basis for invoking fear and uncertainty around this next millennium. The current mood in the United States and Western Europe does not seem cosmically adrift. We're deeply worried, but mainly about jobs and the economy, which are not the stuff of apocalyptic visions.

This mood may yet change before the millennium occurs. Here I must hedge my own forecasting bets, given the uncertain boundarylines surrounding the apocalyptic minority. New Age thinking continues, although its millennial focus is, at the very least, inconsistent, given its greater interest in good health and moonstones. Other small millennial groups, including a new, violent fringe, agitate assiduously. There are unquestionably people in the United States who need to find alternatives to dominant scientific–materialist values. Widespread reports by the mid-1990s of Americans' increased interest in the existence and role of angels show an attitude that could return to some variant of apocalyptic projections. Natural events—for example, a new blast from a volcano like Mexico's Popocatepetl, which last really rocked its region about two thousand years ago (it's easy to get caught up in millennial number crunching!)—could provide renewed support for apocalyptic thinking. More specifically, the millennial idea itself burns brightly in some important Christian sects, at least in the United States. The Church of Jesus Christ of Latter-Day Saints has long emphasized a millennial vision. It has updated the list of apocalyptic signs to include, for example, threats to the U.S. Constitution, and it has added the Elders of the Church as divine agents to right wrongs. But essentially its vision is quite traditional, stressing Revelation's thousand years of peace but carefully avoiding any particular calendar date. Official doctrine explicitly warns against predictions of when the millennium will occur. The millennial emphasis, however, has encouraged some ordinary Mormons (who are allowed to speak up during church services as part of Mormon practice) to build vivid anticipations of dire occurrences to come around the year 2000. Here, clearly, is a spark that could spread in this church, and perhaps beyond, as we move through the late 1990s. Not only among Mormons but among conservative Christians generally, there is an existing millennial subculture that fluctuates in size and visibility.

Even apart from these current signs of cultural diversity, our vulnerability to the millennial legend may still increase. One might argue, somewhat ironically, that our culture, with its belief in rationality and our ability to control the natural and social environment, may be more open to an attack of millennial anxiety than would a more religious society. We have seen that, in fact, a less developed calendar sense and religious assurances, combined with theological opposition to any millennial extremism, worked rather well around the year 1000 to preserve a mood of equanimity. Given that we have less faith in divine guidance and that we are faced with active efforts to rouse anxiety over our responses to the coming millennium, one might have assumed a different outcome today. So far, however, a certain tranquillity prevails in our time as well. Rather than asking, "Should we be afraid?" the better question, both for the present and for the year 1000, might be, "Why so calm?" And for both times, although for different reasons, the question can be answered.

Thus, along with the primary insistence on the need for a more disinterested appraisal of the year 1000, it is worth noting that the first attempts to stir millennial anxieties for the year 2000 seem to have misfired even as a fringe interest— and we're now very close to the millennium. It is still provocative to ask if we will be afraid, and if we should be. The historical reminder is that our ancestors, in a more religious age, do not seem particularly to have feared their millennial event. The current indication is that we may not generate much fear either, despite excited talk on the fringes. This means, in turn, that we need to discuss some different contexts for approaching our millennium; dramatic but distorted history will not serve.

Six

ASSESSING AND FORECASTING MILLENNIA: BEYOND THE APOCALYPSE

WESTERN CULTURE (AND SOME OTHER CULTURES) unquestionably harbors traditions that can anticipate catastrophic change or utopian bliss (or both, one after the other). Fears about nuclear catastrophe or an overwhelming global "population bomb" (an image popularized in the early 1970s but now somewhat faded), although they reflect real issues, may have in part reflected this apocalyptic impulse as well. The idea of associating this impulse to a calendar date, such as a new millennium, is less rooted in tradition than might be imagined, as we have seen in the preceding chapters. Nevertheless, evocation of real or (more often) mythical precedents may still create some nervous anticipations as we approach the year 2001. Certainly there are some authors and groups that would like to heighten this nervous anticipation, either to correct complacency, as an expression of deep belief, or as an extension of personal motives or stresses. There is scant historical reason for them to succeed because there is no real millennial precedent of this sort, and the mood as we near the late 1990s, although recognizing a host of specific problems, does not seem conducive to widespread, free-floating anxiety. But there may still be a tremor or two as the date looms closer.

Is there an alternative way to understand the millennium as a unit of time, a way that would not seek to apply the apocalyptic impulse and would not try to force the historical record to provide dramatic precedents? Does the millennium now coming to a close have some other kind of meaning? And can this serve as the basis of looking for meaning in the millennium to come?

The best way to approach these questions is to do with the millennium what has often been done, over the past three hundred years, at the close of each century: that is, to see what trends described the past unit of time and on this basis, admittedly more tentatively, discuss what trends may shape the same unit of time in the future. I will describe in Chapter 8 how this was done during the transition between the 19th and the 20th centuries. First, though, I must complete our discussion of the admittedly less wieldy, less familiar millennium.

Historians do not usually think in terms of millennia. Whereas histories of particular centuries abound—"England in the 18th century," "the United States, 1900 to the present"—one is hard-pressed to find the millennial time frame. In recent decades, French social historians have developed the concept of the *longue durée,* or extended time period, to take into account how very slow change can be in certain basic human institutions and habits. The great Fernand Braudel thus wrote his massive history of Mediterranean society over the *longue durée,* focusing particularly on some of the stubborn rhythms of peasant life, but he organized his work in terms of several centuries, not a whole millennium. I know of no serious history, in fact, that has used a millennial time frame. Even world history textbooks, which do normally cover many thousands of years, eschew any organization by millennia. Their key periods are usually shorter—for again, even societies that cling to tradition usually change too often for a millennium to be meaningful. I do expect that some histories of the millennium will be produced to grace coffee tables over the next few years—one ambitious entry has already appeared—and it is certainly valid to play off even passing public interest. But there is no extensive basis for looking at the past millennium as a meaningful unit, as opposed to an arbitrary, if long, collection of things that happened.

Furthermore, even if an overview does embrace a thousand years or more—as one might in dealing with ancient Egyptian or Mesopotamian history or China's imperial government, which lasted well over two thousand years with only periodic interruptions—the starting and stopping points have nothing to do with a tidy millennial calendar. A few basic patterns—the Bronze Age, the Iron Age, or even the duration of the Chinese concept of the emperor as the Son of Heaven—last two millennia or more, but these provide background frameworks for the real stuff of history, quite apart from their stubborn failure to align with any single calendar millennium. Most historical trends—the patterns that really shape a particular historical period, including the present—have a shorter life span, particularly as change has accelerated over the past several centuries. And whether in ancient or modern history, major new regimes or wars or even economic and social developments like changes in the birthrate or new family forms rarely coincide with calendar regularities.

Events are particularly untidy. Their resolute calendrical randomness bedeviled efforts to tie predictions to precise dates a thousand years ago (remember Joachim of Fiore, not to mention the few millennial ventures), just as the distraction of major developments between 1989 and 1991 has stolen some of the thunder from our own imminent turn of the millennium. Consult any standard historical chronology: Relatively little happened, of major import, anywhere in the world during the years 1000 and 1001. Just to stick to Western Europe: The date of the great French event closest to the millennium is 987, the date of the ascendancy of the Capetian royal house; the English date is 1066, of course, and the event, the Norman invasion; the German, 1024, the advent of the Salian house of emperors; the Spanish, 1031, the death of the last single caliph to rule Muslim Spain. The year 1000 is sometimes used as the date for Scandinavian conversion to Christianity, but it is a century too late for Sweden and a bit too early (1014 is better) for the completion of the process in Denmark; only Norway works out more closely. The point is obvious: Historical changes are too helter-skelter even to be tied to a century, much less to a millennial focal point.

If, then, we are presented with efforts to find coherent meaning in the second Christian millennium, skepticism is abundantly warranted. The specific year 1000 (or 1001) is not historically significant, although this may be a somewhat carping point. Because few major trends last a thousand years, the millennium now closing does not meet the analytical criterion for a historical period: It cannot be coherently described in terms of consistent internal trends.

There are, however, two exceptions, two trends that have lasted a thousand years, worth noting even if we must return then to the more general point about incoherence. Without using an explicitly millennial framework, and certainly with no apocalyptic references or obscure numerical correlates, various historians have identified two trends that run through the preceding thousand years reasonably consistently, despite a host of twists and turns. One is strictly Western European (although with international repercussions particularly during the past 150 years), the other more global.

The Rise of the Western State: A Thousand-Year Process

From about A.D. 1000 onward (the date is approximate; again, there's no magic claimed for specific years), the Western European state began to grow stronger. This pattern followed about five hundred years of political anarchy in which royal claims were usually hollow (Charlemagne's reign was a brief exception) and in which effective power rested with the local feudal lords. From the 11th century, aided by a more prosperous agricultural economy and the cessation of Viking raids, regional lords like the counts of Flanders or the dukes of Normandy began to use feudalism to build a more solid political order. Random conflict was reduced (the Peace of God movement both emerged from and supported this relief from violence). The same pattern was launched on a royal scale by the Capetians, who very gradually used their control of the territory around Paris plus their feudal claims to build up a small central French state. A tiny bureaucracy emerged, with missions to the provinces; a limited amount of specialization occurred within the royal court. The Norman conquerors of England imposed an even more structured state authority, still within a feudal context. From this point until the present, with only minor interruptions, historians can plausibly trace the growth of France and England as states; they were joined at various later points by Spain, Germany, and so on, and much later still by the United States. Feudalism was further weakened by the rise of professional armies and some direct taxes (14th–16th centuries); then a more absolute monarchy began to develop outright nation-states (17th century); and finally, revolutionary legislation, new technology, and new social issues cleared the way for even further government growth from the 19th century to the present. The interruptions were few, particularly on the European continent. England's trend slowed in the 17th century, amid new assertions of parliamentary control, and England and Norway alone saw their governments briefly shrink under the impetus of 19th-century classical liberalism (only to resume growth with a vengeance as military commitments in England and early welfare activities in both countries expanded).

For Western Europe, then, the past millennium has meant a surprisingly consistent, if very general, political trend. Some medievalists have indeed talked about the beginnings of political "modernization" going back to the 12th, if not the 11th, century. Historians of past periods do tend once in a while to try to popularize their subjects by linking them with what's going on today, so some caution is warranted. But it is genuinely true in Western history (although not in that of China, Africa, or the Middle East) that a focus on the origins and emergence of the modern state over a thousand-year period has some validity. Government functions have gradually (and at some points, quite rapidly) expanded; bureaucracies have developed, gained in self-definition, and grown; taxes have been collected and the size of peacetime military (and later police) forces have fairly consistently increased.

Coincidentally, then—historians would claim no magic in the year 1000, simply a roughly accurate starting point for a long-term governmental change—a political process began a thousand years ago that has to some definable extent continued to this day, despite the huge differences between the modern state and the intentions of the hesitant royal centralizers of the mid–Middle Ages. Perhaps there are other trends in Western society, such as the growth of cities, that can be added in to provide some coherence to our glance back at the past millennium.

A few historians have gone beyond this political statement to argue that a larger process of social change began to take shape in Western Europe around the year 1000 that, again in very general form, has continued to the present day. To quote one study, by Katherine Lynch, of Western family history: "The year 1000 ushered in an extended 'historical moment'; a lengthy and protracted process in which a new social formation took shape. A new kind of society emerged in the centuries after the year 1000 when many novel processes—religious and spiritual, legal and constitutional, social and economic, technological and demographic—created a social mutation." That is, not only the growth of the state but also the rise of cities and greater trade, plus some improvements in agricultural methods and some re-laxation of manorialism, combined to usher in several basic social changes that created a society that we could recognize as the earliest form of a modern society, at least more clearly than would be possible if we looked at the society of the year 900, when cities were still vestigial, agricultural productivity was still held back by rudimentary techniques, and so on. It is also possible, as already suggested, that historians will be tempted into a new look at the year 1000 as the beginning of a wider period simply because the thousand-year unit will attract greater attention as 2000 nears. While it is common enough to see the 10th and 11th centuries as a point of revival in European medieval history, the implication that there is some unbroken chain between this point and modern social and economic forms is less common. And, as we will elaborate below, there are a number of problems with the claim, far more than with the narrower—although still significant—effort to trace political evolution within a coherent millennial span.

Global Connectedness: The Trend Since 1000

The other coherence is a bit less familiar, simply because world history is a newer category, but it has actually become accepted among practicing world historians, and it is the only case where survey texts may take the past millennium as a real unit. By about the year 1000—the date here, too, is simply a point of convenience, to denote a change that had gradually taken shape—contacts among major soci-eties in Asia, Europe, and Africa had intensified to the point that one can talk of the emergence of an international network, or what one historian, William Mc-Neill, calls the *ecumene*, replacing the much less significant, more sporadic con-tacts among societies that had prevailed theretofore.

Prior to this point, various societies had established regional trade: The Mediterranean had some contact with sub-Saharan Africa; India maintained more ample ties to much of Southeast Asia; China traded with Japan, Korea, and Vietnam. There was also the historic trade route that brought silk westward from China. But international trade was limited in extent and impact. Few major civi-lizations had much regular contact with each other. Religions had spread across some boundaries, bringing Chinese visitors to India to gain Buddhist wisdom, for example. Most facets of most societies, however, operated in isolation or with at most regional influences. The exceptions, such as Alexander the Great's contacts with India or China's Buddhist importations, were rare, however significant.

By 1000, the situation changed in degree and in kind. Muslim trade routes extended from Spain to China and the Philippines. They reached into many parts of Africa, both along the east coast and overland. Scandinavian traders pressed through Russia to Byzantium, where they interacted with Arab merchants; large troves of Arab coins from the 10th and 11th centuries have been found in northern Europe. Western Europe participated as well, depending heavily on Muslim and Byzantine merchants. Not only Chinese silk, but also spices, sugar, and other luxury products moved east to west, making a coherent trade zone of what historians are beginning to call Afro-Eurasia. Other contacts were involved as well: Islam converted key parts of Africa, central Asia, and Southeast Asia as well as a minority in India. Western Europe, although hostile to the Muslim faith, gained access to Muslim and Jewish philosophies, along with west Asian holdings of classical Greek learning. While international influences did not yet affect daily lives in most areas, the network was sufficiently vital that when Arab power faltered, other powers moved in to maintain the linkages. Thus, the Mongol conquerors provided vital new opportunities for east–west contact in the 13th century, which, in particular, accelerated the transfer of technology from Asia to Europe (the compass, explosive powder, and printing all came from Asia about this time). Indeed, the British periodical *The Economist* in 1995 named Genghis Khan the "man of the millennium" because of the Mongol role in world exchange. (U.S. conservatives would doubtless prefer a Western millennial man.) When the Mongol moment passed, China briefly experimented with a role as an international carrier with its great trading expeditions of the 15th century. And by the time this brief initiative was canceled in 1433, Western Europe, although still backward in many ways, was beginning to reach out for its own direct routes to various parts of Africa and Asia. Europeans were motivated in large part by the appetites that international trade had stimulated and also by their clear inferiority in the terms of trade. Greater merchant initiative might help compensate for the fact that Europe had few attractive goods to offer on the world market. Thus, the Western European surge, which would sponsor the next steps in world contacts, itself reflected the importance of the network that had already been created.

Although the cast of characters has changed many times—including in our own century with the emergence of Japan and the Pacific Rim as international leaders—the basic pattern is indeed about a thousand years old. Commercial links, and with them significant cultural interactions and recurrent military and diplomatic involvements, have been modifying the essential independence of major civilizations for ten centuries. As with the growth of the Western state, the results by the 20th century would surely be unrecognizable to some of the early international players of the 11th century. The amount, speed, and range of world contact would dazzle and probably terrify the pioneering merchants, missionaries, and scholar-translators. But the evolution has a certain historical consistency even so; it is the second millennial process that can legitimately be defined in a retroactive assessment.

It is not yet clear how much attention will be given to coherent millennial trends as we wrap up one thousand-year span and prepare for another. Again, we have no traditions to guide us. Clearly, evocations of the apocalypse, particularly if they are not constrained by historical accuracy, are much flashier than more sober assessments. And the apocalyptics don't really care what happened in the past thousand years; what counts for them is the future, or rather, its imminent absence in terrestrial terms. Nevertheless, in case we shift toward more systematic assessments, it is worth knowing that, however unfamiliar, the thousand-year period now passing has spun a few durable threads, with each new period building on preceding developments that can be traced back to approximately the 10th century. Certainly we should be wary of any millennial account that merely stresses how different we are from our 11th-century ancestors.

The Messiness of Historical Time

Nevertheless, most of the trends that really shape our time are of fairly recent vintage. Again, we come back to the stubborn fact that relatively few of the basic features of modern history have been around for more than three or four centuries. Without venturing anything like textbook thoroughness, let me mention a few obvious cases in point:

- Virtually all the technologies we take for granted, particularly those dependent on power sources, are less than 250 years old, and most are newer still. The Industrial Revolution, which took shape from the 1760s onward, totally transformed the technological environment, for better or worse, creating a huge divide from the earlier centuries in this millennium.
- The dominance of science in Western culture and education goes back only 350 years. Although it is risky to pretend to define a modern mentality, one historian, Paul Hazard, has plausibly argued that characteristic modern intellectual trends date from the 1680s, including a tendency to believe in secular progress, a clear official disavowal of beliefs in witchcraft and magic, and

a reduction in the valuation of religion, as well as the commitment to science itself. The modernist counterpart in the arts, and particularly the idea of great individual stylistic freedom and the value of innovation and nonrepresentational forms, is newer still, going back to the 1820s at best. As in technology, the importance of fundamental and fairly recent changes in Western and world cultures makes it impossible to find any substantial meaning in longer time spans.

• The demographic structure we are accustomed to, with very few infant deaths and a long life expectancy, is only a century old. Although the birthrate began to decline in the United States and Western Europe a bit earlier (1790s in the United States), the unprecedented shifts in infant mortality unfolded between 1880 and 1920. Here again, a vital facet of life has surprisingly recent origins.

• The separation of work from the household began to become common only during the 19th century. Contemporary technology, particularly computer linkages, may modify this separation in the future, but for the moment, the idea of "going off" to work and its implications for other aspects of family life, including care of children, is another crucial characteristic of daily life that is less than two hundred years old, and more novel still, of course, for most married women. Ironically, this relocation of work occurred only a bit after a major redefinition of the home (from the 17th century onward in Western Europe and North America) to include more family-centered and elaborate meals, conversation, and furnishings.

• The importance of hospitals in medical care—another for-better-or-worse modern phenomenon—dates to the 1870s; before then, hospitals were rare and almost always rejected by any ill person who had enough money to arrange for care at home by the family. The probability that one will die in a hospital, instead of in one's own home, is scarcely half a century old in the United States and less than that in Western Europe.

• The notion that a vitally significant aspect of life consists of acquiring new objects and that certain kinds of goods express one's personality and passions—that is, the essence of consumerism—seems to have originated in the 18th century. Of course, it has accelerated since, but historians are making a pretty good case that the roots of the phenomenon—another taken-for-granted aspect of modern life—can be seen almost three hundred years ago. There is, however, no millennial pattern here.

• Substantial capitalism in Western economic operations—that is, the idea that maximization of gain constitutes a valid and accepted economic goal— has somewhat older credentials. Although not dominant, it began to gain ground by the 13th century. By that time, Western European Christianity had started to loosen its strictures against profit seeking. Again, however, even in rudimentary form the system is well under a thousand years old. Widespread capitalism emerged as European trade expanded internationally and internally in the 16th and 17th centuries. Although the American colonies were wrapped up in this larger capitalist order, a comparable internal conversion to a capitalist market economy in the United States occurred only 180 years ago, in the early 19th century (and, as a number of recent histories have indicated, was achieved amid considerable stress and self-doubt). This staple of modern Western life does antedate other key features, including essential cultural and technological strands, but it is hardly millennial.

- And a humble final instance. The idea that urine is disgusting, to be dealt with in private, seemingly such a deep impulse in our private habits and in our treatment of infants and the elderly, is only about two hundred years old in our culture. Only three hundred years ago, many Dutch people brushed their teeth with urine, noting is cleansing effects, while in parts of Wales a courting custom had young men urinating on the dresses of their intended brides as a sign of possession and commitment. How much has changed, even in human disgust and sensory reactions, and by historical standards how recently!

The point is obvious and doubtless readily accepted: Most of the features that define life today go back to a series of changes in Western history that date variously from the 17th to the 19th centuries; a few are more recent still. Of course, the 20th century has ushered in important variants of almost all the modern trends, from technology to culture, and it has introduced some key new directions; we must return to this issue in a later chapter. But even though a day-before-yesterday approach to the origins of contemporary life is seriously misleading, given the persistent importance of the cultural and capitalist transformations of the 17th century and then the Industrial Revolution of the early 19th, change has accelerated in modern times. The same point also applies on a worldwide scale, although the origins and precise contours of modern trends would differ from the Western model sketched above.

Even the two trends that do offer some millennial credentials underwent important modern redefinitions. A growth of state and bureaucracy patterns did begin to emerge a thousand years ago, but it has been altered almost beyond recognition by the advent first of constitutional, parliamentary government and then of political democracy (17th–19th centuries); by the technological changes in the capacities of the state, including its weaponry; and by revisions in the functions attributed to the state in the areas of economic planning and social welfare (19th–20th centuries). No discussion of the modern state can rely on a straight-line evolution from the 11th century to today.

The same holds true for the emergence of an international network. It is important to realize that international contacts took on a new and in some respects modern importance well before the "rise of the West." But the inclusion of the Americas in the international network, beginning in the 1490s, made a huge difference in the nature of world contacts, not only to the American continents but to the Old World centers now open to American crops like the potato and to other new influences. And, of course, the impact of industrial communications and transportation technology, in shrinking the world from the 1830s onward, introduced yet another redefinition.

There is no need to belabor the point. Most Americans accept, sometimes far too readily, the idea that our world is of fairly recent vintage. The impulse to make sense of our whole millennium is probably not great. While a few trends that shape our lives do date back, in an original but genuinely recognizable form, about a thousand years, most of the factors that actively create our social environment cannot be traced to such remote sources. Historians and theorists who talk of the "modernization" of Western or world society or of specific features like government never go back more than a few hundred years. In the face of superficial, presentist impulses that see even the 19th century as an irrelevant, archaic past, it is important to note that a few forces active in our society are roughly a thousand years old; nevertheless, no serious historical case can be made for millennial coherence.

Perhaps, if only to find some alternative to the apocalyptic approach, some end-of-millennium reviews will attempt to build a case. I can well imagine some historians, aware of the trends that can be defined and eager to challenge the depressing born-yesterday approach to the past so characteristic of contemporary students and probably of the public at large, trying to build a larger edifice, seized with a scholarly version of millennial enthusiasm. But I don't think it can be done. Our vital origins are scattered, certainly not all brand-new despite our frequent conviction that no society has ever been called upon to change as much as ours has. But, save in a few aspects, our origins are centuries, not a millennium, old.

The relative newness of the trends that shape our lives has two further implications, less obvious but possibly more important in guarding against millennial overexcitement. The first implication has to do with progress, the second with prophecy.

A Millennium of Progress?

A dominant strand of U.S. culture has long been its commitment to a belief in progress. The authors of our independence believed in progress and justified the institutions of a new republic in terms of the human capacity to craft a better political society. Our school systems have long taught the virtues of progress: For example, we once had slavery, now we do not, and although there still may be some racial problems, a commitment to harmony and decency will alleviate them in our better future. History has been taught progressively, whether implicitly or explicitly. The past is worse than the present, a few nostalgic points perhaps aside.

Whether we still really believe in progress is an interesting and difficult question to which I will return in Part II in talking not about millennia but about centuries. There is enough vestigial commitment that a journalistic approach to the millennium may seek to cast aside apocalyptic visions as outdated but replace them with the terms of progress. We can tell ourselves how much better off we are now, near the year 2000, than our benighted ancestors were a millennium before. Progressive views of history have long been comforting: If we have some uncertainties about our present and future, at least we can be sure we're superior to the past. Given the difficulties of finding millennial meanings in other respects, the progressive temptation may be hard to resist.

Whether one finds the idea of progress over the past thousand years useful or not is partly a matter of taste. Even a guide to the millennium that seeks to anticipate nonsense cannot resolve everything. But there are at least three dangers in the progressive approach that should qualify any overeager embrace.

First, of course, is the problem of standards: By what standards do we measure progress? If we are to claim progress in any meaningful way, we need to acknowledge the magnitude of any assessment effort. Selectivity is a constant but misleading temptation. Of course modern technology surpasses that of the year 1000; score one for progress. But how does one factor in the dark side of technology, the environmental degradation and the massive increase in the deadliness of war? Wars in the year 1000 could be devastating and terrifying for the small regions affected, but nothing like the total war experience of the 20th century was imaginable. And even if by the standard of technological change the present emerges on the plus side, how does it compare on standards that our ancestors would have valued more, such as spirituality or comforting rituals? It would be hard to argue for progress in these areas unless one is a confirmed rationalist who argues that we are better off without these crutches in any event. Many Muslims, with standards different from those of most Americans, might well argue that there has been a pattern of deterioration since the year 1000, recalling the strength of the faith a thousand years ago and the high tide of Arab dominance in Afro-Eurasia. Henry Adams, just a century ago, made a similar point about the losses since an age of greater faith, in his nostalgic *Mont Saint Michel and Chartres,* a book worth a renewed glance once in a while.

Take a more neutral topic, like child rearing (the technology assessment tends to pander to what our culture finds important, whereas religion and ritual assessments automatically favor the Middle Ages). Historians have contended that modern society has gained ground steadily in its enlightened treatment of children, and although the most extreme argument has been disproved—medieval people loved their children, too—some vestiges remain plausible. We beat our children less than medieval parents did. We force them to work less. We certainly spend more time worrying about whether we're doing right by our offspring. But does this add up to progress? Beating, some experts note, is not necessarily harmful if it's consistent and moderate. The separation of work from home may do more damage to many children, thanks to parental absence, than a harsher system of discipline. Our constant worry about our treatment of children may indicate more guilt and aimlessness than benevolence. The claim that child rearing and attitudes toward children have changed over time is quite valid, and it is important. The assertion that change has definitely constituted an advance, either in the experience of childhood or in children's preparation for adult roles, is much less secure.

To be sure, most Americans would not care to go back to the year 1000 for more than a brief visit (our medieval ancestors definitely did not take American Express). But this is a misleading way to measure claims of millennial progress, for we are trapped by our own habits and cultural standards, especially in the area of creature comforts. Unquestionably, for a consumerist or even someone fussy about toilet arrangements, the late 20th century is better. But a real judgment of progress must shake off this presentist trap and consider a wider range of gains and losses from a more neutral vantage point: Both the range and the effort at neutrality are vital. It cannot be an easy call, beyond the obvious fact that the year 1000 loses if the criteria focus on the production of goods and the ability to sustain large (perhaps overlarge) populations.

The first point, then, involves a recognition of the subjectivity of claims for progress and the need to encompass a broad spectrum of developments rather than favoring a few areas in which modern society excels but by whose glitter it can be blinded. There is no science here, and real humility is essential. These are issues that must occupy us further as we evaluate what we're likely to be thinking about at the dawn of a new calendar age.

The second point is much more precise, though in fact it relates to the problem of measuring advance. Any claim of progress must be careful about the historical baseline. If we want to point to an advance over the course of the millennium, we need a solid and empathic picture of how things were a thousand years ago. Facile assumptions about medieval backwardness, of the sort favored by those French historians who perpetrated the myth of millennial fear and gullibility, will not do.

Medieval Europeans, not to mention the more advanced Arabs or Chinese, were not as stupid or credulous as is held by a lingering historiographical tradition that tried to prove progress by vilifying the past.

It is the third point, however, that relates most closely to the historian's concern about the millennium as a real unit of historical time. Assertions of a thousand years of progress may make pleasant reading as we plan our third-millennium party, but if they imply a coherent, purposeful evolution since the year 1000, they are almost surely wrong; as we have seen, there really was no coherent evolution. The comparison between the years 2000 and 1000, however provocative, is essentially random because there are so many twists and turns in between. Not even material culture moved continuously forward: The Western European economy was much more capable of sustaining its population and even providing for growth in 1000 than it was in 1300, when stark famine returned, soon to be joined by a several-century cycle of plague. Of course, conditions later improved. Serious gains in agricultural capacity began in the late 17th century; by then, the worst of the plagues had ended as well. To be sure, since the mid-1970s, as per capita income has slipped in the United States, we might wonder about renewed oscillations even in basic material life. While a comparison between A.D. 2000 and 1000 shows progress, then, it was not, in fact, along any straight line. And if this is true in the material sphere, it applies even more vividly to more amorphous facets of life. Bonds of male friendship, often tight in the Middle Ages, may have suffered deterioration in the more commercial, competitive environment of the 17th century. But they revived, at least among young adults, in a distinctive pattern of very expressive friendships in the 19th century, only to deteriorate again in our own age. Again, a 2000–1000 comparison would show differences but would conceal the vital zigzags that make up the real historical record and (for those left cold by historical niceties) the real background for our life today. The point has already been made: Apart from all the other nuances, claims of progress or deterioration for a whole modern millennium reach for a coherence that is not there. Only an assessment that involves the development either of bureaucratic capacity (in the West) or of international contacts—neither one usually at the head of our list of progress claims—can accurately envisage the whole time span.

I do not mean to argue against using the turn of the millennium to provide a useful point to talk about historical trajectories and how their qualities should be assessed. Century turns have involved exactly such open-ended discussions for the last several hundred years. But facile evaluations, including those that claim a character for the second millennium that it simply did not have, are mere assertions; they carry no weight except perhaps in mirroring what we wish were true about our capacity to improve steadily upon the past.

Millennial Forecasting: A Nonstarter

The complexity of the millennium now ending also cautions against forecasting about the millennium to come. We actually have no tradition for millennial predictions other than the apocalyptic one, which reflects the real impossibility of looking so far ahead in the terms by which we usually think about the future (apocalypse aside). Shorter-term projections have a lively role in our culture, just as they did at the turn of the past century; this range we can take up later on. But what will life be like in the year 3000? No harm inventing for a bit, so long as we know it's merely a guessing game. Even science fiction adepts, one of the real sources and mirrors of our vision of futures, have not tried to reach so far. No one in the year 1000 could have foreseen the complexity of intervening trends—the changes in culture, demography, and technology—that formed the real context for what turned out to be the millennial future. And despite all our gains in knowledge, there's no reason to think we can do better now. Perhaps some latter-day Nostradamus will give it a shot, and Godspeed. But what we do know about the way history works must inhibit anything more than educated, almost surely inaccurate, speculations. Major changes supervene too often, not just adding new and unanticipated details but providing totally new historical directions. If, as many believe and as can be plausibly argued, the pace of change has accelerated, our crystal ball is even cloudier now than it was a thousand years ago. We simply have no real idea of what the technology, the basic culture, the family habits of our millennial descendants will be.

Even prognostications about the two trends that can be identified as running through the past millennium must be chancy; merely because they lasted for one thousand-year span is no assurance for the future. It seems probable that international contacts will continue to intensify for a while—the collapse of the Iron Curtain shows how difficult it is to remain even somewhat apart from the international mainstream. But vigorous forces of cultural particularism, from Bosnia to Quebec to Islam, may complicate this assertion even in the short run. And who knows what kind of international contacts a possibly intergalactic next millennium will hold?

Predicting some continued increase in the power of the state and its bureaucracy might be another fairly safe short-term bet. Western states have expanded over the past century, thanks to wars and welfare, and most states in other parts of the world have tried to imitate Western forms (even if they shun Western ways in other respects). But here, too, the clouds of unpredictability quickly form. Recent efforts to cut back on welfare obligations and the even wider international trend toward reducing the state's role in economic planning (not only in former Communist countries and China but also in India and Latin America) may open a much more uncertain prospect even for the 21st century. In the United States, the Republicans may succeed in cutting back rather than merely slowing modern government, although they rather like its massive military arm. Ronald Reagan and Margaret Thatcher failed to reduce the role of government, but maybe the new push will last longer. And after that, who knows?

Even if we could point to coherence in the past millennium, trying to guess what a comparable coherence would be in the future would be risky in the extreme. But what we do know, based on modern history, immensely heightens the risk. Fundamental shifts in direction occur too often and too unpredictably to allow precise predictions, even though contemporaries are sometimes too glib in claiming that everything is changing once again. There is historical coherence, but over shorter terms. Perhaps historical complexity is widely enough recognized that debunking erroneously precise projections will not be a necessary part of an enlightened embrace of the new millennium. Perhaps those people who want headline glamor will stick to the apocalyptic mode, warning of some sort of divine challenge in our future rather than claiming to assess trends. But in case there is an effort to outline the next millennium in a more standard forecasting mode, we can be properly warned: However entertaining, however much we might wish to know what will happen over that expanse of future, it can't really be done. Millennia, past or future, do not have that kind of meaning.

Seven

TRANSITION: FROM
MILLENNIA TO CENTURIES

I NOTED IN THE PREFACE THAT I HAVE LONG BEEN FASCINATED with the prospect of living into a new century and when I later became aware of it, a new millennium. As I matured, I also came to view the process of getting from one age to the next with a certain amount of dread. The possibility of an inordinate amount of journalistic or commercial balderdash seemed distressingly great.

A look at the historical perspectives available on the millennium confirms the need for a cautious approach. We have ample precedent for wholesale fabrications about what happened the last time a millennium occurred. We are offered enough nonsense in our various media; there is no need to add spurious "fact" about the coming millennium to the list. Thus, an anticipatory skepticism seems warranted. We need to beware of claims that the millennium is somehow a preternatural unit of time—a simple comparison to the views of other times and cultures reminds us of the artificiality of our calendar, and a reading of Revelation and Christian theology cautions against invocations of divine sanction. We can also be skeptical about claims—should they surface—to find coherent patterns in the past millennium, beyond a not uninteresting but minimal set of trends, and certainly about claims to stake out patterns likely to define the millennium to come. The actual history of apocalyptic prophecy also seems to be unencouraging to those who seek to rouse a special nervousness today, particularly when they so often distort the past in the process. Here, to be sure, a special kind of faith may defy sobriety, arguing that it doesn't matter what actually happened in the year 1000 or whether Nostradamus really predicted future events, since there's magic in the millennial air. But if we can't make this kind of leap of faith (or sensibly don't wish to), then skepticism surfaces again.

A skeptical approach has limits, of course, quite apart from the fact that there are complexities in talking about past prophecies or the actual coherence of the second millennium. Carefully debunking fanciful claims is undramatic, and although this book takes a distinctive approach to the millennium, I can't deny some desire to grab a headline or two for myself. It's tempting to ignore my own advice and venture a more spectacular claim about the portents that will lead up to 2001. And perhaps we won't need to debunk anything. We have noted that attempts a decade ago to fan the millennial flames seem to have sputtered badly, as anxieties have not clearly continued to crest. The drama of recent events, our own preoccupation with more prosaic issues like health care or the foibles of sports heroes, and perhaps even a certain ingrained historical sense that makes us conservative when it comes to grandiose futurology may continue to combine to keep the nonsense down.

Skepticism need not spoil the millennial party. Merely because we don't have quite such dramatic precedents for millennial celebrations as might be imagined does not mean that we can't be creative. Merely because we should be aware of our limited ability to find millennial patterns does not mean that we cannot enjoy and learn from attempts to discuss progress or even to venture guesses about what the year 3000 will be like. Improving our knowledge about the millennium guards against the manipulation of our minds and against the trivialization of our approach to past and future, but it need not deter flights of fancy. Some of us might even choose to indulge in some apocalyptic tremors, despite the fact that in our sober selves we know that the precedents are shaky.

Furthermore, the millennium is not all that looms. We also have a new century to contend with. At the turn of the century, apocalyptic visions have a smaller role to play. But in this case we do have a considerable if fairly modern history of looking at what time means. This history has conditioned most of us to think that centuries are important units of time, far more open to exploration and meaning than is the unfamiliar millennium. The last time the Western world greeted a new century, it made quite a fuss. Mistaken optimism was rampant, but so was an odd mood of gloom.

So there is another set of perspectives to contend with. Like our perspectives on the millennium, they invite thoughts about past patterns and future probabilities. But the scale is different, and so is the relevant history. We have seen that thinking about centuries, although a surprisingly recent development, is solidly anchored in our culture. The unit is artificial, to be sure, but there are no massive myths to contend with. Thinking about century turns offers some additional guidelines toward organizing our own celebration and receiving the various vantage points sure to be offered. Comparing what appears to be our current mood to the mood of a hundred years ago in anticipation of the 20th century promotes some further assessment of what our state of mind is and what it should be as we greet a calendar marker with which we have no direct experience but that we all know about.

Whatever the meaning of the new millennium, 21st century, here we come.

PART *two*

TURNING THE CENTURY

Figure 2 "Portrait of a Calculating Gentleman (not at all a bad looking chap) who has solved the problem as to whether we are in the Nineteenth or Twentieth Century." From *Punch* (January 10, 1900).

HAILING THE 20TH CENTURY: FIREWORKS AND FIN DE SIÈCLE

WE HAVE AN ADMIRABLY CLEAR PRECEDENT for measuring our celebration of a new century. The advent of 1900 was a big deal. The tradition of celebrating centuries, now firmly established, advanced in the midst of growing prosperity and among massive urban audiences. Few could miss a sense of excitement, whether encouraging or anxiety provoking. In contrast to the fuzzy picture of the medievals' experience of a new millennium, our nearer ancestors' thoughts on a century's passing can be easily studied. Their parties need not detain us long. They were loud and lengthy, and ours will be too. What was interesting was the mood—or rather, the moods, for people greeted the new century with great collective ambivalence.

Historians have long known about the contradictory feelings that focused on the advent of the 20th century, although there has been some tendency to emphasize one phase or the other instead of grappling with the odd combination. On the one hand, there was unusual celebration—because of urban concentration and new industrial wealth, the opportunities for display went well beyond the parties that had opened the 19th century. This celebratory mood was accompanied by statements of extraordinary optimism in looking back on the century past and, sometimes with mild qualifications, in anticipating the century to come. The unalloyed pride must strike us, as observers from a century later, as naive, possibly charming, but certainly different from anything we are likely to muster in a more jaded age. Accompanying the optimism, though, were statements of surprising pessimism and uneasiness, suggesting that the world was decaying visibly or at least that some disaster lurked in the new century. This was the fin de siècle spirit, which emerged well in advance of the century's turn. It heralded a marked dichotomy in Western culture, and it also anticipated some of the themes that would help lead a part of the West during a part of the 20th century to fascist attempts to strike a different course. Some celebrations participated in both spirits:

Many banquets and public events in the late 1890s referred to the coming new age with rituals that reflected confidence, wealth, and trepidation.

The messages for us today amid these divided reactions are several. We can certainly anticipate some of the same sorts of celebrations as greeted the dawn of the 20th century. Indeed, as we have seen, huge parties are already planned. We can expect some of the same journalistic retrospectives, spiced, of course, by our greater multimedia ability. We can surely expect some personal combinations of eagerness tempered by anxiety about what may seem to be a new age aborning. But will we also face a similar dichotomy? Can we, and should we, muster up either the optimism or the fin de siècle lassitude that so strangely combined a hundred years ago? I must first describe what actually developed and why, and then in Chapter 9 I will explore the possible analogies and departures that our own century's end may generate.

One point, by the way, was generally accepted in the English-speaking world: The century ended on December 31, 1900 (not 1899). This old dispute was not laid to rest, however. The Catholic church attempted to generate a special celebration at the end of 1899, although its U.S. branch repeated a ceremonial gesture in 1900 as well. Germany held out for 1899 as the century's end. We may well encounter similar national differences this time around, and with them disputes over who was really first to do what in the 21st century. At least, judging by the past precedent, we can avoid civil strife over the issue.

The Newspaper Bonanza

The outpouring of words was immense, quite apart from the fussy calendar debate. The expansion of the press and the increase in popular literacy guaranteed that turn-of-the-century verbiage would surpass any precedent. Newspapers and periodicals competed to produce balance sheets of gains and losses during the 19th century and often extended these into predictions about the character of the 20th century.

This sheer quantity promoted diverse visions. The *London Daily Mail,* a brand-new mass daily created only four years earlier in 1896, chose an optimistic course, claiming that the turn of the century was celebrated "all over the world by demonstrations of thankfulness and gratitude." Its lead article of the end of December was entitled "The Golden Century: One Hundred Years of Glorious Empire," and it began with these proud words: "The genius of a masterful race turns instinctively to forecast more readily than to retrospect; its leaders are ever more prone to prophesy than to search for precedent."

Not surprisingly, different views came from other places less blessed by empire. A Madrid newspaper reported that "the nineteenth century has not been kind to this country, and prayers are being universally offered tonight that the twentieth century may be more felicitous." (On balance it was not to be for Spain, although things have been looking up recently.) A Russian paper cast its greetings in gloom, with more than a hint of self-fulfilling prophecies for its upper-class audience: "One fears for the future of mankind. The most ominous sign is not the fact that the cook, servant girl and lackey want the same pleasures which not long ago were the monopoly of the rich alone, but the fact that all . . . rich and idle as well as poor and industrious, seek and demand daily amusements, gaiety and excitement—demand it all as something without which life is impossible."

But the clash of views was no mere matter of geography. Leaders of the Anglican church disputed the existence of widespread optimism. One canon voiced the "widespread sense of disappointment and anxiety among those who care most for righteousness and truth in the world." Mark Twain offered a bitter salutation speech for the new century: "I bring you the stately maiden named Christendom returning bedraggled and besmirched, dishonoured from pirate raids in Kiaochau, Manchuria, South Africa and Philippines, with her soul full of meanness, her pocket full of boodle, and her mouth full of pious hypocrisies. Give her soap and towel, but hide the looking glass."

The *Daily Mail*'s evaluation of the passing century admitted some problems, such as the decline of British agriculture and rural life and the growth of huge cities. But it could not hold back from its pride in material achievement:

> We have girdled the oceans with our harbours and encircled the world with our cables; we have crossed the sea with our ships; we have harnessed the forces of nature, and achieved over her victories which have only ceased to be wonderful because we are so familiar with their result. Chemistry has resolved matter into its elements, and seems to stand upon the very threshold of yet more stupendous conquests. The spectroscope has transported the analyst to the sun and stars. Photography has caught forms as they are. The phonograph has perpetuated transient sound. Steam and electricity have revolutionized the means of communication as machinery has revolutionized production.

To be sure, as the paper admitted in a genuinely insightful aside, this does not prove that mankind is happier. And the paper projected new problems because of worldwide hatred for Britain's empire and because "in some inscrutable manner the old fire of energy seems to be waning within us" (again, a perceptive shot). "We are entering stormy seas, and the time may be near when we shall have to fight in very truth for our life, 'neath noble stars beside a brink unknown" (not a bad foreshadowing of World War I, although admittedly the war clouds were already gathering in Europe's alliance system; one did not have to be Nostradamus to venture this rueful prediction). But the sense of confidence derived from a glorious past century was merely challenged in this view, not overturned. In contrast, the British Christian or intellectual view could be quite different, blasting the disappointments brought by the 19th century's issuance of universal suffrage (which, one government official claimed, "had disappointed its advocates and its opponents alike") and the results of mass education, which spread a trivial popular literature and led to "an enormous number of persons wishing to be clerks." Cultural leadership, it was claimed, inevitably decayed in this process, amid changes that undermined popular character as well.

Clearly, judgments about the 19th century became something of a battlefield for different perspectives, with scant common ground. What some considered gains were shocking losses to others. All that could be agreed was that an assessment was inescapable because of the magnitude of a new century's dawn.

Festivities

Dispute did not dampen celebration, where at least for a moment the optimistic current clearly predominated. The *New York Times* hailed the "Twentieth Century's Triumphant Entry." New York's City Hall was elaborately decorated, and an unprecedented crowd gathered to bury the old century and welcome the new. Lights flashed, bells peeled, sirens of harbor boats screeched, the crowd sang, and a huge fireworks display was set off. Lights and music were everywhere. City Hall was festooned with more than two thousand new lights, outlining the city's coat of arms and spelling out a gigantic "Welcome 20th Century." A variety of dignitaries offered speeches, which could not be heard.

However drowned by the din, the president of the City Council set a characteristic tone:

> We look back [on the previous century] as a cycle of time within which the achievements in science and in civilization are not less than marvelous. The advance of the human race during the past 100 years has not been equalled by the process of man within any of the preceding ages.
>
> The possibilities of the future for mankind are the subjects of hope and imagination. We shall soon be not only citizens of a Nation recognized throughout the world as the greatest, of a State pre-eminent among States, and of a city not only the metropolis of the Western world, but of the whole world. Our advance in all directions which make a city great already places our city without a parallel in the Western hemisphere, and the same progress continued will make New York without a peer among the cities of the earth, its citizens unequalled in intelligence, in education, and supplied with all the benefits and advantages which flow from civilization.

The president closed with hopes for individual rights, while urging that the "crowning glory" of the coming century should be the end of poverty and wrong amid peace and good will. His speech was followed by a song, "Der Tag des Herrn," from five hundred members of the united German singing societies of the city (German Americans played a striking role in American life at this time, before the national attack on the Huns) and the band played a Sousa march (both of these offerings were easily heard, to great crowd approval), and then the People's Choral Union closed these ceremonies with national anthems and songs of thanksgiving, including the "Hallelujah Chorus." Meanwhile, the official fireworks display was supplemented by rockets that white-collar workers dropped from the tops of office buildings. And an Irish couple was married, the first (?) of the new century, just as the clock struck twelve. Although the crowds were dense and some panic occurred, everyone seemed good-humored and the large police force had no calls to intervene; a police spokesman termed the crowd "one of the largest and best-natured that they have ever been called upon to handle." Enthusiasm reigned.

Similar scenes played out elsewhere. Organized labor gave a dinner, complete with orchestra and "partaken of by over 200 handsomely dressed women." At fifty cents a plate, the "surroundings were much the same as those at the more elaborate feasts of people of wealth," or so the *New York Times* reported. Speakers hailed labor's gains in the 19th century and predicted that in the 20th century the "march of progress" would continue until it was triumphant. As one speaker noted, religious and political freedoms had been expanding and "we shall attain the largest industrial freedom." It was realized belatedly that the roster of speakers had included fifteen men and no women, but a Mrs. Fred Nathan was asked at the last minute to give a speech on woman's economic influence, in which she took labor to task for its omission in the coming "age of the new woman": "A woman's tongue is her strongest weapon, and she ought to use it at every opportunity."

Church services maintained the festive and upbeat tone. The Catholic church offered midnight mass throughout the country, for only the second time in U.S. history. Congregations were surprisingly large given the competing celebrations elsewhere. Prayers, music, and bells spiced most services. Several Protestant ministers related the dominant themes of the century's turn to those of religion. The Reverend Dr. R. S. MacArthur, a Baptist, in his last sermon of the old century, intoned: "The world was never so good as to-night. The Bible was never so studied as now, and science has become docile and reverent. All discoveries—steamships, railways, telephones, and telegraphs—are ministers of civilization and religion. Early in the twentieth century they will girdle the world, making it a whispering gallery, voiceful with praise and radiant with the glory of God."

Ethnic groups met to celebrate. The German Liederkranz in New York sponsored a grand march with hundreds of participants. An old-fashioned German *Nachtwächter* (night watchman) heralded the end of the old year, while a handsome maiden appeared as a symbol of the new year and new century. Guests were handed wine cards complete with cartoons warning of drunkenness. Hungarian and other groups also celebrated, as did various YMCAs.

Golfers also scheduled tournaments specially to open the 20th century, although they waited for daylight and showed less inclination to make speeches than other groups. A variety of tourneys took place on Long Island, in New Jersey, and around Washington, St. Louis, and Baltimore. Cyclists and cross-country runners also sponsored events. Lexington, Kentucky, offered an elaborate torchlight parade to greet the new century, with culminating speeches at various parts of the city. Churches there conducted special services, including the first-ever midnight mass at the Catholic church; the Masonic order held a long banquet.

Similar activities occurred in most cities in the Western world, although in England, speeches took a more mixed tone compared to brash trans-Atlantic optimism. An archdeacon at Westminster Abbey gloomily predicted war pitting England against a combination of European powers. He referred to the "serious trade competition of Germany and the United States" and appealed to England to rouse herself. He also blasted national drunkenness, claiming that one American had told him he had seen more inebriation in a year in England than in a whole lifetime in the United States.

Germany stubbornly insisted that January 1, 1900, launched the new century, so its major activities occurred earlier. (In New York, a German American couple married a minute after midnight that day, claiming to be the first couple wed in the new century; as we have seen, an Irish couple later disagreed.) Berlin celebrated with church bells and massive, cheering crowds, a "dense multitude of joyous people." A thirty-three-gun salute welcomed the new century while trumpeters played from the roof of city hall and a massive fireworks display occurred. The emperor and empress appeared, Wilhelm in full military regalia. The tone was decidedly upbeat, even as the royal couple quickly returned to their gala private party.

Even Japan was beginning to celebrate New Year's in a big way (having recently westernized its calendar). Schools met, but only to sing the national anthem, to cheer, and then to disband. Various official and professional groups met again to exchange salutations. Here was the beginning of what has since become a major national holiday. But because the larger dimensions of the Christian calendar were still irrelevant to Japan, no commentary was offered on the new century; even the ardent Christian missionaries were silent on this theme, hoping to use the festive day to convince Buddhists of Christianity's superiority.

Evaluating the Century Past: The Main Themes

In the West, however, there was an outpouring of articles around the turn of the century that focused on assessing what the 19th century had achieved but that had implications for prediction as well. These articles generally (although not without some qualification) echoed the celebrations' predominant optimism, and they certainly recognized that this transition was a special moment, a time to take stock as well as to hope and perhaps to worry.

The *New York Times* ran a major feature on January 1, 1901, summing up what had gone before. It noted, with impressive sophistication, how contrived a century was as a unit of time: "The world's progress cannot be scanned by the artificial prosody of the calendar." Many vital trends began before 1801, others took shape only in midcentury or later; talking of the 19th century risked implying an orderliness that the newspaper insisted on rejecting; not for the *Times* to "pillage all past time to tickle the pride of the present."

Yet despite this hesitation, there was a strongly affirmative major theme: The 19th century did not begin progress, but it advanced it greatly. "We call it a century of marvels, and it should be marvelous, for it is the flower of all the others." Although the skein of progress started with the first caveman who picked up a stick and used it as a club to kill game, the 19th century did nothing to interrupt this purposeful flow of human history.

Much of the long article reminded readers of its major people and developments, particularly early in the century, including a clear designation of Napoleon as the century's leading (although horrific) single figure. Factual tidbits about Metternich and the Holy Alliance (bad) and the Monroe Doctrine (good) fleshed out much of the presentation. We need not linger over these elements, now part of textbook history, except to note their presence and later to ask what our 20th-century counterparts will be. But in addition to the selective school-history review (an amazing number of developments that we now consider to have been crucial in the 19th century were omitted, another salutary warning for us in planning our 20th-century reviews), the newspaper offered clear criteria by which the century was to be judged a milestone in the human march upward.

The *Times,* and as we will see many other thoughtful observers as well, painted a surprisingly broad canvas, which must challenge our evaluation of our own century and which reminds us of the many reasons 19th-century optimists thought they had to congratulate themselves. The wide scope of the review also demonstrated how many coherent trends could be discerned, trends that were not just scattered about in one decade or another but that ran through much of the century (at least in the progressive view). The *Times* evaluation was saturated with the 19th-century liberal view of history that in the history trade is called "Whiggish": Trends not only moved forward, with progress accelerating in one's own century, but they moved forward with a purpose, toward some well-defined and desirable goals.

First and foremost on the *Times*'s list was the transfer of power to the people, the strides toward democracy. At the century's outset, Europe (which for this New

York daily still served as the prime measure of history) was mired in conservative repression, though the new United States proudly set a different standard. By 1900, "The people themselves, under trusted leaders who knew and loved and served them, have changed all that, or much of it." American popular suffrage had demonstrated its "indestructibility"; only a "few sad pessimists" could doubt this. England, the other most advanced government, was equally secure in its constitution. Other areas lagged a bit, the *Times* noted WASPishly, but "the progress of other races than our own has been marvelous when we consider how late they made their beginning, and the dreadful weight of royal resistance and monarchical tradition that has hung about their necks at every step." A great part of the globe had moved from monarchy to republic (why Britain ranked so high, if this were the criterion, was not specified). Latin American independence could be hailed. Only two years earlier, the United States had expelled the last remnant of Spain's control from the hemisphere. Except for Canada and a few small colonies, "the flag of no monarch now floats anywhere in the New World." Liberty's gains in Europe could be measured by the decline of "Turkish" control, from Greek independence onward (though Greece then disappointed its liberal friends). Germany had yet to secure full freedom, but it had gained ground, and the people had also spoken in Italy, providing national unity and great strides toward liberal, constitutional government. Clearly, if freedom were to be measured by national independence as well as by constitutionalism, and if the world consisted mainly of Europe and the Americas, the 19th century provided a steady story of progress. (Asia nowhere appeared in this long survey essay, except for Siberia.)

To the confident editors, constitutional progress meant more than mere politics: "We may therefore say without fear of dispute that men are freer at the end of the Nineteenth Century than at its beginning. Are they for that reason happier? Demonstrably, and beyond the possibility of doubt." Granted, some aspects of democracy go awry, but, the editors held, it remained true that the people could govern themselves better than a king could, and freedom would only continue to gain ground in future.

Political change also meant peace. The *Times* saw a great change in the concert of Europe, now that petty princes could no longer declare war on a whim. Europeans would work out their problems in harmony. (Interestingly, a similar belief that democracy is antithetical to war surfaced in the early 1990s. Some beliefs are either correct or die hard.)

Freedom was also the basis for material advance. The great inventors and discoverers of the 19th century would have been publicly hanged, so this review claimed, in the bad old days of the Inquisition. "We renew the expression of our belief that the sum of human happiness has been most largely augmented in the last hundred years by the transfer of the control over the destinies of nations from the hands of Princes to the hands of the people." Freedom had existed before, but it had always been transient and fragile. Now it was firmly established and could never again perish.

Political gains headed but by no means exhausted the list of advances. Commercial advances came next. Despite some problems, including debates over currency standards (the adoption of the gold standard seemed a major plus in this context), world trade had soared. The advances of the United States were particularly striking, as a country initially neglected as an economic backwater became a great world power: "Her National wealth increasing at such a rate that from being the borrower of enormous sums she now easily supplies the needs of Old World Governments, municipalities, and private corporations, who have begun to come here whenever they are in need of funds." Again, there seemed no reason not to predict continued gains to come: "It 'expands the imagination' to attempt a forecast of the commercial future of such a country." A separate section, with less editorializing but still with considerable pride, noted the steady continental territorial gains of the United States through the century.

Knowledge had advanced. The *Times* highlighted the immense gains made by the theory of evolution, which for the first time correctly revealed the origins of the species and the workings of nature. The fact that the theory supported a more basic idea of progress, from worm to mankind, was congenial as well. But the review also noted major advances in physics and chemistry, including knowledge of atomic structure, which had "enlarged human knowledge of the universe." The review applauded the gains in technology closely related to science, with the improvements in transportation and communication heading the list here: "The railway and the steamship . . . are the most important contribution of the Nineteenth Century to the commercial development of the world." "The removal of the barriers of time and space [have] given men a chance to know each other better," which in turn greatly improved the prospects for peace, although there were still imperfections to iron out in international understanding. Progress in medical science formed another related category, with the *Times* particularly hailing the discoveries in pathology that explained the nature of disease. Although specific therapies could not be given great play (because there were in fact so few), the germ theory provided a key to progress in health: "We can escape disease by keeping out or destroying these germs." Doctors' ability to treat was advancing: "It is possible for us to escape the enemy where we formerly in perfect ignorance put ourselves at his mercy." And here, too, still better days were yet to come: Surgery would advance further, and overall "we have made only a beginning" in the steady advance of medical care.

Culture had improved. The newspaper did not advance very clear standards of what cultural progress consisted of, but it hailed the number of major writers throughout Europe and the United States, and the rise of art in America somehow added up to a plus. Here however there was hesitation: The *Times* had to note the confusions of the controversy surrounding impressionism and the fact that, in its august judgment, the "masterpieces of long ago remain unapproachable." But it quickly turned from this blot—"it is probably needless to say much"—to a list of achievements through the invention of philology and other gains in knowledge.

Discovery and exploration formed the penultimate category of progress, with advances in Western mapping of Africa particularly noteworthy: "the chief conquest of exploration during this century." But the mapping of the American deserts, of Alaska and British Columbia, and of Siberia was also noted.

Finally, there were humanitarian gains. Hospital service and the advent of the Red Cross directly showed the expansion of mercy. Treatment of war wounds and charity for the poor had both advanced: "The principle that man is his brother's keeper has gained new recognition." The recent Arbitration Conference at The Hague seemed to portend further gains for peace, although the *Times* (again not lacking some commendable historical perspective) admitted that this was too recent to factor into the assessment of a whole century. Gains in both popular and higher education won mention. Lest anything be excluded, the review noted that other kinds of progress were too well known to merit comment and that a few things made a great stir in their own time but did not change the course of history and so were omitted.

And then the concluding exhortation: "Men will cease to wonder at the works and the progress of man in the Nineteenth Century only when the Twentieth shall have surpassed them." Belief in a skein of history, with the 19th century the best yet but the 20th sure to move farther and faster, showed through clearly. Aside from its fussing about art and a few (soon to be improved upon) political imperfections among races like the Germans and the Russians, the *Times* admitted confusion only about what to do with the new U.S. acquisition in the Caribbean— here was a lien on the 20th century, although surely a modest one.

It will be interesting, of course, to compare this review with the one certain to appear in the same newspaper as it looks back on the 20th century and ahead to the 21st. Potshots and nostalgia surely war in our reactions. How could a paper be so blind to so many existing problems—among the poor, American blacks, women, the massive colonial areas of the world—not to mention to the possibilities of the wars and depression that would soon make such a mockery of its claims to peace and steady commercial progress? How could freedom be so confidently trumpeted a mere two decades before the rise of fascism? Surely there are warnings here against complacency, against a too-selective list of progress and against a too-confident faith in the ineluctability of progress itself. But nevertheless, how sweet it must have been to be able to look back on a century for which so many consistent gains could be plausibly claimed. It really was not entirely stupid to camp at the end of the 19th century and note fairly steady improvements, at least in key parts of the world, in political structures, in the decline of war, in commercial wealth, in technology and science, and even (if one's blinders were firmly fastened) in the humanitarian spirit.* I doubt that the same sweeping claims of progress can be made about our own century, and although this is probably all to the good in terms of accuracy and historical sophistication, one can spare a moment to lament the passing of simpler assumptions.

Other Voices: The Criteria of Progress

Other progress reports focused on a somewhat different set of priorities from the comprehensive approach taken by the *Times*. They shared, however, the delight in the century past—one was simply entitled "Wonderful Century"—and a belief that improvements would surely accelerate in the age to come. They might cite problems, but characteristically they quickly and confidently asserted that the problems could be overcome with just a bit of adjustment along with the beneficent tide of modern history. These reports are worth noting, if more briefly, to establish the variety of criteria by which the 19th century could be judged good and by which further progress could be anticipated, and also because some, precisely on the grounds of their greater narrowness in scope, may seem more replicable today.

Science and technology were particularly featured, although their mention was often accompanied by gestures toward greater idealism as well. Technological criteria had figured strongly in more general forecasting efforts in the later 19th century, including the emerging genre of science fiction, and they were usually associated with more generally beneficent gains. Edward Bellamy's *Looking Backward,* published in 1888, envisaged Boston in the year 2000 as a paradise in which technological advances allowed the nation to guarantee education and material well-being to all citizens, with women as liberated as men. French writers such as Albert Robida and Jules Verne looked to massive technological change, including space travel and radical new medicines. Not everyone saw such a rosy future, of course. Mark Twain, testy in his later years, reacted bitterly to Bellamy's portrayal, arguing instead that by the year 2000 feudalism would have returned, along with a new papal Inquisition, and that the United States would now lag behind a more

---

* The failure to highlight the abolition of slavery and serfdom in the 19th century in this and most other reviews was an interesting omission, probably due to ongoing social and racial nervousness.

progressive Europe. H. G. Wells's futurist novels, on the other hand, foresaw the removal of want and the conquest of disease, guided by a new educated elite capable of thinking in worldwide and technologically visionary terms.

In this context, it was small wonder that specific comments on the turn of the century were often rivcted on technology and science as keys to the kingdom. Seth Low, in an 1898 *Atlantic Monthly,* found the main achievements of the century not only in the gains but also in the democratization of knowledge: "The trend of the century has been to a great increase in knowledge, which has been found to be, as of old, the knowledge of good and evil; [and] this knowledge has become more and more the property of all men than of a few." The resulting increase in opportunity did exacerbate certain problems—presumably where aspirations raced ahead of social gains—but their solutions would be found in the "patient education" of the masses of men. Technology headed the list of the century's achievements for a labor spokesman, who argued that despite appearances to the contrary, things had improved for working people because of "inventions; sanitation and hospitals, and education." Frank Parsons, in *The Arena,* tumpeted technology pure and simple—"the increase of wealth and power through invention and discovery, steam and electricity, manufactures, commerce, railroads, telegraphs and machinery"—although he made some vaguer bows to new knowledge and education, liberty and democracy, and what he saw as a growing trend toward cooperation; Parsons also liked "the spread of civilization around the globe by colonization, commerce, and conquest." He worried about the concentration of wealth at society's summit, but he felt that public ownership and cooperation would advance to mitigate the problem unless the aristocracy of wealth maintained a successful stranglehold.

Other themes received some attention. An article in *The Century Magazine* argued that thanks to the challenge of science and greater freedom against sheer religious coercion, the spirit of religion had actually improved. Many authors argued, if vaguely, that there had been steady improvements in justice through the century thanks to the gains of liberty, equality, and fraternity.

The progressive tone led naturally to optimism about the future. Dr. Joseph Parker, in a volume on the 19th century subtitled "Review of Progress," predicted that "the coming century was to be almost next door to the Kingdom of Heaven." Another forecast somewhat oddly maintained that the new century probably could not keep up the pace of material progress but that general happiness would improve thanks to a "higher and nobler civilization." This forecast held that the 19th century was a difficult foundation step toward a blossoming of the human spirit. Optimism about the passing of war was another common conclusion. One essay began by hailing the new century: "On its threshold are the footprints of Divine Love. Its banner is the Golden Rule. Its leader is the Prince of Peace. . . . Altruism is displacing selfishness as a social force. A century of honor lies behind us." Achievements such as the abolition of slavery, the growth of democracy, and the creation of an International Court by the recent Arbitration Conference were then noted. To be sure, the United States had just participated in "another altruistic war" (with Spain), but in general war was becoming too dangerous and too offensive to conscience. The new century would see "the complete vindication of arbitration, the abolition of standing armies, and the peaceful co-operation of all the nations of the globe."

In sum, liberal writers, most socialist writers, and even Catholic writers in the popular vein seemed to agree on a hymn to progress and anticipation of more of the same. They defined it variously, some, for example, assuming that the wonders of science would be balanced by a new religious spirit, others excited about materialism on its own. Some worried a bit about the poor; others hailed new machinery without much regard for social consequences.

A Darker Side

Academic comment on the 19th century and on prospects for the future was typically more nuanced, particularly in Britain, where a sense of new global competition clearly dented national optimism. Some academicians took a balanced approach, noting that every gain in the 19th century brought new problems in its wake. Thus, for example, labor-saving machinery greatly reduced human drudgery but also threw people out of work. The progress was obvious and marvelous, but for want of proper moral concern on the part of business leaders and the state it had created monstrous poverty as well. This judgment was compatible, of course, with greater hopes for the future, and one economist did profess to see signs that consciences were awakening so that the potentially unmixed blessings of technology could be fully realized:

> At no period in earth's history has it been possible to have all the legitimate wants of civilization well ministered to with such short days as to afford men and women ample time for growing upward, for developing all that is finest, truest, and most worthy in their natures, and for enjoying life. Thanks to inventive discoveries, to science, and to the spirit of utility, that time has now arrived and only waits on the awakening of the sleeping God in the individual, in society, and in the State.

From England came A. R. Wallace's book, entitled (with only partial irony) *The Wonderful Century.* Wallace, the biologist who had anticipated Charles Darwin and was somewhat bitter about his unseating as the father of the theory of evolution, placed heavy emphasis on an idiosyncratic list of the century's failures: militarism, greed, plunder of the earth, neglect of phrenology, and opposition to hypnotism and psychical research. But he granted important successes as well: He minutely detailed technological gains, including the bicycle and tricycle and safety matches; he was predictably enthused about gains in science and medicine, including anesthetics and antiseptic procedures in surgery. He calculated that overall, in all of previous human history, there had been only seven great inventions, whereas a full thirteen had occurred in the 19th century alone.

Charles Pearson, a former minister of education in Australia, attempted a more systematic trend assessment in his 1894 effort at forecasting. His approach involved distinguishing between the largely innocuous trends of the early 19th century and an imminent watershed in which matters were going to become much worse. He saw three major problems looming: First, the state would increasingly take over life from the family and the church, a trend that Pearson saw emerging all over the world. Not only state schools and medicine but also state nurseries and meals would replace the family in key respects.

The second problem would be a trivialization of culture as a uniform urban society displaced folkways and regionalism. Pearson lamented the substitution of newspapers and books for lectures (an undeniably declining 19th-century cultural outlet), and he saw drama as a dying art form. Artistic standards would become more relative; science would become more specialized and less open to communication. Scientific and medical advance would continue, but here, too, there was danger in the increased survival of older people with "less adventure and energy, less brightness and hope."

Finally, in international relations, Pearson saw the "higher races" about to be "elbowed and hustled and perhaps even thrust aside" by peoples who had been docile through the 19th century. "The day will come, and perhaps is not far distant, when the European observer will look around to see the globe girdled with a continuous zone of the black and yellow races." Africa would gain independence; China would become a formidable military power; Europe's role in the world would diminish. Pearson's book provoked a great deal of discussion in England and the United States. Some leaders, including Theodore Roosevelt, were confident that the West could and would put down any rebellion of colonial peoples with military force, but others, including Henry Adams, agreed that the heyday of whites was probably nearing an end (although Adams added that he rather preferred aspects of African and Asian cultures).

William Gladstone dissociated himself not only from Pearson's predictions but also from the optimism that Pearson attacked; to Gladstone, the future was an absolute blank; he could not guess what was coming. Overall, Pearson evoked a complex if logical pattern of thought in which the 19th century itself might be largely approved (although Gladstone said that if forced to choose, he would take the "age of Homer" over his own time) but in which it was also seen as generating trends that were about to produce a new and decidedly less friendly environment.

The classical–liberal American economist George Sumner, in an essay written in 1901 but not published until later, also worried about the future. He professed to accept some of the key changes of the 19th century, including greater democracy and more social mobility. And he approved of the intensification of international commerce, which would set a material basis for greater wealth in the 20th century. Scientific gains were also promising. But his crystal ball was clouded by fears of a great war—he worried that the 19th century was an exception and that human society would return to a belligerent pattern like that of the 18th century but with much more awesome weaponry.

Sumner anguished particularly about controlling the state. The 19th century had seen the powers of the state increase, which meant that in the future it would be harder to keep it in bounds. Even private business organizations would expand, which would further material progress for most people but would squash their independence. Sumner argued that the state might be taken over by socialism, which he thought would be monstrous, or that it might be controlled by the interests of wealth. This was the terrifying alternative that faced the 20th century: "It is the antagonism of democracy and plutocracy. It is the most momentous antagonism which has ever arisen in human society because . . . it is in the vitals of society."

Sumner also fretted about debased mass culture. Ordinary man is "ignorant, noisy, self-sufficient, dogmatic" as well as bellicose. He was the ironic product of 19th-century progress, which fanned discontent simply because material comforts improved, giving people more time to complain and aspire. Again, after a good century, the future prospects seemed bleak: "The young century inherits turmoil and clamour with little knowledge or sense." The economist saw hope only in a new breed of experts: "We must look for truth and wisdom to the specialists—and the work of society is to be carried on by combining the knowledge which they will bring to the common stock."

It is not surprising that most of the intellectuals who commented on turn-of-the-century trends and forecasts opted for greater complexity than had their journalistic counterparts. We may well see a similar distinction at our own century's turn. Intellectuals, on the whole, juggled more diverse criteria, and they had their own theoretical apparatus to figure in. Sumner's analysis, for example, was obviously colored by his classical liberalism, which led him to find the growth of the state so distressing. Greater concern for international trends may also have distinguished the intellectuals from other commentators, making them less sanguine about peace prospects and more concerned about larger shifts in the balance of power. Yet the extent of agreement between intellectual and popularized assessments was interesting also. It was hard to argue against the material progress of the 19th century, and some bows to increases in knowledge and education were widespread as well.

Cultural Pessimism

Intellectual assessments also related to another turn-of-the-century current, not popular but widely popularized: the mood dubbed fin de siècle. Here is the final component to be introduced in outlining the world's most recent decade of the '90s prior to our own, before we assess the overall combination. And it is an odd component indeed, far less easy to reconcile with journalistic optimism than the more qualified views of the intellectual pundits.

Fin de siècle emerged early, which is already interesting given our lack of a comparable movement well into our century's final decade. The term emerged in France in the mid-1880s. In some early uses, it seems simply to have meant "modern" or "up-to-date," but it quickly acquired negative connotations, suggesting both uncertainty about the results of ongoing change and a fear of declining moral and cultural standards. Shoemakers and other craftsmen might be praised for being traditional rather than fin de siècle. A play in 1888 called *Fin de Siècle* centered around corrupt deals, adultery, and murder. A mediocre 1889 novel of the same name featured a rich young man beset by boredom, given to gambling, and unlucky in love; he ultimately commits suicide. A Parisian financial weekly in 1890, also called *Fin de Siècle,* concentrated on financial scandals; it failed quickly, only to be replaced by a literary review, under the same title, that concentrated on stories of vice. This journal's editor proclaimed that modern audiences wanted stories of corruption and carnal appetites. Art students in Paris organized a fin de siècle dance in 1893, featuring near-nude and completely nude dancers and outraging public morals, which led to several arrests but greatly enhanced the popularity of the dance itself.

"Fin de siècle" became, then, a widely invoked term in France and elsewhere on the European continent. To right-thinking people, the term had decidedly negative connotations, suggesting rapid moral decline. One French observer in 1891 characterized the mood quite simply: "the ignoble spectacle of this fin de siècle." An errant man, accused of blackmail and of living off the proceeds of his wife's prostitution, explained to a Paris court that he was "a fin de siècle husband." The concept generated larger accounts of civilization's decay. In 1891 a Catholic priest wrote a book entitled *Eglise et fin de siècle* (Church and fin de siècle), which blasted the decadence of the age. In 1901, another author predicted the world's end, and a 1904 book pinned the total demise of the world to the year 1921; it quickly sold over 20,000 copies.

France, like Britain, was in some ways particularly vulnerable to this vague if cosmic pessimism. It had lost a major war to Prussia in 1870–1871, and nationalist spirits had not recovered from the defeat. Many observers worried about French population trends, for France's birthrate lagged behind that of its European rivals, particularly that of industrial Germany. Treatises on degeneration had peppered the 19th century, fed in some cases by Darwinian fears about racial losses in the struggle for survival of the fittest.

But the mood was not simply French. A fin de siècle spirit also appeared in central Europe. Commentators in Vienna, including some middle-class newspapers, lamented that progress was at an end. Debased mass taste had taken over, and social life was becoming more brutal. Liberal dreams for a calmly enlightened, progressive world seemed shattered. This led, of course, to some of the complaints about moral decadence and a society that had spun out of control. Even material progress seemed to undermine character, leading to laxness and corrupt values. Uneasiness was widespread, and concern over the approaching end of the century helped focus the uneasiness on the calendar, leading in extreme cases to worries that civilization itself was near an end. (It was not long after this, although not associated with the end of the century per se, that Oswald Spengler wrote his gloomy but influential *Decline of the West.*)

But fin de siècle, as a mood, involved more than gloom and handwringing. It also described a new tone among intellectual and artistic youth, a tone that indeed rebelled against older, rational progressive standards but that also delighted in the atmosphere of moral change and greater license that the end-of-century atmosphere encouraged. In this sense, fin de siècle served as the birth pains of modern art—what one historian, Carl Schorsky, focusing on Vienna, calls "a kind of collective oedipal revolt" by the city's "culture-makers." Artists and authors were rejecting both the Victorian middle-class moral code, with its strong official sexual strictures, and, more important, the progressive, liberal assumptions that emphasized rational inquiry and incremental political reforms. The new artistic vision idealized defiantly novel, impulsive styles that were independent of the past. Psychology began to replace enlightenment as the key to the human animal, and the role of reason was downplayed. In a similar mode, the future was not to be carefully plotted but became free and unpredictable.

The aesthetic element ran strong in the fin de siècle circles despite the lack of a single accepted style. Artists and musicians hoped to redefine beauty, but they also hoped to gain a new place for artistic expression in an increasingly mechanical world. A number of impressive creations were associated with fin de siècle artists.

Fin de siècle did not involve systematic evaluations of the past century or neatly labeled prognostications about the century to come. Implicitly, however, it involved statements—joyous or critical—that the trends that had described the 19th century were being overwhelmed, replaced by a new spirit that would define the next age much differently. The pace of change seemed overwhelming. The French Catholic intellectual Charles Péguy claimed that human history had "changed less since Jesus Christ than it has changed in the last thirty years." He added enigmatically: "This race has seen plenty. It has never seen as much. It has never seen anything like it. It will get over it."

This was the spirit in which many people sensed that one era was ending and a new, very different one being born—with the turn of the century to some extent a coincidental but obviously convenient marker. Another historian, Eugen Weber, dealing with the fin de siècle spirit, has quite sensibly questioned whether anything particularly exceptional was actually going on. Of course, there were new technologies—movies, early automobiles, and airplanes, to mention a few—and a new, larger leisure culture was emerging as people had more free time and took a growing interest in sports and entertainment, but what was really dramatic was the outlook, the anxious reaction, not the pace of novelty. The French intellectual Emile Faguet translated his own hesitations about accumulating change into a hope that the new century might be far quieter than the one that had passed. "True," he anticipated inaccurately, "we travel ten times as rapidly from Paris to Marseilles as we did fifty years ago, but fifty years hence we will not travel ten times faster than we do today."

The common perception was that the 19th century had generated fundamental transformations around the world and that its end seemed particularly agitated. What was made of this perception varied: Some hoped for calm, some found in what they saw as new agitation a source of danger and concern, and some quite simply embraced the idea that the world was spinning off in uncharted directions.

The fin de siècle mood was, by the same token, hard to pin down. A French article in 1886 explained its relationship to change one way: "To be fin-de-siècle is to be no longer responsible, it is to resign oneself in a nearly fatal fashion to the influence of the times and environs. . . . It is to languish with one's century, to decay along with it." Writers in other countries, from Hungary to the United States, picked up the same tone, using the term frequently in articles and even as journal titles (a German dance company even used the name for a ballet). An *Atlantic Monthly* editorialist noted in 1891: "Everywhere we are treated to dissertations on fin-de-siècle literature, fin-de-siècle statesmanship, fin-de-siècle morality. . . . People seem to take for granted that a moribund century implies, not to say excuses, disenchantment, languor, literary, artistic, and political weariness, and that in 1901 the world will make a fresh start." This last expression of American optimism, that the mood was dire but transient and that a new century would usher in a revival of energy, was not, of course, uniformly felt. Particularly in Europe, fin de siècle to many suggested the beginning of a long decline, and in fact this new pessimism or the related frenzy to defy accepted standards did set a tone for one segment of European culture for several decades thereafter.

Causes of the Contradictory Takes on the Century's Turn

What was going on? How could the same trans-Atlantic society generate both such ringing, even naive optimism about the 19th century and the prospects of still greater progress to come and this odd mood of lassitude, anxiety, and artistic nose-thumbing? Without venturing a detailed analysis, we need to tackle the conundrum before asking how the elements of our own upcoming greeting to a century's end compare with those of its closest analogue.

Both positions—the progressive and the defiant/pessimistic—were solidly anchored. Optimistic renderings combined a long-standing belief in progress, derived initially from the Scientific Revolution and the Enlightenment, with the kind of chamber of commerce reactions to key 19th-century trends that had peppered the Western world since the 1830s. The conviction that society could improve through education, political reform, and technical change had crescendoed since its 18th-century formulation. One interpretation of Darwinism (although Darwinian metaphors were not commonly used in turn-of-the-century rhetoric save in the frequent references to the races of man) had also supported the progressive concept. Self-interested, largely middle-class judgments about industrial and humanitarian gains—the stuff of graduation speeches and inaugural talks at commercial expositions for many decades—translated this optimism into specific praise for what were, indeed, some of the key trends of the 19th century. The extension of education, improvements in medicine and nursing, and various political changes, including the spread of constitutions, parliaments, and the vote, along with the drumbeat of industrial and scientific advance, readily lent themselves to a year-to-year instantiation of the progressive view. Even many socialists, although critical of specific aspects of their society, derived their theoretical framework from a fundamentally Enlightenment optimism that could easily identify 19th-century landmarks (industrialization, popular education, democracy) with progress once they were recast in an egalitarian mold.

The deliberate defiance of this optimistic–boosterish approach through world-weary anxiety or artistic innovation had a more complex, and somewhat more recent, pedigree, but it, too, was no superficial interloper. A number of intellectuals and artists had been worrying about the inadequacy of Enlightenment culture since the later 18th century. They variously sought alternatives that would provide greater spirituality, greater recognition of emotional complexity, or simply enhanced attention to the artistic side of human nature. Romanticism was the first expression of this major countercurrent; it promoted the importance of stylistic innovation (rather than adherence to traditional or rationalistic artistic rules), expressed the need to defy straight-laced bourgeois codes of respectability, and emphasized the role of sorrow and despair in human life. By the middle of the 19th century, even as formal Romanticism waned, groups of artists were accelerating their attacks on bourgeois culture, proclaiming the validity of art for art's sake, stepping up stylistic innovations (as in unrhymed or unmetered poetry), and publicly experimenting with alternative lifestyles. Middle-class critics promptly responded with widely publicized criticism of what they considered immoral artistic bohemianism, even as they maintained their interest in purchasing conventional portraits and literary classics instead of the output of the ragtag contemporary crop of artists. Modern artists were wild men, personally and professionally, to the bourgeois mindset—the same mindset that so enjoyed the approved list of achievements of the 19th century.

Offshoots of scientific developments provided a second source of intellectual support to the budding alternative culture. While Darwinian evolution could be taken as a basis for beliefs in progress, it could also be used to highlight the randomness of human existence and the importance of violence and animal impulse. New discoveries about the significance of irrationality in human life—as in the emerging (and often misleading) field of crowd psychology—provided another apparently scientific basis for challenging Enlightenment optimism. By the 1870s and 1880s, one alternative cultural route was coalescing around what a historian of Germany, Fritz Stern, has labeled "the politics of cultural despair"—a quest for authoritarian, bellicose leadership that would better express the complexity of human nature while providing an alternative to the namby-pamby reformism of latter-day liberal optimists. And, of course, there were many 19th-century developments that seemed to provide empirical fodder for this divergent view: the stalled, corrupt politics of many parliamentary systems after 1870; the ugliness and social divisions generated by industrialization; the banality of new cultural forms such as the mass newspapers or popular theater.

The last fifteen years of the 19th century—when the fin de siècle concept was taking hold—may have provided a particularly fertile field for disputes about historical directions because it was oddly devoid of really seminal events. At least on the surface, this was a much less lively period of Western history than were the early 19th century, with the aftermaths of the French and American Revolutions and Napoleon; the middle of the century, with Jacksonian echoes, American westward expansion, and the European revolutions of 1848; or the 1860s and 1870s, with the Civil War and Italian and German unifications. Of course, there were still individual stirring incidents, such as the Dreyfus affair. And the expansion of European and United States imperialism was a truly significant development that produced such rousing clashes as Fashoda or the Spanish-American War. The fact remains, however, that outside the imperial fields, the end of the century was a bit placid, even dull. We can see in retrospect that Europe's alliance system, which did change in the 1890s with the Franco-Russian understanding, was profoundly menacing, and contemporaries picked up intimations of this in their anxieties about British-German rivalry and their fears of some upcoming conflagration. But the surface of things seemed relatively calm; consider the procession of undistinguished U.S. presidents, which gave lots of scope for people to project their visions of the directions of history without too much distraction from specific events.

Eugen Weber, in dealing with the end-of-the-century mood in France, has explained the complexities of the Western combination of optimism and pessimism by emphasizing their common root in reaction to change. Both camps agreed that the industrialization and unprecedented political reform of the 19th century, overall, had brought dizzying alterations to governmental and economic structures and to daily life. What differentiated the groups was their visceral response to change. For some, the sheer amount of innovation, continuing beneath the surface of standard journalistic fare in the 1890s with new inventions, new fashions, and new currents such as a more strident feminism, was becoming overwhelming. The references to fatigue, to ugliness, and to a sense of rudderlessness clearly picked up on this reaction. So did the other element in the fin de siècle mood, the interest in finding a more novel vantage point through defiant styles and behaviors by which to react to change. But change could remain exhilarating, particularly to people like the Andrew Carnegie–style industrialists who would most clearly profit from it. The fundamental transformations of the 19th century had generated a divided spirit in the Western world, between those who moved eagerly with the tides and those who found themselves either drowning or impelled to swim in some different direction. The prospect of the century's end provided the occasion for an unusually sweeping assessment of the modern tides. The fact that the effort at interpretation began a full fifteen years before the calendar demanded was testimony to the desire to take stock. But the same assessment revealed the profound divisions in response.

Much of the division reflected other splits in the Western world; to a great extent, people's view of the century past and their anticipations of the century to come varied according to the great differences in their position in modern society. We cannot pretend to know fully the mood of many ordinary people in Europe and the United States or to know how much evaluation the turn of the century triggered in their thinking. Most formal popular movements, like trade unionism and socialism, were progressive and optimistic about the future on the assumption that major improvements were within reach. But many people, in and out of these movements, faced great despair as they confronted poverty and the huge changes in the work process that attended new forms of engineering and the early stages of the assembly line. Nor do women seem to have been systematically articulate on turn-of-the-century issues.

Even aside from this important unknown factor, however, the social rifts were immense. Different countries, as we have seen, produced different moods, depending on their confidence or lack thereof in their nation's prospects. While many English observers worried about a major war, the *New York Times* was confident that the United States was just getting going as a world force, although it fussed about new imperialist involvements. Within most Western nations, certain articulate groups had structural reasons to dissent from the optimistic turn-of-the-century assessments. In continental Europe, several displaced social elements, including the landed aristocracy, helped generate a reactionary response to modern trends and certainly provided an audience for counsels of fatigue and despair. Many artistic intellectuals and religious leaders felt bypassed by the leading trends of modern society as prestige came to center on business life and on business-related professional activities. Student groups—even those whose members aimed at later professional success—might pick up aspects of this mood, and an impatience among articulate youth was part of the odd end-of-the-century mix. The experience of adolescence (a new concept in the later 19th century) as a time of dependence and school-centered separation from the world of adult work and reality could generate some complex reactions even from comfortably middle-class youth. On the other hand, business and professional leaders had an obvious stake, beyond their genuine intellectual heritage from the Enlightenment, in proclaiming their enthusiasm for modern trends and their eager anticipation of more to come. Clearly, most gurus of the popular press believed that this promise of an ever brighter future was the principal message that most of their readers wished to hear, which reflected at least their own social position and their implicit desire to harmonize with the views of their leading advertisers.

Within the intellectual community of the trans-Atlantic world, divided reactions also reflected the increasing separation between the artistic and scientific visions—the acceleration in the emergence of what C. P. Snow would much later characterize as two cultures. The scientific approach emphasized structure and rational inquiry, building, of course, on the Enlightenment tradition; and most proponents were safely ensconced in industrial research positions and increasingly research-oriented universities. Artists learned much from science about human violence, about relativism, about optic impressions. But their social world was different and far less secure. And their methods of perceiving and expressing were more different still. By no means were all artists cultural pessimists, aesthetic critics, or bohemian rebels, but the defiant mood was widespread and contrasted vividly with the dominant styles of science that figured so prominently in the optimistic renderings of the turn of the century.

Profound divisions among social groups and cultural communities were not, however, the whole story. The complex pull of calendar celebration brought out divergent impulses within individuals. People could be optimistic and fearful within their own souls. Change itself could generate this contradictory response—one could welcome it but still wonder if it would spin out of control.

Furthermore, the end of the century caught many people, mostly middle-class and basically progressive in their normal cultural response, in an inchoate, often implicit crisis of conscience. This crisis allowed both optimism and fin de siècle Angst to win a substantial and durable response beyond their appeals to divergent groups.

Stirrings of conscience had two dimensions. In the first place, many people who were inclined to share in the enthusiastic approval of the 19th century had to perceive several ominous deficiencies in the historical record. The social deficiency was one such, captured by many of the intellectual comments on the century's legacy. The gains of the century had been ill-distributed. Political democracy had not fulfilled its promise, for it was qualified by the huge social gaps between the prosperous and the poor. For some, of course, this was a problem that further progress would automatically alleviate. For others, it was a source of imminent threat: The social peace that had described much of the latter half of the century was about to be rudely shattered. For others still, less sure in their prognostications, the divisions of Western society were simply troubling, producing contradictory reactions to the claims of optimism and the lure of malaise.

The implications of imperialism formed the second looming problem, again, even for people convinced that important elements of colonial expansion fit the progressive mold. Those who saw beyond surface events had a realistic concern about the potential rebellion of the world's people of color, that is, about what the German emperor so bluntly called the "Yellow Peril." This concern also reflected some real guilt, a feeling that the massive empires were not really justified, that they did not really measure up to the progressive image of the century that proponents struggled to maintain. In at least two respects, then, the implications of some central 19th-century achievements—industrialism and imperialism—inevitably created tensions between optimism and pessimism, between confidence and guilt, even within the same observer; these tensions, in turn, could easily create anxiety that the future could not preserve the benign trends that might have characterized the recent past.

Crisis of conscience also reflected the very real changes that were taking place in the moral environment of the Western middle class in the last quarter of the 19th century. A genuine middle-class culture had been created by the middle decades of the century. It emphasized the sanctity of the family, the importance of work, the clear distinction between gender roles and gender characteristics, and the importance of sexual restraint. This culture was not uncomplicated; despite what is claimed by some oversimple renderings of Victorianism, for example, it did not argue against sexual pleasure altogether. But bourgeois respectability did have real meaning.

By the 1880s, however, the widely shared culture was beginning to unravel in some key respects, quite apart from the diatribes of rebellious artists against middle-class philistines. Work values persisted, but the rise of leisure interests could not be denied. Many men also wondered if work values were quite what they used to be, as growing corporations squeezed out many independent entrepreneurs and large law firms bypassed the self-employed attorneys who had ruled the roost in the good old days. Middle-class women were restive with roles that largely confined them to the home. Even men worried about tensions between aggressive and family-centered standards, or between sexual assertiveness in the whorehouse and respectable restraint at home. Here was another source of questions about gender certainties. A rapid drop in the birthrate, although essential to preserving a middle-class standard of living, created real uncertainties about gender and family values—uncertainties that were cresting in the 1890s. Divorce rates, although minuscule by our standards, were going up in many countries. In the United States, the first public debate about a divorce crisis occurred in the 1890s. New sexual interests were gaining ground, spurred by the greater availability of contraceptive devices; it seems pretty clear that American women born after 1870 had more active expectations of sexual pleasure than their mothers had developed, even though discussion of sexuality remained (again, by our standards today) wrapped in respectable restraint.

The turn of the century, in sum, caught the middle class in something of a values transition, which is one main reason (beyond the outright social divisions) that laments about decadence and excitement about new styles could both make sense. The values transition, in turn, generated an audience simultaneously open to hymns of praise and hymns of dissent about earlier 19th-century trends. One could admire Victorian gains while chafing against equally Victorian constraints. Both approaches had appeal to a still dominant social class that did not quite know what future it wanted.

*   *   *

The turn of the last century was a surprisingly grand occasion. Unprecedented celebrations, reflecting new wealth and technology, competed with divided and complicated reflections and predictions. Debates about when a new century actually begins, reflecting a tradition going back at least to 1700, were easily eclipsed by the intensity of public efforts to figure out what recent history meant and what the next stage of history would mean. The divisions and agonies themselves foreshadowed something of what was to come, if not for the 20th century as a whole then at least for its initial decades. Social divisions did accelerate to become para-lyzing social battles. The colonial revolt did take place. The dominant moral code did change. New movements that sought to translate some of the impulses of cultural despair and a desire for alternatives did form under the banners of fascism and Nazism. The turn-of-the century debates in no sense caused any of this future. They were interesting, and they clearly captured public attention, but they passed. In France, the dominant mood of the decade after 1900—labeled the belle epoque—seemed to shake off some of the uncertainties of fin de siècle. But the divided reactions and the complex reasons the century's turn stirred such varied responses were significant. Here, the calendar event did produce a genuine, revealing, and on balance, deeply troubling mirror for a society in motion. Will our mirror—the mirror we still must polish before 2001—cast a similar image?

Nine

WHERE IS OUR
FIN DE SIÈCLE?

ANY SIGNIFICANT COMMENT ON THE END OF THE CENTURY should stimulate some serious contemplation about what meanings we should seek, if indeed the prospect of a new century is still the occasion for such quests, before we are rushed into purely journalistic and most likely transient commentary. In our public discourse, we don't yet have definite bases for a discussion of how we should assess where we've been and where we're heading, and by the standards of the 19th century we are late in getting started. One of the perspectives that can advance our thinking—even if we decide that turns of the century are no longer very special—involves juxtaposing the conditions of the turn of the last century with the ingredients that seem to be available today.

The history of the buildup to 1900 provides a clear precedent for wondering what we will do at the end of our own century. In contrast to what we know about the turn of the millennium, for which, despite some imaginative efforts at historical reconstruction, there is simply not much to go on, we know that turns of the century can be symbolically meaningful, even tense. The dire prognostications about the world's end that were generated around 1900, although not the predominant tone, had something of the apocalyptic flavor that we more commonly associate with millennial thinking.

The fact is, however, that we already know that the rich history of the last turn of the century is not going to be very faithfully repeated in our case. We may yet generate a meaningful pattern of our own, and we can certainly anticipate a spate of retrospectives and forecasts that will contain some of the ingredients that were present the last time around. Perhaps, in the few years remaining, we will get really excited about the turn of the century, in ways later historians will find quite revealing. It is important not to pretend to false certainties about reactions yet to come; there is plenty of time for a complex mood to emerge. But it is also possible that one of the interesting features of this turn of the century, even as it is combined with a millennial change, will be its relatively humdrum quality.

What is incontestable is that the buildup to the turn of the century, whatever it turns out to be, is going to be much shorter than the buildup that prepared the last end-of-the-century public for its celebrations and ruminations. To be sure, one of the millennial productions of the late 1980s (the book by Hillel Schwartz) included comments on the century as well, but as already noted, this current seems not to have generated any mood at all, century-focused or otherwise. Perhaps the millennial excursions distracted from a more concrete turn-of-the-century outlook, and this distraction may continue; but there wasn't much response in any event. Last time, a full fifteen years of recurrent discussion and lamentation preceded the actual turn of the century. The extensive utilization of the fin de siècle concept revealed a surprisingly protracted need to get a fix on what was happening as one century yielded to the next. To be sure, articles that focused on Whiggish assessments and forecasts clustered more immediately around 1900 itself, and we have ample time for an equivalent reaction here. But our mood does seem to be different. If we are going to manifest a significant amount of end-of-the-century anguish, we'd best get started.

There is no reason, of course, to expect the two periods to be equivalent. Historians and the public at large often search for analogies—that is, past developments that might guide us in our assessment of possibly similar developments yet to come. But the search is often misleading, for too many factors shift for real resemblances to be very common or more than loosely instructive. In this case, there may be little analogy at all. Rather, our understanding of the interesting tensions surrounding the last turn of the century provides a baseline for comparison with conditions today. Within this comparative context, we can legitimately ask how much replication we might expect, and we can certainly already ask why so many features are different. It looks like we are not going to have a fin de siècle, in the sense of the 1880s and 1890s, and it is historically reasonable to seek the reasons for this difference.

To be sure, we have references aplenty to the 21st century. We know the new century is coming. A host of programs, including educational offerings, aim at preparing people or products for the 21st century. And the references surely have a meaningfully futuristic ring to then. The content of most invocations, however, differs little from that of the slogans of the 1980s that were bent on readying consumers or students for the next decade. We've invented "1990s" standards for this and that, and we can easily pin some equally facile labels on the next century and leave it at that. It might be enough just to pompously intone that something "will take us into the 21st century," and we hear this formula ever more frequently. But while this sloganeering taps our sense that a new century is a new age, it has no real heft. The 21st century, apart from its prospect as our next relevant future, has not taken on a great deal of substance. Again, we have not yet moved into the stage of thinking very much about what the new century will bring in terms of new trends or about how it will relate to what we will consider the trends of the century now ebbing away. The fact that a computer or a car or an undergraduate curriculum will help take its users into the next century hardly matches the sense of anticipation and assessment that had built up a hundred years ago. Even a few book titles that are now using the phrase "fin de siècle" remind us how different the collective intellectual mood has become.

In this chapter I explore not only some of the ways in which elements of the last turn of the century may resurface but also the differences in context that explain why reactions have already differed and may continue to differ even as we draw closer to the great divide. Each of the main ingredients of the last turn of the century provides a standard for comparison and often a target for analysis of which constituent factors have changed.

The Candidates for Reuse Around 2000: The Optimistic Camp

We can begin by recognizing some clear similarities between some of the targets of the 1890s evaluations and concerns or hopes that actuate us still. While our vocabulary has shifted in most instances, some of our values have persisted, reminding us that even after an exceptionally busy hundred years, continuities from the past remain quite lively. Our ancestors who celebrated the last century's end could easily recognize some of the themes we are likely to emphasize when we do get around to retrospectives and forecasts.

Our society certainly still resonates to tales of technological and scientific progress. Of course, there are dissenters, who argue that these sectors are not as important as their proponents insist or that they are hardly as progressive as these same enthusiasts contend; there were such dissenters a hundred years ago. But we have many people who think in terms of technological and scientific criteria and who resolutely maintain their centrality to human progress. Engineers who speak at commencements (if they are not too Green, warning of environmental hazards) delight in pointing to the technological gains of our century and in forecasting even brighter tomorrows. Today's admitted problems, such as the high cost of medical care or even environmental degradation, will yield to even larger doses of technological innovation in the future. Such arguments may also be correct; the point for now is to indicate their continuity with many of the turn-of-the-century assessments of a hundred years ago. Pure science has, perhaps, lost some of its panache, not because we dissociate it from progress but because it has become too specialized and too hard to understand. But when associated with technology or medicine, we still readily fall into the habit of speaking of steady advance from the past into an indefinite future. Advances in education are less commonly hailed than was the case a century ago because we are more impressed with the difficulty of keeping pace with economic needs and almost certainly more pessimistic about our youth. This pessimism is another qualification to the argument that science is progress. But there is nevertheless a great deal of continuity, and the continued faith in technology can generate some of the same optimistic renderings of the future that shone through around 1900.

Nationalism has declined somewhat in the Western world, as supranational units like the European Economic Community gain ground, as we realize some of the excesses to which nationalism can be put (for example, by Nazi Germany), and as we see the importance of international interconnectedness. But, particularly in the United States, we surely vibrate still to evocations of a bright national future and will equally surely delight in evaluations of the 20th century in terms of undeniable (but easily exaggerated) U.S. gains. I do not expect the mayor of New York City, in his end-of-century Media Moment (if he offers one), to wax quite as enthusiastic about his city and nation as his counterpart did in 1900. Nor will the *New York Times* so single-mindedly point to U.S. commercial progress in measuring the complex trends of the 20th century as it did for the 19th. But even if not in these settings, in other settings there will undoubtedly be some strong echoes. Popularizers and historians alike have frequently talked about this century as the "American century," and in terms of military and diplomatic ascent and of economic predominance during at least part of the century, the term can be justified to a point. We will certainly see this theme explored in retrospectives, along with some contentions that the next century can maintain the national pace amid an admittedly more complex international context. Again, some of the criteria will repeat those so prominent in 1900. And some of the same nations will be less certain of their modern place and therefore likely to be more guarded in their discussions of the wonders of 20th- and 21st-century modernity. Surely the British will again be less brash than their American cousins, even if the latter confess new anxieties about their own great-power prospects. And surely, although for different reasons this time, many Russians will again look back on the past century with dismay.

Other specific concerns of a century ago will resurface. We no longer refer to the Yellow Peril, but we certainly wonder about the gains and potential further advances of Japan, China, and the Pacific Rim, and what these advances portend for our place in the world society of the coming century. The details have changed greatly. Whereas in 1900 Westerners speculated about possible Chinese or Japanese advance with relatively little evidence, we now know what economic and political strides have occurred. Our news magazines periodically ask if the next century will quite simply be the East Asian century, as this one was supposed to be (and in some ways perhaps was) the American century. Those of our forefathers who worried about the same topics, in more overtly racist terms, would hardly be surprised at seeing these questions in our assessments.

Even the themes of progress through liberal democracy and peace, so battered by the events of our century, will almost certainly resurface. We still like to single out political gains that add up to additional triumphs for recognizably American political values, and some of us still harbor hopes that despite all the wars of our century, a durable peace may yet be right around the corner. The end of the Cold War and the spread of democracy in Eastern Europe and Latin America will surely spark some of the old rhetoric if the new systems hold fast for a few more years.

Clearly, we have hardly jettisoned our desire to measure our age and the next in terms of progress. And when we think of progress, we usually utilize many of the same categories as those so proudly displayed a century ago. Of course, there will be new twists; the progressive argument will surely feature much more discussion of women's advances and future potential, for example, and probably less discussion of organized labor. But our culture, when it comes to celebratory reckonings, has not been revolutionized.

Recurrently, in fact, the 20th century has given rise to popular and scholarly movements that demonstrate how durable late–19th-century progressive assumptions have remained—even apart from our ongoing fascination with the ideas of technological and medical or scientific progress. The ideals of Woodrow Wilson, not surprisingly, still resonated with turn-of-the-century optimism about the importance of installing liberal political regimes as a framework for general progress and about the prospect of permanent peace. Wilsonian goals were naively echoed in the Kellogg-Briand peace pact of 1928, initiated by the United States, another attempt to legislate the end of war by a mere pen stroke ratifying good intentions.

More seriously, in terms of the specific frameworks for our thinking today (for we probably would not put much stock in an international pledge of peace that had no more foundation than its ringing hopes), several scholarly approaches have in essence revived many of the key assumptions that underlay the optimistic rhetoric of the last turn of the century, translating them into another stirring vision of progress. In the 1950s and 1960s, various social scientists, mostly American, worked out a scheme of interpretation dubbed "modernization theory." Modernization theorists argued that recent Western history provided an interconnected pattern that other societies were following or could be expected to follow in the 20th century and beyond. In the West, a host of changes had combined to produce a modern political and economic structure and even a new, modern personality. These changes included the spread of education, the advance of science, the advent of liberal democracy and a more efficient government with trained personnel, humanitarian reforms including better treatment of children, and the rise and eager adoption of new technologies and medical procedures that improved health and living standards. Modernized families practiced birth control and reduced the inequality between husbands and wives and between parents and children. Modernization was accompanied and supported by a new personal style that valued independence, individualism, and progress. These changes, in turn, provided a set of standards that other societies would move toward and were clearly already adopting in some areas, such as the spread of education and new public health measures. Modernization theory did not exactly say why all these changes occurred, although it was assumed that once the West set the pace, mere example and imitation would suffice to goad other areas. But modernization theory read remarkably like the old, 19th-century Whig interpretation of history: Change was progress, and one change linked to the next in creating a better society and better individuals. The only real complexity allowed for was the possibility that some societies might not modernize as quickly as they should; here was a lag that had to be explained. Otherwise, with a sweeping scholarly apparatus, the progressive view of history and the near future was reincarnated. Our society had improved over its own past and would probably continue to improve, and now the whole world might follow in our wake.

Even though modernization theory was a bit too scholarly for widespread penetration, its assumptions were broadly shared. Indeed, the theory not only promoted but also reflected post–World War II U.S. confidence that a large dose of technology, democracy, capitalism, and consumerism was just was the doctor ordered to create a better future. Furthermore, ideas derived from modernization theory entered into a series of popular forecasts in the period, such as Peter Drucker's 1959 *Landmarks of Tomorrow*. In 1964, Dennis Gabor, in *Inventing the Future*, wrote optimistically about imminent world economic advance. Industrial advance was assured, he argued, whenever a society invested a tenth of its revenue beyond that necessary to cover population growth; and this, surely, should not be difficult. To be sure, a few problems, like energy supply, might loom in the future as world industrialization accelerated, but the future would take care of these issues in ways we could not now know: "The problems of fifty years hence will not have to be solved by our present-day technology but by that which we shall possess in twenty or thirty years' time." The exponential increase of scientific knowledge, which Gabor thought he could demonstrate, would easily take care of the needs of progress. An age of leisure based on improved mass education would dawn around the world, and peace would be sustained by widespread prosperity and the balance of terror among the most powerful, nuclear-armed states.

Modernization theory faded from fashion. Its tenets were dented by American failures in Vietnam, where it had been assumed that Vietnamese villagers could quickly be converted to modernized, liberal, rational–economic men and women with a bit of American guidance. Scholars attacked the theory for its oversimplifications, ethnocentrism, and teleology. Other prediction scenarios developed, scenarios that pointed to the dire implications of world population growth or environmental exhaustion and discouraged hopes for easy progress—an issue to which we must return. And it remains popular, to this day, to attack the approach. But modernization theory assumptions continued to be used and may certainly have entered into, or reflected, widespread public consciousness, at least in the United States. The idea that U.S. standards were progressive and might define the future has been hard to shake (and, of course, some would doubtless add: because the idea makes a lot of sense in defining both modern history and the future).

Ask almost any bright American undergraduate—as I recurrently do—if Japan will be more or less like the United States fifty years from now, and he or she will unfailingly answer: more. And not because they believe that Americans will move toward Japanese ways. Rather, they believe that the Japanese will have developed fuller women's rights and more active feminism, less traditional deference and community sense, more generational rifts, and more avid consumerism. They believe that the Japanese will, in sum, continue to modernize along the trails that Westerners have blazed. The theory lives in our minds, whether we know it or not. Given the continued world importance of our culture, it's hard not to think of our patterns as goals for mankind generally, organizing history to come.

Finally, whatever the hold of implicit modernization theory assumptions, yet another round of progressive history and forecast emerged after 1989, with the fall of communism in Eastern Europe and the spread of democracy not only there but also in Latin America, South Korea, and elsewhere. In a widely noted book, *The End of History,* former State Department analyst Francis Fukuyama contended that liberal democracy was the "end point of mankind's ideological evolution." Along with capitalism, the motor of economic progress, it would create a world in which massive political change and war would become unnecessary. Fukuyama was a self-conscious optimist. He knew how naive some older views of progress could seem, including those popular at the last turn of the century. He incorporated a formidable scholarship into his book, with frequent references to Marx and Nietzsche, as he fit his projections into a larger historiographical tradition. Simultaneously, he argued against critics who had tried to oversimplify his ideas. And, finally, he acknowledged the possibility of psychic breaks and regressions in the future.

But despite all the complex apparatus of Fukuyama's theory, the basic picture was clear and familiar: The French and American Revolutions had launched a trend of political democracy and respect for human dignity that could not readily be reversed and that was now gaining global adherence. Efforts to shore up illiberal systems had been destroyed by the needs of economic development, for only democratic systems could sustain material growth. This same liberal triumph would lead to world peace, for in democracies the sovereign people would realize that there was no need to risk lives, that wars and battles were folly. The future of the world rested on the same advances through democracy and material gain that had described our recent past, and peace was now added in as an inevitable concomitant of worldwide democracy.

Whatever one's views of the "end of history" idea, its emergence demonstrates how lively essentially 19th-century beliefs about the direction of modern history and the future remain. We will almost surely see them blare forth in assessments of the 20th century and in projections for the 21st, a few years hence. As a result, some portions of what we will say, hear, and hope, as we hail the new century, will strongly resemble not just the tenor but many of the particulars of the last celebration. We will taste a variety of recipes, blending different mixtures of technology, science, democracy, and peace; but the basic menu will be both similar and familiar. We love to celebrate ourselves on ceremonial occasions—even presidential candidates have a ritual of praise for the world's greatest democracy and so on—and we'll surely wish to indulge that love at the turn of the century. And with this, of course, again the nagging thought: Perhaps this viewpoint represents not only what we should hope for (who can publicly argue against a new age of peace?) but what best describes the trends of our time.

Despite these strong echoes, however, I think it is highly probable that neither the amount nor the range of optimism will match that so vividly available a hundred years ago. This is a guess, to be sure. We have the potential for another orgy of progressive hopefulness. We retain many of the beliefs and we certainly retain the taste for self-affirming rhetoric. Further events between now and the year 2000 (the greater success of democratic agitation in China, for example) might, however briefly, fan the flames of optimism further.

New Elements: Limits on Predicted Progress

There are, however, a number of reasons to speculate that the depth and range of optimism will not match that of the 19th century. The very frequency and diversity of the forecasts to which contemporary Americans and Europeans are subjected may promote a certain generalized skepticism—they certainly should. The penchant for forecasts, both Whiggish and dire, unquestionably increased in the 19th century but not to the current level. We are regularly told about our economic prospects, about coming technologies, about new or forthcoming trends in our sexuality or art, about the impact of an aging population—the list can seem endless, and all sorts of real or would-be social scientists queue up for the parade. Even our habit of trying to pin novel labels on each succeeding decade or generation—the silent generation of the 1950s, the hippies of the 1960s, the me-generation of the 1980s, and now, for lack of any analytical clarity, the generation X of the 1990s—suggests a sense of chaotic and almost random change. The images of current shifts and future trends are numbing. In this atmosphere, seizing on any single forecasting trajectory, and particularly one that seeks to characterize the century past and project the pattern of a whole century to come, may prove to be tough sledding. This very difficulty may also be a useful prod toward realism, protection against the touching naiveté of some of the liberal wish lists of the last turn of the century, but it definitely adds new complexity. Clearly, as a society, we still crave predictions; and clearly we are still somewhat open to the old progressive diet, including the commitment to advancing science and technology. But as an audience we may be harder to sell than our ancestors of a century ago were.

Research on reactions to forecasts is not extensive, and it does not include a clear historical component that would allow definite statements of contemporary skepticism versus earlier receptivity. What research there is, dealing with forecasts ranging from weather reports to warnings about the future impact of global warming, does suggest that there is a wide range of latitude in interpretation. People read their own meanings into statements about the future, and they easily identify overgeneralization in the forecasts offered. Many people find predictions ambiguous or imprecise. They correctly note that many forecasts lose relevance because they artificially narrow the range of inquiry. The United States government, for example, spends over a billion dollars a year predicting the climatic effects of global warming but pays no attention to its social and economic repercussions or possible compensatory adjustments; small wonder that the results of the forecasts often seem remote. The forecast deluge, in sum, may ironically have blunted our response, which in turn can constrict the confidence of traditional optimists and new-style pessimists alike. We may not hear as much sweeping rhetoric about the future, come the year 2000, or at least, we may start squirming pretty quickly if we do.

Jaded audiences are not, however, the main point. The two biggest reasons to hypothesize a more muted diet of progressivism involve the new complexity of the world balance of power and the checkered experience of the 20th century itself. Optimism around 1900 rested heavily on the West's dominant position in the world. This same position generated some guilt and anxiety, to be sure, which showed up in the bitterness of a Mark Twain or even in aspects of the fin de siècle mood. But optimists seized eagerly on the West's imperial leadership and on what that leadership seemed to assure both for the West itself and for the "inferior" races who were now subjected to the West's benevolent tutelage.

It is hard to imagine more than traces of this imagery in our upcoming turn-of-the-century assessments. From writers like Francis Fukuyama we will hear about the world's turn to liberal democracy under the guidance of Western example, which is quite a plausible latter-day extension of forecasting based on Western leadership. And we will certainly have to assess the role and prospects of the United States as "the world's only remaining superpower," a phrase that our politicians and pundits already repeat endlessly. But we cannot assume a world subjected to Western or even United States control. We have to recognize about diverse reactions to Western predominance, including outright hostility to Western directions, as is felt, for example, in part of the Muslim world. One of the leading themes of the 20th century has been the diminution of imperialism and Western dominance; even the surge toward power of the United States, an undeniable complexity, has not diverted this trend. This development may well be a cause for rejoicing as we assess the 20th century, but it certainly makes for a much more nuanced picture both of our own century and of prospects for the future than that which could still be painted in 1900, in the heyday of imperialism.

Mixed in with the hopes for a spread of democracy must be some uncertainties about the future of U.S. power in the face of the economic surge of East Asia. And while some Western Europeans may—again plausibly enough—paint a bright picture of their own regional future under the European Economic Community, they can hardly equate the world and the West as was so often done a century ago. The basis for this kind of simple optimism has clearly eroded. Again, the result may be greater realism in our end-of-century assessments; the "West is best" theme of the pundits around 1900 rings today not only politically dubious but painfully inaccurate, given the imminent retreat of colonialism. The decline of Western predominance does not prevent optimism of a more complex variety, optimism that extends to hope for various of the world's peoples amid new independence and greater opportunities for diverse cultural expressions. But the West's relative slippage will surely mute the trumpet section of any simplistically Whiggish orchestra.

Furthermore, although this may be a more subjective note, observers who do claim a continued leadership role for the West must deal with the tawdriness of some of the lingering remnants of Western leadership. The theme of the spread of democracy harks back to the tunes of 1900; so, perhaps, will some stirring portrayals of the United States as policing the world in the interests of peace. But the West and the United States retain their most pervasive world role in the commercialization of taste—in the spread of Cokes and cigarettes, Hollywood and game shows, McDonald's, and (due note taken of European resistance) Disney. This commercialization is an interesting phenomenon, and although open to obvious criticisms, it is not necessarily a pattern that dooms the world to some inevitable degradation of taste. But it is hard to claim this kind of lingering cultural imperialism as the basis for liberal or humanitarian progress. The new complexity of world power relationships, even granting a still-disproportionate Western role, provides a much different framework for projections than that available a century ago.

The second great impediment to systematic optimism, particularly in a turn-of-the-century context, when we must look a hundred years backward as well as forward, lies in the difficulty of describing the 20th century in consistently progressive terms. In 1900, compiling such a description for the 19th century required no small selectivity, and it is not easy to compare one's own century to a period in the more distant past for which some of the rough edges may be less visible. Optimists in 1900 ignored the urban miseries of early industrialization, the attacks on African Americans and Asian Americans after Reconstruction, the new limitations placed on many women with the separation of paid work from home, and the brutal incursions of Western military might and commercial exploitation into Africa, Asia, and the Pacific. It is possible that some observers in 2000, bent on upholding the standard of progress that clearly has not died in the West, will exercise similar selectivity to come up with an ultimately glowing picture of our own century, on the basis of which further hopes for the future will seem reasonable.

But the selection will be more difficult because inescapable (or nearly inescapable) 20th-century events get in the way. Whigs in 1900 could look back on almost a full century of considerable peace after the end of the Napoleonic turmoil in 1815. Of course, they could not entirely ignore some European wars in the 1860s and 1870s, the U.S. Civil War, and some bloody skirmishes outside of Europe amid imperialism, but they could legitimately argue that the European wars were fairly minor, that the U.S. Civil War was clearly heroic and liberating, and that imperialist bloodshed (most of which affected people of color in any event) was part of a larger advance of civilization over "inferior" races. At the end of the 20th century, we simply cannot similarly wipe away not one but two unprecedentedly horrible world wars not to mention other major conflicts such as the recent contest between Iran and Iraq. Nor can any but the most fervid neo-Nazi extinguish memories of the Holocaust or other instances of 20th-century mass slaughter and genocide. Of course, the diehard progressives—neo-Whigs?—may note that the United States did nothing so awful in these calamities; the worst 20th-century evils came from other sources (assuming, of course, that we don't look too closely at our decisions affecting Hiroshima and Nagasaki). And it is always possible to contend that as dreadful as 20th-century wars and atrocities were, they lie in the past; that we can learn from them to set a more firmly humanitarian path in the future. Certainly, the record of wars of the second half of our century has been much better than that of the first, and the record of atrocity a bit better, which may be a cause for renewed optimism. But at a date when we will be called upon to look at the full century, it is hard to imagine using the 20th century as a springboard for systematic confidence in ongoing progressive trends. Even that staple of progressive forecasting, technology, which in the 20th century has been so clearly associated with a massive increase in the power to kill in war and to exterminate civilians, must look more complex in 2000 than it did in 1900.

It is doubtful, then, that our celebrations of the coming turn of the century will be quite so gloriously optimistic as those of a hundred years ago. We will have banners and fireworks aplenty, simply because we still like to party. We retain a strong streak of Whiggish optimism, so we will doubtless entertain some of the same kinds of progressive rhetoric that so dominated official commentary in 1900. Even some of the new complexities may play into a rebroadcast of Whiggish optimism. If Western dominance can no longer be touted—a clear change—then we can hail the enlightened independence of so many parts of the world and the capacity of the West to retain or revive its internal strengths even as its empires have been stripped away. The combination of decolonization and European renewal has indeed been an impressive achievement during the past thirty-five years. Even if the horrors of war and totalitarian oppression must be acknowledged as an incontestable part of the 20th century's legacy, we can nevertheless restore our faith by noting the long world peace since 1945 and the retreat of totalitarianism over the past several decades. But it will be harder to be an unqualified optimist. Hopes and beliefs in progress will more commonly be tempered by some doubts and historically derived anxieties than was true in the resounding reassurances around 1900. Or at least, they should be; this has been a very messy century.

Opinion polls in the United States at various points in the 20th century have noted a clear wavering of faith in progress. Granted, we have no corresponding polls for the 19th century, which makes any comparison flawed. But it is probable that a commitment to progress would have shown more consistently during the previous century than it has in our own, despite diversity of opinion and some probable oscillations (for example, at the outbreak of the Civil War in 1861) during the earlier period as well. American belief in progress was certainly tempered in the wake of our confusion about the international scene following World War I. We believed in American progress, but we were unsure about progress in the rest of the world. The depression was another check to our optimism, although a commitment to future progress in principle suffered less than might be imagined. It was from the 1970s onward, amid declining U.S. international economic power and growing income stagnation at home, that polls showed a particular turn away from cosmic confidence in the future. At some points, ironically, belief in the possibility of personal advance persisted even as judgments about the larger society nose-dived. Again, our recent bouts of uncertainty don't prove that we won't enjoy some stirring turn-of-the-century optimism to lift our spirits at a symbolic passage of time, but they do raise doubts that we can or should replicate the public confidence of 1900.

Why Not Pessimism Instead?

But if our turn-of-the-century celebration must include some recognition of the world's new complexity and the dark shadow of unspeakable horrors in our own century, as well as some more recent concerns about developments in the United States itself, why do I not anticipate an updated version of fin de siècle lassitude and uncertainty? Here, for analogy fans, is the more interesting puzzle. It is not at all hard to explain, in anticipation, why optimism has changed. The gap between the rhetoric of 1900 and what actually happened just a decade and a half later, with World War I, encourages us to be cautious in our optimism. The main complexity here is that we must still make allowance for cultural persistence, for the reminders that Whiggish beliefs can still surface. But it would seem to be much easier to make a case for turn-of-the-century pessimism. If lots of people in the 1880s and 1890s were seized with anxieties or revulsions about their own time and the prospects for the future, why is the same not happening in spades today? With doubts about new world power alignments, with structural economic problems seeming to dog us even in nonrecessionary years, with weaponry available to kill both in war and on the streets, why is there no fin de siècle mood today?

For, fairly clearly, we don't have one. We don't use the term to describe a current mood, and we haven't invented a new term for a similar mood. Only the dubious "generation X" label, describing the strivings and value confusions of young adults in the 1990s, might be seen as remotely comparable. A hundred years ago, fin de siècle was in full flower. Efforts to describe and disseminate a mood of artistic rebellion and disenchantment had been gaining momentum for over a decade already. We simply do not see a comparable phenomenon today, which means that we cannot expect the pessimistic characteristics of the last turn of the century to be repeated, either. It is striking, given our delight in catchy slogans, that we have neither reintroduced the term "fin de siècle" nor invented some alternative. It is legitimate to ask why.

Explaining the reasons a development has not occurred is inevitably speculative. In this case, we first need to come to some agreement on what caused the fin de siècle mood a century ago, which already opens some territory for dispute. Then we must go on to suggest how these or comparable causes are absent from the contemporary scene. Needless to say, there is no precise science here; rather, we face a terrain for raising additional questions about the contemporary mood.

Pessimists of various sorts abound in the 1990s. We are routinely flooded with laments about crime rates, educational decline, and other serious national and international problems. Environmentalists, although losing audience attention in the middle of the decade, can certainly point to a host of disasters waiting to strike if we don't mend our ecological ways. The 1994 World Population Conference brought forth a related range of dire predictions about what will happen if we don't get population growth under better control. To be sure, none of these gloomy anticipations is uncontested. There are scholars who point out that world population growth rates are easing and that existing growth has not overwhelmed us or that American crime rates are actually if modestly declining despite public fears. But there is certainly a basis for a grim view of many world trends, and pessimistic scenarios will undoubtedly surface among the optimistic throwbacks to 1900 when the pace of end-of-century assessments and projections accelerates.

Americans do worry about declining moral standards. We have seen that morality, along with environmentalism, is a key theme among post–Cold War apocalyptics. But the concern goes further. Conservative William Bennett's *Book of Virtues* had sold 1.5 million copies by the mid-1990s. A bit earlier, Allan Bloom's *Closing of the American Mind* had appealed to buyers who thought U.S. intellectual values were disintegrating. But many of these same American buyers are quite upbeat about the nation's prospects: In 1994, 68 percent of those polled contended there were no limits to potential U.S. progress. This juxtaposition signals an odd mood, to be sure, with some overtones of the ambiguities of the 1890s. But some worry about decay is common in many societies. Sinclair Lewis sold a lot of copies of *It Can't Happen Here,* warning of moral issues (of a slightly different sort) in the late 1930s. Laments about misguided youth are part of adult pleasure, and not only in our own time. Lacking, in any general way and especially among bellwether artists and intellectuals, is the sense of despair, crisis, or confusion that fed the distinctive fin de siècle of a century ago.

The fin de siècle mood remains absent. Pessimism has not yet coalesced into clear new forms of artistic rebellion or declarations of hopelessness and lassitude or even systematic protest against the degeneracy of our times. We are less optimistic than our ancestors of a century ago, but we don't quite match their complex cultural ambivalence, either. Although historians looking back on our decade may find otherwise, it seems quite probable that we have no particularly distinctive mood to label or convey.

One reason for the nonemergence of a new fin de siècle disgruntlement, at least in its continental European centers of origin, lies in the aberrant political use that was ultimately made of some of the themes of cultural despair. The sense of hopelessness, focused into attacks on simplistic liberal trends and institutions and on other aspects of modernity including mass taste, unquestionably fed into fascist and Nazi movements after World War I. The discrediting of these movements in turn legitimately generated hostility to too much vague, antiliberal cultural anxiety.

Three other factors are more generally significant in preempting a revival of the fin de siècle mood: The late 20th century has seen a pattern of events and implications different from that of the 1880s and 1890s; the relationship of artists and intellectuals to the wider society has shifted; and the kind of sea change in mainstream values that supported the more defiant aspects of the fin de siècle outlook does not seem to be repeating itself as we near the end of another century. Each of these elements can be briefly explored.

The late 19th century did not have many events that could lay claim to fundamental importance. French political life was jolted by the Dreyfus affair; the Spanish-American War raised understandable concerns in the United States and Spain alike; key imperialist clashes were unquestionably exciting at the time. But the events that shaped the 19th century had occurred earlier. This slack period left space for various observers to ponder more basic trends, and although some saw the years of calm as grounds for optimism, others picked up a sense of drift and aimlessness. Furthermore, some of the events and trends that were occurring might (correctly) have seemed ominous. The division of Europe into two competing alliance systems, with Britain still independent but locked in growing competition with Germany, produced uneasiness even beyond those prescient commentators who directly foresaw a coming great war. The rise of Japan suggested new complications for the West's dominance over the world at large.

In contrast, the late 20th century has been filled with genuinely fundamental events, and although all sorts of problems beset us, it is harder to tease out a sense of impending doom from the contents of the daily press. The collapse of the Soviet Union and the rise of democracy in Russia and other parts of the world captured general attention in the late 1980s and early 1990s as no events a century ago could have done. And to all but the most diehard Communists, these events did more than redirect key aspects of contemporary history; they also promised a better future. To be sure, change of this magnitude raises questions and uncertainties; we must ask about the solidity of some of the new democratic institutions and even about the possibility of new forms of Russian aggression. Furthermore, we unquestionably have not enjoyed the glow that emanated from the collapse of European communism as long as we expected five years ago. Other problems and worries have intruded. But the fact remains that our anxiety about the prospect of war has greatly diminished. Our confidence in our own political institutions, however diminished by the year-to-year morass of U.S. congresses and presidencies, has been given a delightful lift by the desire of new areas of the world to take lessons from us. At the end of the 20th century, it is harder than it was a hundred years ago to be bored, fearful, or dour about the headline news items.

Americans do fret, with good reason. They see the endless crime reports on nightly local television, and they actually exaggerate their perceptions of crime rates in the process. They know about drug use and the collapse of the inner cities. The average American has been suffering from a stagnating real income since the early 1970s. Concerns about high structural unemployment, summed up in the common concept of a new underclass, and about the U.S. competitive position in a difficult world economy, figure high on the list of anxieties as well. Evidence that U.S. students lag behind other nations in educational performance, particularly in the secondary schools, raises another set of worries. Furthermore, as the changing results of polls about prestige and confidence clearly suggest, Americans have demonstrably lost faith in their politicians and in many once proud experts such as medical doctors. But with all this, we do not seem to have fallen into a national mood of despair or even substantial alienation. Enough vestigial optimism remains to prevent a clear American variant of fin de siècle. The fact that we have no overwhelming international rivals, at least in the military field, and are facing no prospect of major war surely cushions the various problems we do identify. And in Western Europe, home of original fin de siècle, conditions are even less conducive to a mood of lassitude or anxiety. Despite a number of problems, including some of the same structural unemployment that besets the United States, Europeans have to be pleased at the prospects for peace and the tremendous surge that their region has made over the past forty years, capped and perhaps furthered by new strides toward economic unification. The despair, not just of the last turn of the century but of the interwar decades, has substantially subsided.

Recent events, then, and the implication of current trajectories—particularly in the diplomatic and military arena—differ greatly from those of a hundred years ago. This is not, of course, a universally valid proposition. One might look for something closer to a fin de siècle mood in Russia, if the current political and economic confusion persists to the century's end. In other areas, the end of the Cold War may be less significant, but the establishment of national independence—such a pervasive theme of the second half of the 20th century in Africa and Asia—may still generate enough excited pride to inhibit fin de siècle doldrums.

The second factor limiting the prospects for a distinctive, pessimistic end-of-the-century mood in the Western world involves changes in the position of artists and intellectuals. Disgruntled figures still remain, but on the whole the 20th century has seen a fuller integration of artists and intellectuals into middle-class ranks than was true a hundred years ago. In the 1890s, the leading artists were preoccupied with the development of new styles designed to pull art away from traditional constraints and, in the process, to shock the conventional middle class. Beyond the artists were various other intellectuals who felt alienated from their society—sometimes even from the artists, whose avant-garde styles seemed a sign of decadence—because they lacked an established place. Minor writers of various sorts fell into this category. Both facets of this alienation have changed considerably. Artists still try to shock on occasion, as recurrent quarrels with public patrons amply illustrate. The depiction of graphic sexual materials can still prompt an uproar, although the shock value is greater if the material is homosexual rather than heterosexual. But the middle class has accepted the principle of artistic innovation. Audiences may respond eagerly to a new style (witness the fairly quick acceptance of Andy Warhol's pop art), or they may be merely resigned, still preferring more conventional taste. But the pitched battle between innovators and the general public has receded. As museum collections attest, diverse forms of modern art have arrived. At the same time, artists have often been incorporated into more established settings. Some have academic positions; others, like Warhol in his prime, mingle with high society. Finally, as postmodernism, poststructuralism, and other currents vie for attention, artists and their audiences have become more relativist than their counterparts of a century ago were. Lack of agreement on standards of beauty makes it harder to recapture the aesthetic hopes of fin de siècle, although some would argue that a revival of aesthetic canons is just what we need to make this turn of the century culturally meaningful.

The number of unaffiliated intellectuals has dwindled. In Western Europe and particularly the United States, more and more facets of intellectual life have been taken over by universities. Poets teach writing; Marxist critics define the new genre of cultural studies. The "public intellectual," eager to comment on the state of society but dependent on the vicissitudes of noninstitutional patronage and so at times easily swayed to melancholy, is no longer common. Of course, bitter intellectual controversies still brew; we've just come through a period of open battles over "political correctness." The gay rights and feminist movements have channeled a great deal of intellectual energy into a variety of attacks on mainstream conventions. But the worst fights occur on campuses rather than in society at large, and although they rouse intense passions, they are also conditioned by the fact that most of the participants are or hope to be academically employed. The possibility that a larger pattern of intellectual alienation will develop has dwindled, at least for the moment.

A final ingredient of the past century's uncertain mood also seems largely absent: Feeding into the fin de siècle atmosphere was a sense that sexual and leisure habits were changing—and the sense was accurate. Uncertainty about standards in these areas fed the allegations of modern degeneracy—one element of the fin de siècle reaction against modernity—while also prompting some groups to display their sexual or lifestyle progressivism as yet another way to shock the bourgeoisie. Social observers are not always correct when they think they can identify a contemporary lifestyle watershed, but a hundred years ago they were. Victorian shibboleths about the dangers of sexuality and the absolute primacy of work were beginning to yield, without, however, yet disappearing; hence the dispute and confusion.

We can now realize more precisely that what was happening in the sexual arena was a transition from Victorian preoccupation with controlling sexual habits, as a means of birth control and as a central moral focus, to a greater interest in sexual pleasure along with more extensive use of artificial contraception. Middle-class women, particularly those born after about 1870, were beginning to seek more consistent access to sexual enjoyment, at least within marriage. Restrictive costumes and courtship habits were easing. Public discussion of sexuality was changing to include more graphic sexual representations and more open discussion of alternatives. The installation of these changes was very halting, because the Victorian standards had been profoundly internalized. Even as sexual interests grew, new anxieties about homosexuality or venereal disease served to complicate the process.

Similar basic change generated matching hesitation in the more general leisure area. Leisure life expanded with a decrease in work time and with the greater availability of commercial sources of amusement, from the new genre of amusement parks to professional sports to vaudeville and early films. But the middle class had long defined itself in terms of the delights and rewards of hard work. It participated in the new leisure, but it worried greatly at the same time. Again, the resultant confusion in values helped to define the darker side of the turn-of-the-century mood.

We can say—tentatively because, again, it is so hard to grasp one's own time as part of a historical continuum—that we do not seem to be facing a comparable set of dilemmas in values today. Disputes exist, to be sure, and they can be bitter. We have entered a period of greater sexual conservatism thanks to the power of vociferous Christian groups, the renewed concern of some articulate feminists about the impact of undue sexuality on women, and the threat of AIDS. Certainly, different factions disagree about appropriate sexual behavior and about sexual trends, and as noted, there is some concern about the often evoked "family values." But as a society, we still accept the importance of sexual expression, and we remain fairly committed to a high level of sexual innuendo and representation. We are still operating, in other words, along many of the trend lines that were just taking shape a hundred years ago. Our last big fight about a shift in values came in the 1960s, recently enough to limit another pitched battle despite skirmishing around the edges. We look openly for sexual satisfaction in marriage and understand when marriages dissolve on grounds of incompatibility. Rates of marital infidelity are not high (and it is conceivable that they have declined from the steamy 1960s; evidence is not clear), but marital sexual activity is considerable, by 19th-century standards and, given the widespread adoption of birth control practices, openly designed for pleasure. Among adolescents and young adults, we are not really surprised at news of premarital sex, despite important controversies around the margins. We have not tried to roll back the costumes and habits that began to open up sexual behavior by about 1900. As a result, the mainstream middle class is harder to shock in this area than was its counterpart of a century ago, less likely to sense degeneracy right around the corner; at the same time, fewer groups—although of course some remain—feel obliged to demonstrate their own sexual indulgence as part of expanding the boundaries of modernity.

To be sure, certain religious minorities dispute the terrain. And concern about teenage morality persists amid high rates of illegitimate births. During the mid-1990s, some newscasts began to highlight chastity pledges by various teenagers, occasionally claiming that here was the "morality of the nineties." But evidence was otherwise. Rates of teenage sexual intercourse, which had first gone up as part of the early marriage age of the 1940s and 1950s, continued to be high even though the marriage age itself had risen. Even adjustments in teenage sexual activity in response to AIDS were surprisingly modest. Amid some contention and ambiguity—and in a society that in fact remained somewhat more prudish than its counterparts in Europe or Japan—Americans stayed committed to the high stake in sexuality that had begun to emerge, amid much greater uncertainty, about a hundred years ago.

The same partial resolution of earlier tensions applies to leisure styles more generally. We have worked out a combination of work and leisure that seems to be fairly widely accepted. A few critics aside, we no longer rail against some of the most common forms of mass leisure; instead, comment is aimed at specific manifestations, such as particular television shows or some objectionable feature of the latest Disney park. We certainly do not defend a rigorous work ethic against any significant leisure outlet. We worry about people who do not have or claim well-defined leisure interests. We are, in sum, still relatively comfortable with major aspects of the culture that first began to take shape around 1900. We don't need to focus on the turn of the century as a means of expressing our anxieties about changes in values or of demonstrating our freedom from outdated standards.

For all our worries, we appear to be somewhat better able to operate in an industrialized, consumer-focused society than our ancestors were a hundred years ago when the basic structure of the economy was so much more recent. Perhaps this adaptation is not good; adjustment has its costs in terms of the loss of critical perspective. Perhaps we have been sex-ed and leisure-d into complacency, which is after all a criticism still levied against modern mass culture. But the fact is that, either in our reactions to modern art or in our handling of sexuality, we do not present the diffuse field needed to generate such a mood as fin de siècle. Probably, in this sense, it was the 1890s that were unusual in associating an important set of intellectual and values issues with a coincidental anticipation of the calendar.

A mood of uncertainty could still coalesce that would give our end of century some distinctive tone. The most ardent critics of sexual looseness and degenerate values in the Western world are Christian conservatives. Few of them are intellectuals, and virtually none seeks to experiment with new art forms or with serious aesthetic issues; this already inhibits them from generating a fin de siècle atmosphere. Most of these conservatives—a violent minority aside—are still optimistic about America's future if only a few trends can be reversed, like big government, abortion, and (tacitly) the pressures from racial minorities. This mood (which is echoed in Europe by groups such as the French National Front) is interesting, but it is simply not as sweeping as its counterpart was a hundred years ago. It doesn't invoke the end of the century, and it doesn't embrace such a sweeping reevaluation of modern society. Conservative success is generating liberal pessimism, however. American liberals, reeling after their congressional defeat in 1994, worry greatly about a conservative, business-dominated future. Some point to the need to address moral issues, including violence and sexual license, here belatedly agreeing with conservatives that we must reexamine our spiritual core and that merely arguing about economic and welfare policy is not enough. This group does include intellectuals. Faced both with a crisis in values and the ascendancy of anti-elitist conservatism, this group might yet generate a searching, pessimistic mood, providing a subterranean echo to the strange fin de siècle stirrings that occurred before 1900. But none of this has yet coalesced. For now, Western society awaits the next century divided in many ways, but without the odd mixture of beliefs and quests that greeted the last century's end.

*   *   *

The combination of outlooks that marked the end of the 19th century was fascinatingly complex. Our moods, a hundred years later, are less extreme. Both naive optimism and fin de siècle anxieties were confounded or tainted by developments during the first half of our century. Although acknowledging our recurrent impulse toward sweeping optimism, it is hard to lament a contemporary context that constrains both unadulterated pitches for progress and disoriented carping.

We may be just as confused, certainly just as worried, as were the last heralds of a new century, but we no longer greet the ongoing elaboration of industrial mass society either with rejection and frontal conflict or with a wishful glorification of every modern trend. In our narrower range of debate, we may also be a bit less flamboyant. Certainly we do not seem to be leading up to the celebration of the 21st century with a great drumbeat; our parade thus far has no particular direction and no dramatic floats. Unable to match the unique drama of the 1890s, in hailing and lamenting simultaneously, we will have to carve out a different path. One way to start might be to take a deep breath and figure out what the 20th century has been about, free from the compulsions either to boast endlessly or to sulk that distorted the efforts of those who tried in the 1890s to capture what their own century had meant. Warned by the last turn of the century but driven again to use the occasion for evaluation, perhaps we can do a better job.

Yet there is another angle as well. Contemporary society also shows a rift, in many ways as striking as the optimist–fin de siècle divide of the 1890s, although perhaps more shallow. On the one hand, religious doomsayers provide their version of a critique of the dominant culture, encouraged by millennial apparitions. On the other, a certain vestigial optimism combines with a contemporary party-on spirit, of the sort that has led to the reservation of London's Savoy or the Seattle Space Needle for turn-of-the-century revelry years in advance. As the ball drops, some moderns will huddle for the world's end while others will seek the mother of all benders. Might we be better off with the more intellectualized optimism–pessimism of a century past, despite the confusions and exaggerations involved? How much does the contemporary division reflect disagreements about how to escape reality, while oddly sharing a common sense that some flight is essential?

THE 20TH CENTURY:
GUIDELINES FOR THE
RETROSPECTIVE

EVER SINCE THE IDEA OF CELEBRATING CENTURIES became firmly established in 1700, looking back on the past hundred years has been an inescapable and desirable feature. Retrospectives of this sort refresh our collective memories—much like year-end reviews on a grander scale—and encourage us to think about trends and meanings. Precisely because we have no grand end-of-the-century mood and because our century has been so full of turmoil, we can expect assessments to be complex and controversial. Some ingredients, nevertheless, are clear enough as we prepare for the welter of evaluations that will vie for attention. After some general orientations to the century that is now slipping away, we can turn to several categories of developments that do give the 20th century some clear historical directions.

Like any good century—and perhaps more than most—the 20th has been full of diverse events and patterns. Large textbooks have been written spelling out the complex web of developments on the world scale, for Europe, for the United States—almost literally, for every major region. There is no point in trying to re-hearse this level of detail. Rather, in advance of the newspaper summaries that will surely attend the turn of the century, we need to ask about basic trends and meanings. This chapter both cuts under the sweeping megajudgments about whether the century should be viewed in terms of progress or of a fin de siècle disengagement and sails above the meticulous textbook accounts. As we think about what this century has added up to as we watch its close, or perhaps as a basis for thinking about what will come next, what major themes can we accurately identify?

Who, for example, has been the most important individual in the 20th century? If the *New York Times* or some less-sophisticated outlet should ask this question in their retrospective, what might the answer be? The *Times,* of course, unhesitantly pointed to Napoleon for the 19th century, while immediately indicating its distaste for his warlike, autocratic ways. Perhaps a case could have been made for Karl Marx or Charles Darwin. It would certainly have been possible to argue that the idea of designating a single most important personage for a whole century is silly. But surely, if one were willing to indulge the conceit, the answer would have been a European male from a fairly short list. I find it much harder to come up with a plausible list for the 20th century. Surely a male still, for male power has continued to surpass that of women. Almost surely not a European (unless perhaps Albert Einstein), for Europe no longer pulled the strings during the century as a whole. Mao Ze-dong or Mahatma Gandhi? Henry Ford? The difficulty in coming up with a name reflects our proximity to our own time, and it may be accidental that a single individual ever stands out as much as Napoleon did. But the difficulty may also reflect how hard it is to pinpoint what our century has been about, to find any coherent theme.

At the same time, of course, we are quite accustomed to thinking in terms of centuries. Our history courses and textbooks are typically organized this way, reflecting how deeply ingrained the concept of the century has become. Material on the 20th century is commonplace, and this implies at least that there are some central threads, for the world as a whole, for our society, or for specific topics like youth or fashion. At times, to be sure, the century label is merely a convenience, an arbitrary definition that provides starting and (soon) ending points that have no inherent significance but that allow us to focus our inquiry. Most of us, however, when we think of a 20th-century history of this or that, probably do assume that more than random opportunism is involved. And despite the complexity and the difficulty, this is probably correct. Although not all centuries have definable characteristics, ours does, and it will help to review these characteristics as part of making intelligent use of the end of the century in taking stock of where we've been coming from and where we are.

A signpost: Even though it is hard to choose a "most important person" for the 20th century, choosing the decisive event is relatively easy. World War I set many of the century's main developments and tensions in motion, particularly Europe's decline in world power and the increasing chorus of voices from outside the West. The war also launched redefinitions of government roles and huge new uncertainties about the power of modern technology. Decisive people or events do not always emerge early in a new century—the 18th century would be a recent example—but they have appeared early in both the 19th and the 20th centuries, which helps orient any larger interpretation.

Three preliminaries before tackling the main analytical task: We must, of course, note (as the *Times* did in its panegyric to the 19th century) that not every major trend of our times began with the 20th century. Many aspects of the rise of science that started in the 17th century are still with us. There are some specifi-

cally 20th-century features in the role of science—including its growing specialization and inaccessibility to a literate public—but the dominance of scientific
prestige, assumptions, and methods is not a peculiarly 20th-century feature. Our
continued attraction to the idea of progress, although newly beleaguered in our
century, goes back to the 18th-century Enlightenment. Many themes of our own
time—for example, the importance of technological innovation or the tensions
between work and family—were launched with the Industrial Revolution, which
took shape between 1770 and 1840. There is no need for an exhaustive list, so long
as we remember not to overemphasize the stand-alone qualities of our century.
Any definition must fold in traits that persist from prior periods.

There is also the problem of deciding when, for analytical purposes, the century began. Most definitions of the 19th century actually take in almost 150 years,
beginning with the early Industrial Revolution and the political revolutions of the
1770s and 1780s, and running up to 1914. Many 20th-century histories, in turn,
take 1914 as their starting point. On the whole, this breakdown makes sense. Giving centuries a character depends on some flexibility in dating. At the same time,
a case can be made for considering the last quarter of the 19th century to be the
beginning of the 20th century, and thus including the new linkage of the world
through European imperialism; the rise of advanced industrial technology, including the electrical and internal combustion engines; and the development of
many of the attributes of consumer society, such as mass advertising and a more
open sexuality. Here, too, there is no reason to linger over a debate, so long as the
necessary suppleness is maintained. Some "20th-century" trends are clearly a century and a quarter old by now; others only began with World War I. Almost none
actually started between 1900 and 1905, which was not (some exceptions made
for eastern Asia) one of the really interesting half-decades of modern history. Beyond this range—suggesting a roughly forty-year, variable, start-up time between
the dominant trends of the 19th century and those of the 20th century itself—
further precision or debate would quickly become academically petty.

The eminent historian Eric Hobsbawm has recently tried to cut through uncertainty by defining a "short" 20th century (which followed the "long" 19th century
that lasted until 1914) in terms of the shake-up of world alignments that began
with World War I and ended with the fading of the Cold War in 1989. This is tidy
enough. But as we will see, other defining trends, such as low birthrates, feminism, or consumerism, originated in the 1870s or 1880s and show no sign of let-
ting up even today. We need to admit the necessity of flexibility, even in identifying when, in terms of trends and not mere calendar, our century began.

Finally and most important, it is vital to remember that although the 20th century does have definable traits that we can legitimately assess and ponder while
waiting for the next century to kick in, it is far too long a time span to be entirely

coherent. Some of the same caveats offered for the millennium must be repeated even for a period a tenth as long. A hundred years provide ample space for many internal changes of direction, and these must also be noted even as some overarching themes are identified as well.

There has, in fact, been a strong temptation to equate the 20th century with just one of its parts. When I started teaching, I was involved in a survey course run by older Europeans who had come to maturity in the interwar years and then fled to the United States. For them, the 20th century was unadulterated horror, defined by the decline of Europe in two world wars, the rise of Nazism and Soviet communism, and (although they were too kind to say so explicitly) the saccharine surge of American-style mass taste. There was no reason to teach such an awful century explicitly; they assigned Dostoyevsky's *Grand Inquisitor* and left it at that. For many people raised between 1914 and 1945, the searing experience of war and depression, exacerbated by intellectuals who warned of the West's downfall, marked the whole century. More recently, there have been those, like Francis Fukuyama, who want to see the 20th century defined by the hopeful events of the past decade, which they see as picking up on older trends. To these analysts, the 20th century means the rise of liberal democracy and material advance under capitalism. They define the whole span by trends that have been far more visible since 1945 than they were during the dreadful decades of world war, when both democracy and capitalism declined.

Clearly, the whole century cannot be captured by either of these truncated approaches. In gross textbook terms, the century divides into three subperiods (four, if one begins the century in the 1870s for analytical purposes). Period one is defined by the world wars and the depression. Period two is framed by the Cold War, decolonization, and the unexpected revival of Europe; it runs from the late 1940s until 1985. Then a new period opens (perhaps it will turn out to be best regarded, analytically, as the beginning of the 21st century) with the spread of democracy and the collapse of European communism and the Soviet empire.

Major facets of political and diplomatic history do not have a century-level periodization, in sum. The analysis of these facets requires the century to be broken down into smaller units, for the causes that actuate them are powerful for only a few decades, not beyond. Thus, the decades between 1914 and 1945 are defined by the preconditions for fascism and Nazism, by the causes of the depression and its social and political consequences, and by the rise of Germany and Japan and their clash with their European and U.S. opponents; but just as dramatically, these factors receded rapidly after 1945, to be replaced by other shaping influences. To be sure, residual worries persisted, fears that Nazism could rise again, that a classic depression might recur, or that Germany would once more get out of hand. Even in the 1990s it is possible to drum up some scary scenarios about history repeating itself. But nothing of the sort has happened, nor (except the worry itself and the sensible attempts explicitly to prevent recurrence) have these possibilities been a major factor in the history of the past fifty years.

A whole set of assessment categories, as a result, cannot be applied to the 20th century as a unit. Political systems form one such category. There simply is no political trend for the whole century, aside from flux and variety spiced by an extraordinary number of revolutions. The 20th century does gain some coherence if it is seen as a century in which traditional systems were cast aside, extraordinary widely, and in which innovation had to ensue. With the major exception of a handful of Western democracies—the United States, Canada, Australia, New Zealand, Britain, Scandinavia, and the Netherlands—no major country has enjoyed the same basic political system through the whole 20th century. Moves toward democracy early in the century were swamped in Italy, Germany, Japan, Spain, and the smaller states of Eastern Europe, only to be later restored. Monarchies were replaced or downgraded almost everywhere, most notably, of course, in China, where an imperial system dating back several millennia decisively gave way. A bit later, the colonial regimes so dominant in much of the world in 1900 were definitively dislodged. But the replacement systems were just as likely to be totalitarian or authoritarian as democratic. So although the 20th century is full of political change, founded on the need to experiment with novel systems given the rejection of more traditional structures and of colonialism, variety and instability seem to the only identifiable characteristics of the century's political systems worldwide. In the last quarter of the century, a nearly worldwide turn toward democracy may set the stage for a more uniform political experience in the 21st century, but this democratic shift is not yet well enough established to pass muster as a durable political trend.

Diplomatic flux is just as obvious a political trend, particularly in terms of great-power interaction and the advent of war. The rise of the Soviet Union and the United States does run through virtually the entire century, taking different forms, of course, between the world wars and afterward. In this category, there is a bit more to work on in defining the 20th century in the international arena than there is with political systems. Even at the century's end, some of the leading questions about world affairs relate to uncertainties about the future course of these two great powers. And a few diplomatic alliances have been reasonably stable—the United States and Britain, for example. Finally, the question of rebalancing overall world alignments to take the quests for freedom and the independence of Africa and Asia into account does provide a consistent backdrop, a point to which we must return. But it is risky to venture generalizations much farther. Japan was a major belligerent power at one point, but then it changed its stripes dramatically. Germany, so obviously central from before 1900 until 1945, declines without disappearing as a diplomatic pivot after World War II. Relatedly, several decades dominated by world wars or the fear of world wars yielded to a period of armed, uneasy peace punctuated by severe regional conflicts but also characterized by unprecedented coordination efforts in Western Europe (here, the deliberate contrast with the interwar years could not be more striking). Even the vital theme of the relationship between the West and the rest of the world takes on radically different contours between the period of striving for independence, the period of outright decolonization and decolonization conflicts (1946–1970s), and the period of independence (overlapping the conflict decades) in which major states like Egypt, India, Nigeria, and Indonesia begin to play a significant role.

The volatility of political and diplomatic currents may seem unsurprising, although it does obviously caution against sweeping characterizations of our century. But themes a bit farther beneath the surface of events have also shifted direction frequently in our century, again bedeviling the generalizer.

Four examples may suffice. First, technology. Obviously the 20th century has seen the fairly steady generation of increasingly advanced technologies for transportation, communication, and production. In this sweeping sense, then, there is a unifying theme of innovation (which goes back, in fact, at least one century further, to the advent of the Industrial Revolution). But many analysts argue that the nature of technology decisively shifted in the 1960s and 1970s, moving away from advanced industrial technology (characteristic of the new machines of the 1920s) to the postindustrial technology that centers on the computer but that also includes a new emphasis on genetic engineering, robotics, and high-speed energy transmissions. This shift, it is contended, was more than a recurrent acceleration in innovation. The new technology greatly streamlined the production of goods, but because it focused on information exchange, it fundamentally altered the labor force. The number of blue-collar workers, the focus of previous new technologies, now began to shrink, while white-collar and technical workers faced rapid technological change for the first time. Relatedly, educational requirements for dealing with the postindustrial technology went up, leaving a group of workers, both in Western Europe and the United States, structurally unemployed. Factories as centers of technology receded in favor of offices, and thanks to computer linkages, some work even returned to the home. In sum, a new technological context broke the 20th century in two in the economically advanced areas of the world.

Demography is our second example. Here, too, there is a case to be made for an underlying 20th-century theme in societies like the United States (world demography will be handled later). A major demographic transition had begun late in the 19th century with a dramatic reduction in birthrates. This transition was completed in the decades 1880–1920, in Western Europe as well as the United

States, by an almost-as-dramatic drop in infant mortality. The result was a trend toward low birthrates, rising life expectancy and a resultant aging population, and very slow population growth. This complex trend, visible already in 1900, moved steadily through the interwar period, enhanced, in fact, by the pressures of the depression, and this is the trend that we are familiar with again today, with societies like Japan joining in. But there is an obvious problem: Right in the middle of this tidy trend came the startling, portentous baby boom, running from the mid-1940s to the mid-1960s. Family size increased notably, in Western Europe and particularly the United States, as the middle class nearly doubled its birthrate and the working class stopped reducing its own. Pundits at the time wrote persuasively about a "third phase" of demographic history. In the first phase, high birthrates and death rates prevailed. Then came the demographic transition, compelled by limited family resources plus the pressure of falling infant morality. But then came another transition as a more prosperous society deliberately chose to expend its new resources on the joys of child rearing and expanded family life. Of course, this argument was flawed because there was no durable new demography, only the monster blip of the baby boom. After 1963, the pattern of restrained birthrates resumed, dipping lower in some places (Germany, Italy) than it had during the 1920s and 1930s. But this dramatic oscillation clearly imposes real caution in talking about "the" demographic trend in industrial societies during the 20th century. The unexpected happened, and its results, in creating a large and sometimes querulous baby boom cohort, have colored the whole second half of the century. Even societal aging, a major trend early in the century and again at its end, was reversed for several decades thanks to the boomers—another development that complicates generalization and bedevils our social policy toward the elderly. In Western demography, in sum, the 20th century does not really operate as a unit; a more precise, shorter-term periodization is essential.

Religion forms the leading cultural example of the zigzags of the 20th century. Through much of the century, formal religion has seemed to decline. Marxist attacks joined with the lures of nationalism or consumer culture to replace or limit religious commitment. Not only Europe, the Soviet Union, Japan, and China but also important sectors of the Middle East and Africa seemed to be rejecting or weakening religious leadership. The trend was complex, as the large fundamentalist minority in the United States demonstrated, but a prediction that secular loyalties would gain further ground seemed safe enough until the 1970s. But the dramatic revival of Islam and Hinduism, a new Protestant missionary current in Latin America, and signs of religious vitality in post-Communist Eastern Europe have created a much more varied picture. At least for a time, diverse cultural currents, rather than inexorable religious decline, dominate the international scene. In this area, too, the 20th century has broken its own initial mold.

Finally, consider the fortunes of the trade unions. For the United States and Western Europe, the first half of the 20th century can readily be described in terms of the rise and growing impact of the trade union movement. Brief oscillations and setbacks, as in the "Red Scare" period of the 1920s, must be acknowledged, but they do not seriously qualify the larger trend. There were good reasons for growing union strength: the maturing of the labor force, the impact of full political democracy, and the new pressures placed on the work process by growing corporations, new and faster equipment, and speedup procedures such as the assembly line. But this trend peaked in the late 1950s, only to be replaced, again throughout the Western world, by increasing trade union decline and disarray. There is no single "20th century" for the trade union movement or labor politics. (Note the rise and fall of Communist parties in the United States and Western Europe.) As in the other cases of internal periodization, for which dramatic shifts in direction prevent any centennial generalizations, this lack of a unitary "20th century" means that different questions about causation arise depending on what part of the 20th century one examines. For the first half, explanations for the rise of trade unions gain pride of place, but after 1957, the wheel turns full circle as the question to be answered becomes why unions begin to fail.

No century, even if its designation is refined so that it begins with some real change (like the events of 1914) rather than the accident of the calendar, has full unity. Major internal shifts have to be recognized. It is possible that the 20th century involves more such internal shifts than the 19th century did, although it would be otiose to spin this comparison out in detail. If the 20th century includes a major redefinition of industrial life shortly past its midpoint, it is hardly surprising that it becomes difficult to convey the full hundred years as one entity. Another obvious complication is the need to keep in mind an international focus vastly more complex than that of the 19th century, when the rise and abusive intrusion of the West did impose some surface simplicity on the world at large. For the 20th century, the growing if incomplete autonomy of key regions imposes a serious requirement for greater nuance in any generalization scheme. In women's history, for example, although the 20th century has seen some consistent movements toward greater voting rights and legal equality, generalizations break down in the areas of work and even of effective political voice when the international arena is taken into account. The spread of mechanization and commercial agriculture has displaced many women in the production sphere, in Africa for example, and the growth of state functions has reduced women's informal political powers. There is no tidy, straight-line trend in the world as a whole, although perhaps one will emerge, thanks to growing feminist pressure, for the next century.

In sum, the 20th century simply does not work as a unit for a number of key topics or as a means of adequately capturing the world's diversity. Trends carried over from earlier times complicate any attempt to hail the century's originality, and major internal shifts in direction and a massive new dose of regional diversity hinder the same attempt from within the century.

The Hazards of Labeling the Century

Internal subperiods constitute one of the reasons that some efforts to define the 20th century have missed the mark:

- Early in the century, well-meaning social workers tried to characterize the new age as "the century of the child." In terms of lower birthrates, better health, and new concerns about individual children, the label seemed to have meaning. But how can the title be defended, even for the Western world, for a century that has seen rising divorce rates with scant concern for the effects on children, considerable parental loss of interest in children as a measure of family success (as determined by polling data in the United States from the 1950s to the 1970s), and, again in the United States, massive increases in children's poverty at key points amid more general affluence? Changes in children's situation, particularly after World War II, nearly overwhelm any single, benign description.
- Another common label, "the American century," may have more going for it, but here, too, there are marked changes in U.S. policy and position during the course of the past hundred years that qualify, at least, any sense of a sweeping, coherent trend toward ever greater U.S. power and influence. Certainly, the impact of international involvement on the United States altered greatly with World War II as an effort to preserve isolation shifted to the massive military effort that, admittedly along with growing global economic stakes, has so altered our society in the last fifty-plus years.
- Another plausible label—the title of a fascinating book by a French pundit, Raymond Aron—"the century of total war," also does not fit, save in noting the continued technological and organizational potential for war. The years 1914–1945 saw the birth of total war, in the sense of massive citizen involvement and unprecedented weaponry. But with the exception of the Iran–Iraq regional conflict, we have not seen a total war since. Changes in the nature of war unquestionably influenced the entire century, even in peacetime, but they have not really defined it. Internal shifts, from hot war to cold and then to the new peace we are currently attempting to chart, force the century out of some of the more dramatic characterizations.

It's not easy to reduce our era to advertising jingles because there have been too many different developments and too many sea changes along the way. Yet as we look for meaning at the century's end, a real case can be made for evaluating the past one hundred years in terms of some overarching trends and for considering these trends to be fundamental in changing much of the context in which most people of the world live. This characterization does not neglect the important internal confusions and complexities; it does not apply to every feature of our social lives. But talking about 20th-century history is not hollow; it conveys some rough but real meanings, applicable to the whole time span, conveying real analytical coherence. Even if the century has not tidily defined every major facet of historical change, it does actually seem to have been one of those seminal points—far rarer than centuries themselves—when a number of key new directions took shape and moved from infancy toward greater maturity.

The Perspective of World History: A New Power Balance

For world historians, the 20th century stands out as a major turning point in the relationships among the major societies of the world, a time when trends going back to the 15th century began to be reversed. Simply put, the dominance of Western Europe was initially challenged by new nationalist movements in various places—like the Congress movement in India, which had emerged by the 1880s—as well as by the growing economic and military influence of the United States and Russia. Early challenge was supported by basic shifts in the demographic and, more gradually, industrial patterns of many non-Western societies, and it was then greatly accelerated by the internecine warfare within Europe during the first half of the century. Europe paralyzed its own capacity to respond. The 20th century, then, although in successive iterations, gains unity as the stage for the replacement of the "rise of the West" by the "rise of the rest." This has not meant an absolute decline within Western Europe itself, although this seemed to be occurring into the 1950s and was often foretold by intellectual pessimists like Oswald Spengler. But Europe's relative decline is undeniable. Here is one of the main reasons the 20th century stands out not only in contrast to its immediate predecessor but as the launching pad for a new, larger period in world history whose full contours are by no means yet clear.

Changes in the world balance, as the century's leading theme, help explain why political innovation has been so widespread. During the 20th century, most regions of the world have needed to find some political alternative to Western dominance or to older regimes, such as the Chinese imperial system or the Ottoman empire, that proved to be incapable of regaining national freedoms. Even some Western countries have experienced changes in regimes as part of their adjustments to a new world position; France, for example, was forced by Algerian rebellion to redefine the republic at the end of the 1950s. Again, during the century as a whole political systems have varied, but the widespread problem of finding new kinds of legitimacies to replace old colonial or tainted structures relates directly to the fundamental shift in power alignments.

The toppling of Western dominance has had at least four facets, each running through the 20th century and all in combination reinforcing each other. The most obvious facet has been the cessation and then the reversal of European colonialism, that process of acquisition that began even before Columbus and continued just beyond 1900. By 1900, most of the world had been carved up by the West, save for some parts of China and the Middle East that were a bit too challenging to bother with and where Western interests themselves clashed dangerously. Japan stood apart, of course, as did most of the Americas, although in Latin America the West continued its economic dominance despite the fact that political independence had been achieved. The West showed some ideological hesitation about colonialism when it listened to Wilsonian preachments after World War I and converted certain territories to League of Nations mandates rather than outright colonies. More of the Middle East was divided up, however, in what was technically the high-water mark of Western control.

Agitation against Western dominance was already gaining ground. Pressure in India mounted steadily, spearheaded by the famous campaigns of Gandhi. There was an increase in Arab nationalism, whose intellectual origins lay in the 19th century. The first Pan-African nationalist meeting occurred in 1919. China's 1911 revolution put new pressure on Western enclaves, which were gradually reduced. As early as the 1930s, concessions had to be offered to the major Arab states in the Middle East, although full independence for this region did not occur until after World War II. Western exhaustion and still greater local nationalism, from Indonesia to Algeria, simply compelled rapid decolonization from the 1940s onward. The bulk of this process was completed by the 1950s, although a few particularly complex holdouts persisted for another two decades. By the 1970s, Europe's colonial empires had almost completely disappeared. Only scattered holdings in the Caribbean and the Pacific, such as French Tahiti, bore witness to the once mighty structures.

Decolonization was paralleled and in some cases furthered by the West's relative military decline. From the 15th century until the early 20th, Western nations had gained a decided edge over the rest of the world in the tools of war. The first advantage, chronologically, focused on ships and naval gunnery and allowed the West to control the seas plus many ports and islands. Then, in the 19th century, more mobile artillery and more automatic small arms brought Western preponderance inland, such that small European forces could easily defeat larger armies of Africans or Chinese. This increased firepower was the technological basis for the final round of imperialism. But in the 20th century, this long trend began to be modified although it was not completely eliminated. First, a few non-Western nations, notably Japan, began to develop armaments levels comparable to those of the West. Then innovations in warfare, particularly in guerrilla tactics utilized in places such as Mao's China, Vietnam, and Algeria, gave non-Western forces the ability to hold their own against technologically superior arsenals from the West. Finally, newly independent states, as in the Middle East, were able to manufacture or buy enough advanced weaponry to make it impossible for Western states to pick them off easily. To be sure, the West could still outgun the forces of a nation like Iraq, but it now had to prepare massively and might even in victory hold back from outright invasion. Militarily, the tide was turning, at least in terms of the relative balance of power around the world.

The West also began to be decisively outnumbered demographically. Western Europe's share of the world population had grown fairly consistently from the late Middle Ages through the 19th century. The huge population spurt of the 18th century had propelled a final surge, providing enough Westerners to support expansion into North America, Australia, and New Zealand. By 1900 this pattern was shifting. One of the great trends of the 20th century has been the massive expansion of the populations of Asia, Africa, and Latin America, based on improved food supplies and new public health measures, along with the rapid reduction in the demographic growth rates of the West. Some observers may wish to pull out the overall world population trends as a separate factor in the evaluation of the 20th century, for it is certainly true that total growth rates increased massively in this century, beyond all precedent, straining available resources, producing teeming cities far larger than those of the West, and further threatening environmental quality. It is also true that these same trends fit into the rebalancing of world power relationships, putting new pressure on the West from immigration and creating issues of social and economic inequality at a new, global level. Again, these basic patterns have filled the whole century. It was early in the 20th century, for example, that India's persistent population surge began. It was in the 1920s and 1930s that Muslim immigrants from North Africa began to filter into France, a foreshadowing of the more massive movements that after World War II would create a huge French Muslim minority. Centuries of Western population outflow have now been replaced by a century of more complex pressure from non-Western demography, and there is almost surely more still to come in the future.

Finally, the rebalancing of the world has involved a shift in economic dominance. Here is the most complex aspect of the relative decline of the West, for it mixes some familiar changes with shifts that have sometimes been obscured by the indiscriminant use of labels such as "Third World" but that build on developments visible from at least the 1920s onward. The baseline, of course, is familiar enough. From the 16th century onward, the West steadily gained in manufacturing sophistication over the rest of the world. This pattern was given a quantum boost with the Industrial Revolution, which for over a hundred years created a massive gap between the technologically advanced West and virtually the entire rest of the world, much of which actually lost industry as it faced cheap, factory-produced imports. Only Western-populated societies, such as the United States, Canada, and Australia, complicated the picture, for they proved to be capable of integrating industrial equipment fairly rapidly and joined the ranks of the industrial West during the 19th century itself.

Since 1900, the gap between the industrialized West and the rest of the world has narrowed in several ways, even aside from the tremendous advances the United States made on Europe's leaders from 1900 until the 1970s. Several non-Western areas have managed to industrialize either fully or substantially, which means that they have rapidly gained on the West or caught up outright, in technological levels, per capita income, nature of manufacturing, and so on. Japan, whose catch-up process began in the 1880s and reached fruition in the 1960s, is the great success story in this category, but the more recent industrialization of South Korea and Taiwan fits in the same category. "Advanced industrial" and "West" are no longer coterminous, and this is the culmination of a process of industrial rebalancing that has gone on through the whole century. At the same time, other areas, although not yet matching the West and Japan, have managed to sponsor a significant industrial evolution that has modified the world economic gap and reduced the West's relative edge. During the 1920s, Iran launched a policy of selective modernization focused on developing its internal capacity to produce basic industrial goods in order to limit dependence on Western imports. Turkey followed suit soon afterward. During the 1930s, key Latin American governments in Chile, Brazil, Argentina, and Mexico, for example, adopted much the same policy of import replacement, using state initiatives to foster manufacturing in ways that would halt the growing imbalance between Latin America and Western Europe and the United States. India has pursued a similar policy since 1947. In none of these cases has a full industrial revolution occurred. Continued economic problems often earn these nations the dreaded "Third World" label. But in fact, the label is misleading, for it masks significant change. Large industrial sectors have developed, often commanding about a quarter of the total labor force. Significant manufacturing exports have emerged: India sells widely to Southeast Asia; Brazil has become the world's fourth-largest computer manufacturer while also competing directly in international sales of steel. High growth rates have often resulted. India has managed a growth rate, at 5 percent of its gross national product per year, in advance of its admittedly burdensome population explosion. Mexico and Brazil have experienced several periods of rapid growth, and Brazil, at least, is currently expected to enjoy a roughly 7 percent annual growth through the 1990s. China, since it modified its strict state planning in 1978, has also surged forward, with annual growth rates up to 10 percent. This pattern of development is not worldwide; it has not yet embraced much of Africa. And it is subtle, in the sense that it fails to overcome massive poverty and it preserves some of the previous gaps with the global industrial leaders. But it is among the basic trends of the 20th century—what might be called an "industrialization of the world" replacing the West-centered Industrial Revolution of the previous period. Here, too, a clear pattern of Western hegemony, stretching back before 1800, has been modified, creating a much more complex set of interactions among the major world regions than had prevailed when the rise of the West so simplified global dynamics.

The 20th century, then, is one of those relatively rare moments in world history when the balance among major societies alters in fundamental ways. Most of the processes involved in this rebalancing have been operating during the whole century, although the specific manifestations have unfolded in stages, notably with the burst of decolonization coming around midpoint. As the century closes, all parts of the world are still adjusting to and building on this pattern of change.

A Century of Internationalization

At the same time, the century offers a second, somewhat confusing theme: As world leadership has become more diffuse, international connections have on the whole intensified. Internationalization is the second major theme of the century, by definition on a global scale. International contacts have been increasing fairly steadily since an early point in the history of agricultural societies and civilizations. I have already noted that there was a major redefinition and acceleration of these contacts a millennium ago. Determining clear breaks in this trend, moments when the intensification of contacts becomes a change in kind and not just degree, is not always easy. Nevertheless, a good case can be made that the 20th century is one such watershed, if only because of the tremendous strides in connective technologies, from the late–19th-century undersea cables and wireless radio onward. The increased speed of transportation thanks to the airplane, the steady expansion of capacity both for international communication and the movement of goods, and more recently, the development of satellite and computer linkages set a clear basis for vastly increased connections among virtually all the inhabited parts of the globe. When over a quarter of the world's population can watch a single event on television—such as World Cup soccer—a new level has clearly been attained. Organizational developments have paralleled the technology: From the late 19th century onward, international organizations have proliferated, and although many—such as the International Postal Union—were initially Western-dominated, they soon came to have genuinely international leadership and impact. The rise of the multinational corporation, originating from the overseas expansion of European and American businesses in the 19th century, was another sign and promoter of growing interconnectedness. International scientific conferences have created links among experts who share a common specialized training that often transcends regional affiliations and allegiances. International sports interest constitutes another unprecedented development that crosses almost all regional lines. Not only soccer but also the Olympic Games—reestablished in the 1890s and gradually shifted from initial Western dominance to global participation—both symbolized and promoted this facet of global cultural contact.

In sum, the 20th century has seen a dramatic acceleration of the technical capacity for international exchange, a variety of organizations capable of promoting contacts in areas ranging from business through science to sports and popular entertainment, and something of an international culture, with a host of people heavily committed to the importance and validity of an international approach. As two world wars themselves attest, never before has the global framework harbored such a capacity to affect the course of individual lives on a regular basis in societies on all the inhabited continents.

Regionalism and Internationalism: Two Trends of the Century in Conflict

The two major world trends that define the 20th century have coexisted uneasily, which has also contributed to the character of our time. Freedom from Western domination—the global rebalancing—has promoted and been promoted by a host of nationalisms and regional loyalties. With a larger number of separate governments and with growing demographic and even some manufacturing strength around the world, there is more opportunity for conflict between varied assertions and expressions. Yet the impact of world contacts usually operates in the opposite direction as international businesses and other organizations work toward growing coordination. Much of the content of global communications is, in fact, Western-dominated. The worldwide (though uneven) influence of U.S. films and television, of Euro-American fashions or rock music, of Euro-American skyscrapers and hotel chains, or of U.S. fast-food eating habits has been an obvious fact of the 20th century. Western cultural influence has accelerated since World War II, but it was clearly launched by the meteoric rise in the 1920s of Hollywood as the dominant source of mass movies and by the spread of the "international" style in modern art and design. Popular culture exports became one of the staples of the U.S. economy, second only to aircraft sales. Global connections here war with newly independent regional power bases. At the same time, Western popular cultural and stylistic leadership (supplemented, to be sure, by Japanese and other business backing, as foreign capital promotes Hollywood movie companies or Disney resorts) complicates the pattern of relative decline of the West in other respects.

Reactions to the tension between heightened internationalism (with its homogenizing potential) and more decentralized political and economic power have been varied, and the oscillations form a major part of the complex coherence of the 20th century. At times, major countries have attempted to pull back from the international web, to go it alone in order to protect regional autonomy and self-expression. The Soviet Union adopted this course under Stalin; China did so under Mao's Cultural Revolution. By the end of the 20th century, these dramatic gestures seem to have been unsuccessful, although small individual countries, such as Burma, continue to take this path. Regional particularisms—ranging from subnational independence movements in various parts of the world to the separate film industries of nations like India (the world's largest movie producer, although Indian films are not for export) to gestures such as the Japanese government's subsidization of training in the use of chopsticks (against schoolchildren's preference for the more efficient fork)—dot the 20th century; they are attempts to combine participation in the international arena with the preservation of adequate space for smaller, individual identities. Nazism was an attempt to break away from the pressures of international connections; it asserted a unique German identity and created a mythic past in the process. Part of this checkerboard is formed by cultural reactions since the 1970s, and particularly the rise of religious fundamentalisms in Islam, Hinduism, and some parts of Christianity, on the part of people empowered to express their own values (not all of them traditional; there are some newer ones as well) yet constrained by the web of international connections. The fact that in many areas elites have participated more readily in an international culture than ordinary people have adds an important social tension to the brew. Conflict between an internationalist elite and a more proudly parochial heartland certainly defines an important recurring 20th-century theme in the United States.

The 20th century is thus marked by two decisive trends at the world historical level and by the uneasy relationship between those trends, which underlies some of the more dramatic passages of the century's cultural trajectory. Although some of this interaction was foreshadowed by 19th-century developments, revolutionary technology plus multinational business and the decline in the power of the West have been decisive new elements. Where the future lies, in this complex balance, is unclear, but this is precisely what one would expect from a century that launched unprecedented trends at the global level.

Any historian looking back on the 20th century will surely see the breaks in world patterns as the leading characteristic of the age precisely because so many long-standing trends were reversed and because such a difficult interplay, between powerful internationalism and new-found particularisms, was established. Closer to home, however, we can also identify another set of patterns that give the 20th century some coherence and some real claim to innovation.

A Domestic 20th Century:
Developing the Consumer Society

We can begin, in this domain, with a particular example and then move out to the more general. Between 1890 and 1910—that is, as close to the beginning of the 20th century as one could hope for, in terms of a general trend—middle-class Americans began their ongoing battle against body fat. After a period in which stoutness was esteemed as a sign of prosperity and good health, not only in successful businessmen but in women (for example, a feminist leader was praised for being "plump as a partridge"), mainstream opinion turned decisively toward slenderness and (in men) muscularity. Dress styles and women's magazines touted the new image; "pliant, willowy grace" became all the rage. Even pornography shifted to a uniform interest in slenderness: "Lucia was just a little above the middle height for girls . . . she was full in her bosom without being too plump. . . . She had a waist naturally small." Doctors warned about the dangers of excess weight and the character flaws that underlay them. Diets and diet columns began to proliferate. The *Ladies' Home Journal* installed a feature called "Side-Talks with Girls" in 1896 in which it regularly commented on the need to lose weight, restrain eating, and live up to the new feminine ideal: "Every pound of fat that is not needed for some purpose is a burden and should be disposed of as soon as possible."

The U.S. preoccupation with weight control, in other words, is roughly a century old. Individuals had doubtless worried about fat before, and there was a much older tradition of Christian fasting that saw emaciation as a sign of holiness. But the widespread popular concern about dieting and the chief manifestations of this concern, including a growing commercial sector devoted to selling diet plans and special foods, are a 20th-century phenomenon. Like all good century-bounded phenomena, it has intensified over time. Scales became common household purchases in the 1920s, thus bringing weight anxieties into the daily routine. The weights recommended by insurance company body tables became progressively more rigorous with each passing decade. Hostility to obesity, although already emerging in the early 1900s, when disgust about fat reached virtually contemporary proportions, seems to have increased. Employer campaigns against fat, although most recently motivated by a desire to reduce health insurance rates, inserted this preoccupation into yet another sphere of life.

So when we're summing up the 20th century, it will be quite accurate to note its status as the century of the "battle of the bulge." Although the phenomenon may seem a bit humdrum, the reasons for the hundred-year trend are not, in fact, trivial. The hostility to overweight emerged as a result of several factors, and the causes have persisted, explaining the intensity as well as the durability of the theme. By 1900, Americans had become increasingly sedentary; this fact alone could prompt a new kind of worry about eating and weight. Doctors, eager to gain status, delighted in finding issues on which their advice was essential. As medical views on sexuality liberalized, reducing doctors' ability to prey on guilt and to sell services in this area (save for birth control), fat became a welcome replacement.

Scientific expertise scored in yet another respect as research uncovered new findings about the deleterious effects of weight and as the decline of communicable diseases highlighted the growing importance of physical degeneration in adult health. In an increasingly service-oriented economy, commercial hucksters were overjoyed to be selling anything. Diet products of all sorts, and ultimately the ubiquitous weight control groups, were ideal candidates for exploitation. In an age when attractiveness increasingly counted in impressing strangers, whether for courtship or business purposes, consumers were open to more precise signals about ideal body styles. (The new rage for cosmetics and for women's leg and underarm shaving, expanding from the 1920s onward, was not far behind the first diet fads.)

Finally, dietary admonitions provided an ideal leaven of daily guilt in a society where old standards of respectability and even religious devotion were crumbling. Weight watching counted not only for what it did for the body but also, even more, for the relief it provided the soul. Fat, to a real extent, replaced sin. If one worried about one's weight, even futilely, surely one was not a hopeless hedonist. Other indulgences could be balanced against the self-discipline required to avoid excess pounds or the humility demonstrated by claiming to need a diet. Fat people could be reviled for their lack of character—a pattern that, in fact, emerged along with the passion for dieting itself. One early advocate of dieting, the Yale economist Simon Patten, directly connected diet and virtue: He urged weight control as a battle against gluttony, a triumph over "crude appetites," even as he praised the new freedom that Americans could enjoy in the consumption of other objects. For a century, dieting has helped U.S. society counterbalance its other indulgent passions, which is the key reason that the weight control motif has survived so well as a 20th-century theme.

The early 20th century saw the installation of a number of patterns suggesting people's growing adjustment to a mature industrial society after the upheaval of the 19th-century Industrial Revolution itself. Weight watching and compensatory worry formed one thread in the broader fabric of industrial maturation.

The dominant feature of the Industrial Revolution itself had been the massive reorganization of work. New production technologies and the rise of the factory compelled increasing numbers of people to a new discipline and intensity in their work and also created new patterns of bossing and being bossed. Urbanization and immigration added relocation to the list of changes. For the most part, these developments have continued in the 20th century, even with the so-called postindustrial changes. Work discipline has grown stricter with developments such as the assembly line and, more recently, computer monitoring. The pace of work, driven by newer, faster equipment, has increased, and with it periodic complaints about stress—called neurasthenia in the 1880s and burn-out today. Factory-style work patterns—including, of course, the daily experience of being supervised by others—have been exported, *grosso modo,* to department stores and offices. And, though slightly modified by suburban growth, the urban focus has been maintained. These persistences and concentrations are themselves important in shaping life in the 20th century and linking it with patterns established in the 19th century.

The emphasis of the industrial economy begin to shift, however, away from the single-minded focus on work and production toward the problems of consuming the goods produced. This shift meant creating new tastes and needs; it meant trying to distract people from the ongoing monotony of work with a variety of commercial pleasures; it meant developing attitudes that, without impeding work, could meet the pressing requirement of assuring sufficient demand. What the 20th century has added to industrial society, and where it gains its more distinctive character in American and, ultimately, Western European history, are the novel opportunities and constraints that now supplement the dynamic of work itself. Here the big innovation is the rise of mass consumerism, including new uses of leisure time, that took shape in the later 19th century and that has, in the main, persisted and steadily intensified through the whole hundred-plus years. Consumerism was itself not entirely novel; historians have traced it back to the 18th century. But there is no question that the importance of acquiring and identifying with things took a giant leap forward after the 1870s, becoming a central feature of most peoples' lives and producing new guilts in the process.

Advertising changed, beginning in the 1890s. Matter-of-fact descriptions of goods in terms of price and utility gave way to terms such as "alluring," "bewitching," and "young and carefree." Kleptomania surfaced as a modern disease, an extreme of consumerism gone mad. Children began to receive allowances, among other things to allow them to prepare for lives as consumers. Leisure time became filled with commercial pastimes. Professional sports, first formed in the 1860s and 1870s, began to become a big business—and not coincidentally, the word "fan," presumably short for "fanatic," entered U.S. English around 1900. Commercial popular theater directly fathered early motion pictures, again becoming a common entertainment form during the first decades of the new century. Consumer levels and interests hardly attained the patterns familiar a hundred years later; among other things, the lower classes were not yet fully drawn in. But the stage was set, which meant the launching of trends that have run through our century, defining more aspects of our lives, perhaps, than we would care to admit.

Growing consumerism, as a balance to intense, often routine work, plus frequently passive leisure in which the doings of professional entertainers and athletes formed the centerpiece, also helped generate a distinctive 20th-century emotional style in the United States. Pleasant emotions were touted over the difficult ones that had often been highly rated as motivators in the more achievement-minded 19th century. Guilt, openly employed in 19th-century emotional life and child discipline, now became suspect, its potentially harmful qualities often seeming to require apology rather than enforcement. There was a direct link here with consumerism as well as with the new emotional divide between pleasantness and unpleasantness: Too much guilt could deter one's indulgence in things. "You're making me feel guilty" became a legitimate response to criticism after child rearing experts in the 1920s began to attack this bastion of Victorian emotional life. Guilt persisted, of course. The fact that by the 1970s one-third of adult Americans regularly claimed to be in some state of dieting at least implicitly announced their guilt about indulgence in food. But the idea of using guilt deliberately, even in the discipline of children—where 19th-century parents had blithely excelled—was now hedged with concern. Guilt became one of those "negative" emotions best avoided, as anthropologist Ruth Benedict noted in 1946. Well before this, parents' manuals had intoned against "traditions of guilt and sin," which could burden a personality lifelong ("laden with their feelings of guilt") and, in the sexual area, "unfit the individual for conjugal relations."

Not only consumerism per se but also new demands in the workplace pressed for novel kinds of emotional restraint and self-presentation as the American economy become more service oriented and as managerial hierarchies became more elaborate. It was in the 1920s that Dale Carnegie began advising salesmen to avoid any show of anger and to present a pleasant front no matter what the circumstances. During the same period, foremen, once told that anger was a great motivator at work, were taught that it was their responsibility to defuse any annoyance on the job, a task that must begin with their own rigid self-control.

Launched in the 1920s, the effort to condemn workplace anger has extended to the faddish "Total Quality" movement of the 1990s, which anathematizes what it calls "attacking" emotions in one training session after another.

"Impersonal, but friendly" became a watchword of U.S. emotional life in many areas. In contrast to the style of the 19th century, this new style involved a great increase in informality. Dress styles and behavior codes steadily liberalized, as in the ubiquitous trend after World War II to address everybody by his or her first name, regardless of prior acquaintance. At the same time, deep emotion became suspect—not only anger but also many forms of love. Mothers, the fount of intense emotion in the 19th-century image of family life, were now told to cool it lest their fervor damage the independence of their offspring. Jealousy became increasingly disapproved of as a sign of emotional immaturity rather than the basis for cementing deep commitments. Again, consumerism helped shape this new trend as more intense attachments to goods and to acquisition corresponded to somewhat cooler emotional relationships among mere mortals.

Changes in the treatment of grief, beginning in the early 20th century and extending with only minor modifications through its course, exemplify the transformation of emotional values that has characterized our era. Grief was highly esteemed in the 19th century, and elaborate mourning practices developed to express it. Grief, after all, symbolized the profundity of human attachments and ennobled those who suffered its bittersweet embrace. It was the 19th century that invented the idea that loved ones would be reunited in heaven, a balm for the grief that any proper person should experience. As Victorian songs repeated, endlessly: "I'm kneeling by thy grave, Katy Darling: This world is all a bleak place to me"; "All night I sat upon her grave, And sorely I did cry." Shortly after 1900, this approach to grief was explicitly attacked in popular magazines in a real deluge of sneering articles: "Probably nothing is sadder in life than the thought of all the hours that are spent in grieving over what is past and irretrievable." Anything more than a brief pause in the normal, upbeat routine suggested "something morbid, either mental or physical." And death practices changed apace. Death was relocated into hospitals rather than homes. Cemetery markers became much less elaborate, even pedestrian. Formal mourning was first reduced and then virtually eliminated. Grief, in sum, became a counterproductive emotion. It went against the pleasure-seeking grain of consumerism, and it also disrupted an increasingly intricate work schedule. This does not mean that the emotion was not still experienced; it simply means that its experience was less tolerated by others and more troubling to the individual involved.

The transformation of values that ushered in the 20th century included, of course, a more open interest in sexuality. The 20th century has seen a fairly consistent escalation of sexuality, interrupted by periodic pauses but never really rolled back. Early in the century, the practice of dating began among young Americans, and it soon generated a complex pattern of sexual expression including "necking" and "petting." This youth culture led fairly directly to the drop in the marriage age of the 1940s and 1950s and then to the increase in premarital sex by the 1960s, which, of course, was then enhanced by the subsequent rise in marriage age. Media representations of sex or sexual innuendo also increased reasonably steadily as sex was quickly linked to hedonistic entertainment and to the sale of consumer goods.

New emphasis on consumerism and the changes in emotional and sexual styles helped redefine family life. Successful families were, increasingly, units formed for mutual pleasure, including sexual enjoyment and shared consumerism. The previous hierarchy between husband and wife began to give way, by the 1920s, to a new, consumer-oriented companionship. Family consumer interests subsequently provided one of the key motivations driving married women into the labor force, first in the working class during the 1950s, then in the middle class—the goal was to earn more money to help the family add a room to the suburban house, pay for a better vacation, or send the kids to college. Consumerism also (along with more open pursuit of sexual pleasure) dictated the widespread adoption of birth control measures and, with the huge exception of the baby boom, the increasingly severe limitation of the number of children born. Children, in fact, became a consumer good, to be indulged in when enjoyable but only to the point that other consumer goals were not unduly jeopardized. Finally, building on a trend established late in the 19th century, the 20th-century family was unprecedentedly open to deliberate dissolution. The first U.S. "divorce crisis" occurred in the 1890s, when the trend of increasing divorce was initially spotted, and the increase in divorce has persisted, with some intervening plateaus, ever since. Marriage was fine, even vital, when it served mutual enjoyment, but it might be judged harshly when the going got tough. Some families failed, indeed, when the consumer expectations of one or both partners were not being met, and the result fueled the rising divorce rate.

Thus in the United States, the 20th century has featured a combination of essentially industrial work patterns, extended even as the economy moved increasingly toward service occupations, with a dramatic set of cultural changes that opened up new consumer and leisure styles and adjusted personalities and family life accordingly. It should be noted that much the same transformation occurred in Western Europe, but here it came later, mainly after World War II, and so it cannot be tidily identified with the 20th century. In the United States, however, the emergence of new social patterns joins the American slice of the larger world trends, including the nation's increasing importance in international business and diplomacy, as a fundamental characteristic of a centennial span. As the United

States also began to export its mass culture, it actually joined its internal transformation to the new intensity of global contacts. As Hollywood became the world's film center in the 1920s, its movies pushed more open sexuality. American-style stores provided models of indulgent, pleasure-seeking consumerism; even the supermarket had this impact, in countries like Switzerland, simply through the luxuriant display of foods. U.S. salesmen tried to convince other societies of the importance of an informal personal style, with at least some success. McDonald's sedulously trained its employees in the techniques of superficial pleasantness—a major cultural chore, for example, in reorienting habits during the 1980s in Russia, where grumpiness had long been seen as the shopkeeper's prerogative amid scarce goods.

Conclusion: Editorial Spins on the Century's Character

The basic trends of the 20th century—the relative decline of the West complexly linked to tighter global connections, the transformation of U.S. and then (to an extent) other societies amid the apparent joys of consumerism and mass entertainment—can of course be stated in other ways. Population growth, the spread of manufacturing, and Western consumerism have unquestionably led to unprecedented environmental degradation and threat. Environmental change was not created by the 20th century, to be sure, and some caution is needed lest the long history of human willingness to mess with nature be oversimplified. Still, when in a twenty-year span (from 1974 to 1994), a forest acreage equivalent to the whole United States east of the Mississippi is cleared (over 600,000 acres), and at the same time, 1.7 billion people are added to the world's population, a distinctive, arguably menacing innovation has taken shape. And, of course, other assessments of the 20th century may seize on different developments; there is no exact science in the process of determining a century's character.

Nevertheless, when the fundamental yet varied changes of our century are combined with the ongoing trends established earlier, such as industrial work patterns, a commitment to technological innovation, and the importance of science, something of a profile of an age does emerge. Our century has added important new trends to the historical stock—however these trends are rated. Some observers, referring to at least certain of the 20th-century trends, have dismissed the century: Leon Kass, in *The Hungry Soul,* calls our century "mechanistic, dehumanizing"—and a case can surely be made that he is right, given technological heedlessness and the superficiality of aspects of mass culture. Yet greater independence for key areas of the world can surely provide a basis for optimism, although such a view contrasts with the confidence in Western guidance that permeated commentary at our last turn of the century; international political oppression has declined. At least some aspects of the cultural changes associated with the redefinition of industrial society can also be defended, including the new roles for women. Characterization of the century, in sum, lends itself to varied editorial judgments, which can be no surprise.

The basic innovations that run through the century have caused some observers to identify one final feature: an acceleration of the pace of change itself. Certainly the 19th century, for those who lived in the West, presented less confusion about world power alignments than our age does. The West continued to rise, which meant God was in his heaven, whereas now we grope for a definition of basic world patterns. The new international connections, including the dramatic technologies that underlie them, have been undeniably striking. The culture of consumerism includes a built-in proclivity toward shifting fads and fashions—one of the ways to sell goods is to make last year's necessities obsolete—which adds to the air of constant flux. It might be debated whether Westerners have actually confronted more basic change in this century than in the one just past, given the startling transformations associated with the Industrial Revolution, major scientific discoveries, and mass urbanization. It is important not to lose perspective even as we acknowledge some of the fundamental new directions of our age. But the new directions are unquestionably substantial, and we are unquestionably still trying to adjust to them.

The three new features of our century, each with many specific facets, all seem quite vigorous at the century's end. Despite the health of Western European society, the relative decline of the West continues to underlie many of the basic issues in world diplomacy and in the global economy. Interconnections around the world continue to accelerate, and the reduction of artificial barriers with the partial opening of China since 1978 and the collapse of Europe's Iron Curtain both reflects and furthers this process. The trends of U.S., and now Western, society in adjusting to a new phase in the elaboration of an advanced economy also persist. Vital innovations, such as the ubiquity of television, have largely confirmed and extended many consumerist patterns. Redefinitions of emotional style and sexuality, launched early in the century, have persisted even amid a new generation of technology (the "postindustrial" wave); there is no sign, to date, of a values transformation equivalent to that which took shape as the 20th century began. A few modifications have been introduced. Although it is still largely confined to private expressions, grief has gained slightly more sympathetic interest in the past two decades than it received during the height of the campaign to suppress it. A few voices have been raised against the tyranny of 20th-century diet standards and body ideals. A few historians wonder aloud if a broader reevaluation might be possible. Gary Cross, a student of 20th-century work patterns and time allocations, asks if the Western world might shake off its obsession with consumer acquisition in favor of a more leisurely pace of life, using technology to reduce work and permit wider horizons rather than insisting that people keep nose to grindstone in the interests of material standards. A good question, but to date the answer is clear: We are not really changing. Americans, particularly, in response to the sluggishness in real earnings since the 1970s and a reluctance to expand leisure time massively (in some contrast to European success in at least gaining longer vacations), seem wedded to the 20th-century drill. Where the century's trends have led to greatest innovation, they continue to set much of the framework for our lives and the lives of people worldwide.

More basic changes will surely come in the future. The current diffusion of world power, in the aftermath of the West's relative decline, might yield to some one society gaining a new lead. Will the 21st century be the East Asian century? The consumerist patterns that took root over the past hundred years must sometime yield to innovation—either because of environmental constraints or some new spiritual quest or some even more unforeseen alternative. But for now, the 20th century seems to be ending on some of the same notes on which it began. We're still trying to lose weight (although, in fact, we keep gaining, another feature of this century's prosperity and frustration). We still embrace new opportunities for faster links around the world. We still suffer superficially cheerful salesmen (some of whom are now machines). But, of course, we also wonder about the future; we wonder whether the next century will have such a decisively new character as the 20th had (granting all the complications and internal inconsistencies). The final assessment that must greet the turn of the century involves our passion for prediction. Here is where the look back at the basic trends of our age meets our unquenchable desire to know what we cannot know—the trends that have yet to occur.

FORECASTING
THE 21ST CENTURY

MODERN SOCIETIES HAVE DEVELOPED A GROWING THIRST for forecasting. Both the apocalyptic expectations of a millennium and the more prosaic, recent traditions of greeting centuries inevitably cast the eye forward to speculate about what is to come. The apocalyptics, of course, know what is to come, although they delight in painting pictures of specific manifestations. Century watchers, however, face a more open-ended challenge: They have to figure out what a plausible future is. We will encounter many ventures at forecasting as we near 2000 and 2001. Although tastes will vary—and forecasting plausibility is partly a matter of taste—analytical procedures are involved as well. Assessing these procedures can be as interesting and certainly as revealing as the forecasts themselves.

When 1900 rolled in, most explicit commentary spent more time dealing with the trends of the century just passing than discussing the prospects for the century to come. The latter approach was not absent, to be sure. A few optimists directly stated their assumptions that the good things of the 19th century would get even better in ensuing decades. A few realists noted ominous recent developments, like the Anglo-German rivalry, and (correctly) predicted a dire upheaval. But partly because of the predominant public confidence that the 19th century had been good and that progress would be assured, elaborate forecasting did not seize center stage.

I expect the balance to be different in the commentary that will accompany the year 2000. Although forecasts about the entire coming millennium (aside from the inevitable apocalyptic warnings) would be silly because the time span is too vast, predictions about a century, or at least about an undefined but not strictly immediate future, will be more common.

There are several reasons to expect the more active forecasting mode. In the first place, I don't think we are as solidly comfortable with what has happened in the century now closing as our counterparts were a hundred years ago. Easy extrapolation—"things have been good, so let's just sit back and watch them get better"—is less likely. Correspondingly, despite some remaining optimism that I think we can expect to see in commentary, broad Whiggism—that is, a simple faith that progress is the wave of the future—has been dimmed by greater sophistication and by the complex realities of contemporary history. Furthermore, many recent events are open-ended, raising not only new possibilities but also vital questions for the future precisely because no clear trend is established. For example, consider the case of the political prospects for Eastern Europe. Can Russia really convert to successful democracy? It's impossible not to wonder about the future in these instances, and for some, wondering leads to forecasting.

At the same time, we have grown much more accustomed to the forecasting genre. As noted before, this has probably increased our skepticism, but it also creates an audience expectation: We may not believe the projections, but we might be disappointed not to hear them. Science fiction, although of 19th-century origin, has become a consuming passion for generations in our own age, and it easily orients many Americans toward speculation about what the future holds. Scientific or pseudoscientific forecasts abound in the daily press. While the public may discount some of this predicting, as research discussed earlier suggests, the idea that the endeavor is legitimate has taken deep root. Quite simply, we expect various folks to tell us about the future, whether we plan to believe them or not. We anticipate knowing tomorrow's weather. We anticipate being told what the economy will be like next year. We count on knowing the future promise of every medical discovery. We anticipate that sociologists and outright kooks will tell us that this family trend is going to shake us to our roots or that that leisure fad means that the next generation will be very different from our own. This kind of prediction has become standard material for newspaper and newscast fillers, and few questions are asked about plausibility: If someone says it is going to happen, it's worth a story. We're also accustomed to being told by environmentalists that this or that dire change awaits us for sure unless we do this or that to prevent it. Some of our institutions mandate forecasting: U.S. social security legislation requires that the government periodically issue fifty-year projections as a basis for setting rates and dealing with possible revenue shortfalls. Current federal research funding requires scientists to explore exactly how global warming will occur over many decades.

What we have done, in essence, is to translate a normal human passion for knowing what is to come into a series of wider expectations and even professional obligations. We no longer read entrails or tea leaves to tell us if we should go into battle tomorrow or the next day (although Nancy Reagan consulted astrologers, and she was not alone). But we do expect certain groups to explore what has not yet happened—economists, for one. We have even constructed a name for prediction, "futurology," that makes it sound like a science (although happily that particular misconception seems to have receded somewhat during the past decade). I was once assured by one of my children's sixth-grade social studies teachers that although the course we were discussing would deal briefly with colonial America, "most of our time will be spent discussing the future." This was supposed to assure me that the material would be on solid ground. And of course, American adults have consumed a host of best-sellers, such as *Megatrends*, devoted to the task of telling us what the next decades hold.

More uncertain about where the future is going than our Whiggish forerunners were and vastly more experienced in receiving forecasts, we can expect the occasion of a new century to spur a spate of predictions. The final perspective needed to anticipate the year 2000, then—along with millennial knowledge, awareness of past century turns, and some sense of how to define the 20th century—is a perspective on the art of forecasting itself.

The Forecasting Mode

We too often receive forecasts right and left without exploring their bases. We may find them valid or silly, but we do not necessarily know how to sort them out very carefully. Although this chapter ultimately ventures a few forecasts—if only because I, too, cannot resist the chance—it is devoted above all to furthering the assessment of forecast types. If we're going to be told what the new century holds, as I think we will be, perhaps to overflowing, we can also gain some sense of how predictions are shaped and perhaps of how some predictions can be judged more interesting and sounder than others.

Four steps stand out in the art of evaluating forecasts. First, we must remember that any prediction is a guess at best, and the guesses will often be wrong. Second, we must decide whether a given forecast is optimistic, pessimistic, or neutral and whether the tone makes sense. Third, we must distinguish between predictions that largely extrapolate from what is already going on and those that chart new directions; each mode has merit, but each contains some different drawbacks that compel attention. Fourth, particularly when some of the more sweeping efforts are involved, we must try to evaluate the range of the forecast, the number of factors that it embraces. Some predictions are mindlessly deterministic, arguing that one set of factors alone will shape our entire future, without explicitly assessing the assumptions on which this determinism is based.

We need not dwell on the first two steps. Despite the assured manner of many forecasters—after all, how else will they be heard?—forecasts are inherently inaccurate and often wildly wrong. A leading sociologist, Seymour Martin Lipset, has calculated that more than 65 percent of all forecasts issued by U.S. social scientists between 1945 and 1980 were erroneous—including, of course, economic predictions. To be sure, his calculation does not count very short-term forecasts based on opinion polls—for example, who's going to win a given election can be called three days beforehand—although even these sometimes err. It also excludes psychic ventures, such as the 1994 forecasts that an earthquake would make Florida an island, that the pope would decree that intercourse should occur only on Fridays, or that Princess Di would acknowledge that one of her children was sired by an appliance repairman.

Psychics aside, there is no science to prediction. Best-selling authors like Alvin Toffler and books like *Megatrends* undeniably command an audience by pretending to massive confidence, but they are hollow at the core. We all can recall striking assertions that proved wrong. Hitler overstated just a bit when he trumpeted his thousand-year Reich. When I was growing up, in the late 1940s, popular science writers looked to a future full of family helicopters. After all, the car had spread in a mere half century, and we lived in a society based on steady technological and consumer progress; a simple extrapolation seemed to make good sense. In the late 1960s, a number of sociologists predicted a future in which communal living would replace the family. After all, communes had gained ground over a whole decade. Other experts, at the same time, told us that youth was becoming the key protest group, replacing the classic working class. Interestingly, one eminent social scientist, Kenneth Keniston, who favored this argument (literally a year before youth protest began to disappear, as a collective entity, in 1973) also contended that married women's work (one social trend that has continued) was an anomaly and would cease as soon as men's wages began to go up. Still more recently, a president of a leading university, Richard Cyert of Carnegie Mellon, predicted in the mid-1980s that by the year 2000 the computer would have changed U.S. education as fundamentally as the steam engine had reshaped manufacturing in the 19th century. Again, wrong—at least in its prediction of the short time allowed for the transformation to occur. And lest historians seem to be exempt from critique (save that they often refuse to predict at all): One British colleague recently noted that the only future that historians can reliably call is the outcome of horse races—after they're over. Jane Bryant Quinn put the same point more succinctly from an economist's standpoint: Give them a number or give them a date, but never both at the same time—the forecaster's survival maxim.

Widely hailed, soon-failed forecasts include: electronic impulses from a supersonic alarm clock enter your brain directly to wake you up (1955); electronic brains will decide who marries whom, making more happy marriages (1952); only 10 percent of the population will work, while the rest are paid to be idle (1966 and recurrently); within a few decades, communicable diseases and also heart disease will be wiped out (again, 1966, clearly a banner year for optimistic technologists).

Some phenomena are almost impossible to predict. Revolts and revolutions always catch the experts by surprise—witness Iran in 1978–1979. We have pretty good ways to interpret protest, including its causes, once it does occur, but all attempts to forecast its likelihood have fallen flat. So in response to the questions "What will the hot spots be in the 21st century?" or "Will the 21st century see the same recurrent waves of revolution that the 20th did?" we can offer some guesses but no real predictions. Russia is a good current candidate for instability, but the 20th-century analogy of France proves that revolutionary societies ultimately settle down, so some caution is in order. Even the decline of Marxism shouldn't be pressed too far; there are other revolutionary ideas available. Anyone who sets up as a futurologist in this vital area is blowing smoke, judging by our track record thus far.

The first line of defense, then, in dealing with any new burst of forecasting at the turn of the century involves a very healthy dose of skepticism, particularly for any prediction that ventures to characterize a whole century. For as we know from our own experience in the 20th century, a hundred years is a very long time and all sorts of trends can turn, reverse, or zigzag despite their apparent strength in a given decade. There are probably a number of trends that will last a century, but figuring out which they are among the myriad of possibilities will be in considerable measure a matter of luck. A forecaster may be most credible if, defying the traditions of the craft, he or she suggests some appropriate humility while picturing the unknown.

Optimism/Pessimism

The tone of the predictions will be interesting as we greet the 21st century. Many forecasts about technology, for example, bear a decidedly optimistic tone. The United States continues to provide a receptive audience for calculations that an additional dose of technology will be good for what ails us. A 1994 commencement speaker: "Do we have a health care problem? The savings possible by applying sophisticated computers more fully to medicine will bail us out. Environmental issues? Give us more machines, appropriately designed, and pollution will quickly diminish." (By this point, engineers in the crowd were wriggling with delight.) Speaker of the House Newt Gingrich urged a laptop computer for every poor family as its way out of welfare (but he quickly retracted the recommendation). Although we have an antitechnology movement as well and although many Americans find specific new technologies menacing, we're conditioned to think that new machines can lead the way to a brighter future. Certainly this is true in the medical field, and it tends to inform predictions about the advance of computers more generally. Even neutral forecasts, like Daniel Bell's classic essay on the postindustrial society, are often taken as heralding better times to come simply because they highlight the probable gains of advanced technology.

But technology is not the only optimistic context for forecasts. Unless we get some bad news in the next four years in the form of the collapse of a major regime, the future of democracy will also be grounds for considerable optimism—just as it was a hundred years ago but now based not simply on general Whiggishness but on the heartening political trends of recent decades in Latin America, Eastern Europe, Africa, and elsewhere.

At the same time, we are also accustomed to predictions that are meant to trigger fear for the future, even though they are sometimes qualified by a hope that decisive policy might yet save us from ourselves. Environmental forecasts emphasize accelerating deterioration. How much of the 21st century, we will be asked to ponder, will be shaped by global warming? The related predictions of the impact of growing world population point in an equally bleak direction. Although the granddaddy of all pessimistic predictions, the threat of nuclear holocaust, has receded, we face some new concerns that can also trigger long-term anxiety. The potent mixture of declining employment for the unskilled plus racial tensions may certainly occasion some discouraging predictions about intractable structural imbalances in the society that will take us through the 21st century. The probable bankruptcy of the social security system in the face of growing numbers of elderly, predicted to occur around the year 2013, might well come in for some anguished comment. We will certainly see further editorializing on the ominous portents of our unstable family structures and the decline of what are called "family values."

The mood of the turn of the century remains hard to calculate. We have already ventured the guess that optimism will be more qualified than it was a century ago. I expect that this will translate, quite simply, into a spate of more diverse predictions, collectively pointing in almost every conceivable direction. *Newsweek*'s December 26, 1994, grab bag of forecasts thus seemed to be almost a random mix of pluses and minuses, with no overall vision—a mix that was not clearly justified by arguments that other trends had been considered but rejected but that had the ultimate honesty of avoiding the extremes of hopefulness or despair. The effort to avoid the most simple-minded Whiggishness may show up in more carefully nuanced statements meant to avoid either optimistic or pessimistic extremes. As an audience, we can still seek to determine whether a value judgment undergirds a forecast, even if that judgment is concealed by a more sophisticated, neutral veneer. We can also ask about our own reactions: If we're told, for example, what medicine will be like a century hence, are we conditioned to assume that this must be progress? Along with healthy skepticism, then, an understanding that both the forecasters and the receivers of their wares frequently go beyond anticipation to evaluation and assume progress or deterioration will help us sort out scenarios for the 21st century.

Trends and Their Future

Distinguishing between extrapolation from present trends and prediction of directional change, the third task in disentangling forecasts, involves a less familiar but intriguing analytical task. The simple fact is that there are only two basic ways to go in forecasting. The first involves determining, or purporting to determine, what's been happening recently and assuming this will continue, although perhaps intensifying or moderating. The second involves asserting that we're about to shift gears dramatically (which can include a prediction that we're about to go back to some situation that once prevailed in the past, although this is not too common an impulse in modern Western culture). Too often, forecasters themselves don't seem to be fully aware of which mode they're using or of what kinds of arguments and proofs each mode requires.

The safest short-term forecasts, and some of the predictions that we're most familiar with, rest on extrapolation or projection: "Here's the current trend, and we'll simply see more of it over the next twenty, or even fifty, years." We "know," for example, that the average age of populations in the United States and Japan will increase over the next several decades, for the birthrate is already low and life expectancy is gaining; the average age in both countries, already unusually high by historical standards, will be even higher by the year 2010. Some stabilization may occur thereafter, but current trends suggest (crisis in health care expense aside) that aging will continue more slowly as the birthrate stagnates and as adult life expectancy rises gradually (people in their eighties already constitute the most rapidly growing age group). This forecast assumes, of course, that present trends will not be disrupted by some new surge in the birthrate, by a higher death rate among adults in late middle age, or by new immigration patterns that alter the demographic structure. On the other hand, the same kind of trend analysis would argue that by the mid-21st century, most societies will begin to encounter the same kind of aging that hit the West in the 1920s and again after the baby boom ended and that has occurred in Japan more recently. Birthrates are slowing. Population continues to gain thanks to earlier high birthrates, but it will stabilize; and life expectancy has gone up. So, by trend extrapolation, the 21st century bids fair to be the century of old age, or at least older age. How's that for a prospect? However unappetizing, it's actually quite plausible. A fair portion of the 21st century may well be defined by the growing elderly segment as older people develop new attitudes and adjustments and as society at large reacts to their unprecedentedly large numbers.

Trend assessment can cast a long shadow, particularly if combined with examples or analogies from relevant past history. Investment bankers currently argue that for the next fifty to a hundred years, the rapid economic growth areas of the world will be East Asia, East Central Europe (Poland, Hungary, and the Czech Republic), and Latin America, plus possibly South Africa and even more tentatively Russia. This projection is based on current trends: the fast growth in the Pacific Rim, including China, and in Latin America. The gross national products of key Latin American countries are expected to grow 7–8 percent a year in the near future, and China has already been generating 10 percent growth. These trends are combined, however, with more general historically grounded assumptions, based on evidence from past history, that younger industrial areas (such as Japan from 1920 to 1960 or the United States from 1870 to 1930) grow particularly fast, compared both to mature industrial areas and to nonindustrial areas. The predictions are qualified by noting the assumption that there will be no new factors, such as a major war. They do not speak to possibly unanticipated potential in Africa or South Asia (remember that Latin America would not have been on a prospect list in 1900, but the region changed unexpectedly from the 1930s onward; the same may well happen elsewhere in the 21st century). Whatever the ultimate accuracy of the forecasts, they show how much can be based on trend extrapolation supplemented by a bit of historical background.* Although the projections seem plausible for the next several decades, the temptation to extend farther, possibly to a full century, may well push beyond what even an enhanced trend assessment can reasonably sustain. Trends, however, constantly lure us in ambitious directions because they originate in clear, verifiable data.

We have already discussed a host of additional trends, in full force, that may well continue through the 21st century. The pervasiveness of the scientific outlook, now several centuries old, is one candidate. So is a spread of the consumer mentality, that is, the set of attitudes that encourage people to acquire material goods and to base part of their personal identity on such acquisition. This outlook, two hundred years old in the West, has clearly been capturing new adherents in China, Japan, Africa, and Russia; this trend is gaining momentum and could well continue to intensify.

Newsweek's 1994 potpourri of predictions was almost entirely trend extrapolations—for example, *Newsweek* predicted that China's cities, already growing, will get bigger and more difficult to govern; that East Africa's AIDS rate, already ex-

---

* The fragility of economic predictions should be obvious, for some historical pitfalls are clear. In 1950, pundits were writing off Western Europe, wondering if the region could ever recover much less grow. Investment forecasts at this point were ludicrously wrong. In 1900, a Rothschild banker, assuming that political stability was the key to future performance, put his money in the three stable empires of his day: Russia, Austria-Hungary, and Germany. None of these empires still existed in 1918. It's a tough field, but it is one in which forecasting is essential if only to guide investment choices.

panding, will get worse. The forecasts even included a squib anticipating sports stardom for several talented fifteen-year-olds who are already proven winners, which is trend extrapolation at an absurdly simple level. The only area where *Newsweek* showed more daring was in its inclusion of what the magazine might call "techno faith": A few segments discussed new technologies that are currently possible but not yet implemented with the confident assertion that those will be beneficent parts of our lives thirty years hence. In this case, our conditioning to believe that what is technologically possible will come to pass and will be good contributes an additional, if logically and historically suspect, dimension to the otherwise common, safe practice of extrapolation.

Trend projection routinely shows up in job forecasts. Occupations beginning to command more employment are seen as offering peak opportunities a decade down the pike. Thus, for example, whereas film projectionists will lose work to automation, jobs for actors and amusement park attendants soar. Medical practitioners of all sorts will be in new demand (although, interestingly, this projection makes no attempt to factor in the current uncertainties of health policy and funding, which could rapidly muddy these waters; trend extrapolations usually cling to simplicity). Paralegals and software innovators will gain, as will security guards. And so the forecasts roll on, telling us that what is now happening will happen even more intensely over the next short term.

Trend extrapolation has two vulnerabilities, of course. It depends in the first place on accurate identification of current trends. One of the reasons it's important to get a good fix on the major patterns of the 20th century, of the sort discussed in Chapter 10, is to provide a basis for plausible projection. Some areas are simply murky. What's the trend in youth sexuality, for example? The age of first sexual intercourse has been going down for at least sixty years, with particularly dramatic premarital results since the 1960s. But currently there's some discussion of a new wave of chastity, and some teenagers are at least signing pledges to refrain from premarital sex; and AIDS and the widely publicized consequences of adolescent parenthood provide powerful reasons to abstain. Where's the trend here? Is there enough clarity to permit even a speculative guess about the future?

The sheer novelty of recent developments in many parts of the world also inhibits trend projection as we near the end of the century. Speculations abound, but extrapolations? Is the democratic trend solid enough in Eastern Europe to plausibly be extrapolated to the future? Is the collapse of the Soviet Union permanent, or should we, with the Russian nationalist leaders, predict a resumption of the older expansionist trend at least to the reincorporation of Ukraine, Belarus, and Kazahkstan? Is the Chinese pattern of combining economic liberalization and political authoritarianism, unquestionably this nation's recent trend, viable for the future? Is the growth of European unity a dominant trend, such that we can confidently anticipate not only full Scandinavian membership but also, as many are now asserting, the adhesion of Poland, Hungary, and the Czech Republic by the early 21st century? The canvas established by the events of the past fifteen years, in South Africa as well as in Europe, Asia, and Latin America, is tantalizingly vast; but can we paint more than question marks?

The second problem with trend projection, even in areas where a current pattern does seem clear and solid, involves the intervention of unforeseen factors. The trend toward an aging population, for example, although entirely plausible precisely because it is already occurring, might easily be interrupted by the sheer cost of maintaining increasing numbers of senior citizens. Even if pension systems are modified (which would be a fairly safe extrapolation from the current trends), the burden of health care may prove to be unsupportable, causing reductions in availability that would actually, however painfully, reverse the trend of increasing life expectancy for middle-aged adults. We are already experiencing a trend toward reduced care in the United States, although it is too recent for determination of consequences. Extrapolation works best when the trend is not only well defined but also explainable in terms of a limited number of factors (like better health and lower birthrates). But over any extended period of time, factors do not stay limited, which is one reason that the mode of forecasting for more than the early part of the 21st century will be particularly risky. Ironically, it may be some of the older trends, such as the prestige of science, that will prove to be most lasting precisely because they are so deeply rooted, so hard to shake without an unusual concatenation of new developments.

A final weakness of trend extrapolation, related to our inability to calculate unexpected factors, involves the difficulty of predicting ramifications. The U.S. trade union movement has been declining for forty years thanks to the rise of the white-collar sector and the migration of jobs to union-hostile regions like the Southwest. Surely this is likely to continue. But will new forms of labor protest arise in the wake of this trend? In a related vein: The drop in blue-collar jobs will almost certainly persist. Here's another trend to bet on. But what the resultant shape of the labor market will be is another matter. Will income gaps between the highly educated and the less educated continue to grow as they have in the past fifteen years? Will a high level of structural unemployment continue to bedevil us? Extrapolating a troubling but plausible trend is one thing; predicting what reactions and compensations will develop around it is quite another.

A Very Different Future: Analogy as Guide

Much of the near future will, in fact, be determined by current trends, intensified or slightly modified; extrapolation is the most accurate form of prediction simply because basic changes in direction are uncommon in any field. The problem is deciding which trends and for how long. Yet what of a future that will be quite different from what we know today, or at least a future based on new factors that we can at present only barely discern? The most eye-catching predictions—and we will surely see some competition for audience here, in welcoming the 21st century—are those that anticipate brand-new directions, something very different from what we currently experience. Trends, after all, we know because we live them. It's the brave new world that fills us with wonder or dread.

Aside from sheer assertion in delineating some startling future utopia, two related forecasting modes are particularly common. The first involves analogy. When we face the prospect of a future that seems uncertain but that has some vaguely familiar dimensions, an apparently ineradicable human impulse is to look for similar cases in the past, cases whose exploration, although not strictly predictive, helps determine some guidelines. Many people who predict that new technologies will revolutionize education or the economy compare the future with the known example of the Industrial Revolution. Alvin Toffler likened his "postindustrial revolution," based on computers, genetic engineering, and robotics, to the two previous human transformations of economic framework: the initial development of agriculture and the replacement of the agricultural economy with industrialization. The analogy conveyed the sense of magnitude that Toffler suggested and allowed him to argue that if the analogy is correct, the "third wave" of technological change would have similarly sweeping impacts not just on the economy but on the functions of cities, the definition of the social structure, and so on.

Western thinkers in the 20th century have recurrently used analogies drawn from the fall of the Roman Empire, contending that the West is about to decline as Rome did fifteen hundred years ago, and for similar reasons of moral decay and inept leadership. Paul Kennedy, more recently, has compared prospects for the United States with the decline of other societies that overextended their international commitments, destroying their domestic strengths in the process. He makes analogies not only to Rome but also to Britain at the end of the 19th century and to other empires, such as the Ottoman, the Dutch, the Swedish, the Spanish, and the Venetian. Kennedy, in fact, almost pressed analogy to the level of a historical law, suggesting that imperial societies push their military involvements and expenses too far and lose the internal drive that made their economies powerful, inevitably falling back in world power.

Another analogy that might be applied to U.S. prospects in the 21st century also comes from European diplomatic history. From the quarreling city-states of Renaissance Italy through the rise of France in the 17th century and again during the Napoleonic wars, a standard rhythm in European affairs has involved one major power growing stronger than the rest, with its strength generating a coalition of opposing states bent on constraining the interloper and ultimately trimming its eminence back to more manageable dimensions. The same process has applied, slightly less smoothly, to Germany in our own time. At the dawn of the 21st century, the United States will be the "world's only superpower," as we've been told now for several years. Will history imitate past diplomatic analogies, rooted, of course, in balance-of-power common sense; that is, will a coalition of states, individually weaker than the United States and not necessarily hostile to our system of government, arise to trim our sails? (Again, some trend assessment may be added; the current move toward the acquisition of nuclear capacity by additional nations, almost certain to continue even if unacknowledged, will increasingly affect the diplomatic climate.)

Analogy of a more immediate sort is being used as another means of illuminating the darkness of the world's diplomatic future. Several analysts contend that now that the Cold War polarization has ended, some other major confrontation must take its place. They don't invoke analogy explicitly, and in fact they use a bit of trend extrapolation as well, but their thinking is clearly colored by the assumption that major culture clashes constitute the natural state of affairs for the modern world, such that when one dies another must be born. Thus, one persuasive scenario has a future world divided among the West, home of good old Western values, embattled Islam, and the Confucian-inspired, group-oriented societies of East Asia in a three-way tug-of-war for world leadership. New levels of competitive tension with places like Japan and South Korea and the undeniable rise of an anti-Western fundamentalism in Islam are the trends on which this scenario is constructed. But the larger future—the notion that these clashes will escalate into a full diplomatic framework for world affairs—is clearly based on the Cold War analogy, just as the Cold War viewpoint was itself based on the analogy of democracy's confrontation with Nazi Germany. Hence, forecasters in this conflict-by-analogy mode urge Westerners to recruit allies with similar values, for example, among the former Soviet states including Russia, just as we once looked for partners against the Soviet menace.

Analogy certainly comes into play, along with some trend assessment, when we think about how the world balance among major civilizations will shape up during the 21st century. The 20th century, as already noted, has seen the relative decline of the West in world affairs despite its ongoing strengths and great influence. The situation bears some resemblance to the 15th century, when Muslim power began to decline slowly while a number of alternative frameworks were explored. As in the 15th century, the decline of the previously dominant civilization was qualified by the rise of a new power: the Ottoman empire taking over from the Arabs, the United States taking over from Western Europe. As in the 15th century, an initial candidate to replace the previous power structure seems to have been a false start: the brief flurry of Chinese trade dominance between 1405 and 1433, the brief attempt by the Soviet Union to grab at least a share of world leadership only to fail by the 1980s. If the analogy is applicable, one would expect the previously dominant power to continue its gradual relative decline (as the Muslim world did during the 16th century before it began to fade fast as a world power by the 17th century) while a new pattern of world leadership slowly emerges. Certainly many observers have assumed that if the West can't continue to dominate the globe, some other civilization will—hence the speculations about the 21st century as the century of East Asia.

Analogy is great fun, and in many situations it is almost unavoidable. We can't help but remember vivid "lessons" from our own past or that of society and ask whether they fit an unfamiliar, essentially unpredictable situation in the future. The popularity of analogy in the field of technology conveys a sense that we're on the verge of another major transformation about which, precisely because current trends will be disrupted, the normal mode of forecasting has little to offer. Analogy in foreign policy reflects, first, the long-standing tradition in military and diplomatic training to look for past example from international affairs or from battle strategy as a guide for future policy. More important in our current predictive climate, the use of analogy in foreign policy also reflects the sheer confusion that the end of the Cold War has necessarily entailed, a situation in which extrapolation is impossible—beyond simplistic comments about the probability of increasing numbers of small regional conflicts, given trends already apparent in the Balkans and elsewhere—because the whole setting is novel. Lack of familiarity breeds analogy.

Analogy is not confined to technology or world affairs. Elaine Showalter, a feminist historian, seeking some directions for women's future as the feminist surge wanes somewhat, makes a direct analogy with the last century. In *Sexual Anarchy: Gender and Culture of the Fin de Siècle*, she notes the parallels between late–19th- and late–20th-century feminisms (and possibly their incomplete success?). She notes other parallels: Syphilis, as a source of sexual peril, did for the 1890s what AIDS may be doing now. No full explanation for the parallels is offered—analogy tends to be longer on description than on causation—but certainly here is another case for some kind of recurrent historical cycle.

Analogy is, however, inherently inexact. It may help organize some interesting questions about the future, pinpointing some possibilities to watch, but it really cannot predict. Two related problems surface here. First, analogy may call attention to points of change, but it hardly indicates precise guidelines for the future. This is true in both specific and general cases. In the 1970s, policymakers concerned about oil shortages trumpeted U.S. success during World War II in accelerating the development of synthetic rubber to replace sources cut off by Japan. The analogy produced a claim that a crash materials substitution program could similarly help solve the oil crisis—in that sense, it provided a general orientation toward the future. But it did not really say what to do next, and in fact the whole scenario was dropped.

Recently, Newt Gingrich has revived Toffleresque "third wave" analogies:

> Where we are right now is not 1933, it's the 1770s to 1800, that just as the English-speaking world went through the transition from the end of the medieval agrarian society to the rise of commercial and ultimately manufacturing society and out of that came waves of change that were very traumatic and very profound, that the transition from the industrial era into the information age is very similar in forcing us to ask the most profound questions about relationships.

Here, big-picture analogy is meant to convey a deep sense of imminent change. But change to what, and how should we proceed? The Speaker (having modified his analogy to argue that today is more like 1760, that is, even earlier in the transformative process) admitted: "We don't yet know what . . . our intellectual constitution for the future is." So, one might ask, aside from a dramatic metaphor and a display of real historical knowledge, what has the Speaker's analogy gained us?

The second problem with analogy actually cuts deeper, for it involves the question of whether two major situations, one past, one present, ever have enough in common to permit the drawing of parallels in a predictive sense. Using prior cases for suggestive questions is one thing; invoking them where policies need to be anticipated is quite another. Even though analogy calls attention to the past, most historians don't like it because of the distortions involved in trying to fit a future prospect into the dimensions of a known past event or pattern. Of course, it is possible that past behavior will resume, for example in reaction to great-power dominance in international affairs, such that the United States will face an increasing coalition of nations hostile to its unique military strength and diplomatic influence. But the conditions of European balance-of-power diplomacy may simply be inapplicable on the new world scene. The United States may learn such caution and benevolence, or it may work international alliance systems so cleverly, that it simply won't rouse the resistance that blatantly expansionist France or Germany did. The comparison between the 20th and the 15th centuries as times of fundamental power shifts is intriguing, but there is no reason to press it too far. Western culture seems to have a world appeal that Islam (despite its great ongoing vitality) never quite gained; this difference already messes up the comparison. And even if the world balance does continue to even out, a virtual cinch for the 21st century on the basis of trend extrapolation, this does not mean that another civilization is destined for a single top spot—there's no inevitable logic for this prospect at all. With regard to feminism, the parallels with a hundred years ago are interesting, but today there is no landmark achievement like suffrage, so where, predictively, does the analogy lead? Again, and inevitably, circumstances have changed. To take another analogy: The "postindustrial revolution" may, of course, turn out to share the magnitude of the Industrial Revolution, even though the latter occurred such a short time ago. But, in fact, many industrial principles, including the detailed monitoring of work, are actually enhanced by new technology, not disrupted; it's not at all clear that the analogy is useful, except in selling books. The AIDS epidemic immediately evoked the analogy of the Black Death of the 14th century—another example of how we respond to uncertainty by this historical recourse—and, as with all good analogies, the example was worth exploring simply because it generated some useful questions about our reactions to contagious disease. But our assumptions about disease have changed so much and the apparatus used to fight disease is so different from that available in the Middle Ages that the analogy had little ongoing utility.

The more uncertain corners of the 21st century may well be explored through predictive analogy. Such explorations can be suggestive. It's important to keep the inexactness of the method firmly in mind and also to realize that some analogies are a great deal more accurate than others. Because it applied recently and in circumstances not totally dissimilar from the current world scene, the European balance of power is a more plausible analogy for predicting the future of the United States as world policeman than the terror of the Black Death is for predicting the cultural or medical impact of AIDS. Above all, receivers of analogy must be wary of the distracting comfort that the method involves. After all, in a real sense analogy urges us not to think too hard about the future but, rather, to pull back toward a much better known phenomenon in the past. Then, reminding ourselves of what we know about the balance of power or the decline of Britain as world policeman or the response to the Black Death, we are invited to take a leap of faith and assume that this very genuine knowledge can guide us in understanding something that has not happened yet. The impulse is understandable; the results can, again, raise possibilities well worth considering; but we must always remember the limitations.

Analogy may be unusually precarious right now, at least in some key areas of politics and diplomacy, precisely because we live amid so many changes and uncertain prospects. One of the main forces of our decade, for example, the continuing economic decline of Russia, has no clear precedent in industrial history. This means that analogies involving Russia and a world order that must still include the giant nation are inherently shaky and inexact because we cannot cast back for another modern case in which such an important player was deteriorating so rapidly in peacetime. Even the U.S. characteristics that depended, for over half a century, on a great-power enemy for identity have become newly tentative, making analogies that predict U.S. political and cultural prospects difficult. Other uncertainties on the diplomatic horizon also strain any analogical effort. What analogies are there for the disappearance of effective states in important parts of Africa (Somalia, Rwanda, Liberia), southeastern Europe, or Central Asia? One must reach far back in history, when other conditions were very different from today's, to talk about states that suddenly become stateless. In a period of new directions, comparisons with the past confirm change but make prediction difficult. Exactly when we might most like to use analogy because we have few other signposts, we should be wary.

Dramatic Forecasting

The second approach to eye-catching new future directions in history (sometimes but not always combined with analogy) usually involves what might be called "Big Cause" forecasting. If the pundit senses that some dramatic new departure is imminent, one that will alter many aspects of the human condition but that has not yet generated clear trends that can be projected, then a focus on a decisive Big Cause is the logical way to go. After all, one of the limitations of trend analysis is its inability to build in major changes of direction—that is, to anticipate the forces that might introduce vital new themes that, however, cannot yet be directly traced. An obvious way to overcome this limitation without venturing a series of scattered speculations is to identify the key Big Cause that will order much of our future.

The claim that the Cold War framework will be replaced by a Western-Muslim-Confucian tug-of-war is one example of the Big Cause approach, although applied to the military–diplomatic arena alone. Forecasters have recurrently projected other dramatic factors that will, in their estimation, change the face of world history to come. Encouraged to think about patterns for a whole century, as part of greeting the 21st, the temptation to seize on a Big Cause may be particularly great—here will be the dominant new force, prompting many other aspects of human life to fall into line.

The Big Cause approach to forecasting has an interesting, and clearly checkered, recent history. In the 1960s, "population bomb" predictions argued that the current rate of global population growth guaranteed increasing misery, environmental strain, and warfare between the haves and the have-nots. Population growth was the new, out-of-control factor that would crush every other aspect of human society in its wake if not brought under control. Catastrophe demographers (reviving Malthus on a global scale) could quite correctly point to the fact that there was no precedent in history for the speed or extent of 20th-century population growth. They parlayed this into the Big Cause argument by going on to insist that other shapers of the human condition paled before the force of this new factor. Interestingly, their arguments are no longer fully fashionable, not because they were entirely wrong or because their concerns do not still apply to an extent but because their advocates overdid the case and probably did not sufficiently examine their own assumptions. It turns out that, to date at least, food supply can keep pace with 20th-century population growth except in parts of Africa. This may not apply forever, but it does weaken the catastrophe argument. Unprecedented population growth has not displaced all other major causes in determining wars or standards of living; indeed, at least where wars are concerned, it has yet to be a major factor. There was also some unexamined racism in many of the population bomb arguments, which (implicitly) suggested that not only is the world exploding, but it is exploding with people of color who must learn the same kind of sexual discipline that the white folks have. This unexamined assumption, it has since been realized, helped distort the predictive claims. For a variety of reasons, then, population bomb gloom, as a Big Cause approach to our future, has declined in favor.

The two Big Cause themes currently most fashionable are environmental degradation (which bears some relation to the population bomb idea) and postindustrial technology. It is fair to note that they don't combine very well, for it is characteristic of Big Cause approaches that they are fairly exclusive, such that one pundit's Cause preempts another pundit's Cause. We will surely be treated to many sketches of the 21st century based on the increasing suffering of Mother Earth. Growing pollution, based on the waste of advanced industrial societies, the heedless travails of new industrializers such as China (soon to be Number 2 in causing air pollution, after the United States), and the sanitary strain of mounting billions of people, will set the tone for the future. It will increasingly force adjustments in economic behavior, in living standards, and in health, and it will also become a leading political and diplomatic concern. Other human endeavors may continue, but they will be dwarfed by this unprecedented environmental crisis. This Big Cause, in effect, will shape our destiny, making our future history increasingly different from any past that we can recall.

We will also be treated to the technology Big Cause, along lines laid out in books like *Future Shock* and *Megatrends* (plus more scholarly forecasts, like Robert Ayres's *Uncertain Futures*). Proponents may note with Toffler that in this case we actually do have a few precedents in human history for this sort of transformation. But because the technologies are unquestionably new and their effects are so sweeping, this future, too, will be different from anything the species has thus far experienced. Some postindustrial enthusiasts use the new technologies currently taking shape, including, of course, the increasingly ubiquitous computer, to sketch how a host of present practices will change stripes. Manufacturing labor, obviously, will continue to shrink as service and information jobs expand (trend extrapolation, this). Cities will change from being production centers to being primarily meeting places and concentrations of entertainment. Command of information, not property or wealth, will determine the social structure. Some forecasters further point to greatly increased leisure (though this is not a current trend, as work hours have been going up); Ayres, for example, urges that machines will provide a growing array of games to take up the slack for work that is more quickly done. Other postindustrialists claim a high-tech future not only for the advanced industrial societies but also for the whole world: Countries like Sri Lanka may, in this vision, be able to bypass the Industrial Revolution entirely, heading directly into postindustrial, computer-driven production and information exchange. Postindustrial work will be more personalized and self-directed than industrial work was (present trends again do not really point this way, but maybe later in the 21st century?). People will once more work at home, commuting by computer; the postindustrial family will be vastly different, as a result, from its current counterpart. Some definitions of the postindustrial family highlight the work and consumer activities of both spouses, which may not seem all that startling (except that children don't figure in too clearly). But this modesty concerning familial futures may simply reflect a lack of forecasting imagination: If work returns home, surely more will happen that we simply cannot presently calculate. Might the divorce rate decline, as the stress of work–home separation eases?

Interestingly, even Big Cause technologists have shied away from many space age predictions because the framework is too uncertain and the prospects too far distant. It will be over a century, for example, before a manned Mars probe is possible even by optimistic estimates, and no one knows what the consequences might be. Still, even without space, technology buffs love to paint pictures of the future.

Big Cause forecasts—and the environmental and high-tech scenarios clearly head the list—assume the importance of a single major factor. They are what historians call "monocausal," or "deterministic": If we know what's going to happen to the environment or to machinery, then everything else will fall into place. They are also by definition ahistorical, in that they urge that the imminent change is so great that most current and recently past patterns will prove irrelevant; at most, analogies with other Big Changes in history provide a rough indication of magnitude. By definition, predictions of major changes in direction cannot be disproved or proved. They have not happened yet, although a few current trends (like the interesting but still small movement toward more people using computers for work in their homes) may be taken as foreshadowing what will blossom in the future. The big problem with the Big Cause approach, however interesting the questions it may raise, is that most historical experience argues against placing so much emphasis on one basic factor. Even major technological changes in the past have intertwined with diplomatic shifts, continuities in cultures, and new population patterns to produce what any given society was actually like. Even if work returns to the home, our expectations of individual satisfaction have so broadened that the impact on divorce may be negligible, or it may even exacerbate the divorce rate by increasing domestic tensions; old trends often persist even as new elements add in. No change is complete—there are always significant continuities, and no single change operates without interaction with other kinds of change. Single-factor determiners, from sunspots to plagues to the advent of industrial equipment, rarely if ever explain the past. This does not prove, of course, that some single determinant will not explain the 21st century. But it is useful to be skeptical.

What is striking about most Big Cause forecasts, and often other kinds of predictions as well, is how they artificially restrict the range of what's being projected. Here is the final component of a sensible assessment of turn-of-the-century futurology. Obviously, if the pundit is only concerned with one phenomenon— What will 21st-century transportation be like? Will the divorce rate continue to rise?—well and good. But if the implications are wider and the characteristics of a whole society come into play, then the breadth issue is essential. Even for the single phenomenon, in fact, the net must be fairly wide, for the causes that affect behaviors such as divorce come from various and sometimes unexpected directions. For example, we may well see forecasts of increasing longevity in the 21st century based on some recent trends and a faith in miraculous medicine. But any such forecast that fails to consider the murky area of growing economic constraints on health care is simply shallow. A single set of variables doesn't make the grade.

Many technology forecasts, even if they go outside the narrowest groove, still suffer from inadequate breadth. The 21st century will unquestionably be colored by the ongoing adaptations of computer technology and genetic engineering. But it will also be affected by the predictable aging of the population, a megatrend that too rarely is combined with the predictions of technological and organizational dynamism. Which will shape lives and societies more, increasing aging or computerization? It's not an easy call despite our cultural delight in technology, for no single causal ingredient is likely to predominate. There is no need to insist on an either–or proposition. Technology will shape the future; so will aging and other demographic trends; so will the ongoing rebalancing of world power given the growing economic and political strength of parts of Latin America, China, and so on. The list, without doubt, is considerable. But any forecast that does not acknowledge and seriously work with at least part of the relevant range, beyond one single component such as the environment or technology, is almost certainly flawed—unless, against almost all historical precedent, one sweeping transformation or catastrophe does make everything else irrelevant as the 21st century defines itself (which is what some gloomy environmentalists and eager technologists do, in fact, assume).

One of the greatest challenges in discussing future trends with the more visionary type of engineer involves overcoming a penchant to believe that any possible technology will surely soon turn out to be a real technology, and that it will reshape lives regardless of other factors. It is vital to insist on the normal complexities in causation, in which even powerful technologies will blend with other factors, including attempts to maintain existing patterns. Computers, to take an unavoidable example, have surely affected education and will surely affect it more in the future. But they have not displaced conventional educational settings nearly as rapidly as some proponents expected. The lag, and probable lags even in the future, result from routine-mindedness but also from costs and from the ongoing convenience of keeping teenagers and young adults in classrooms as a means of limiting their impact on the labor market and demands on parental attention. Multiple causes, including continuities from the past, lie between vision and actual future probabilities. Some historians, in fact, plausibly argue that computers, far from being a Big Cause at all, will simply maintain trends of growing job specialization and bureaucratic control, helping them along with some fancy specific hardware, but not launching anything really new.

The Range of Factors: Other Scenarios

Breadth in forecasting, particularly in any efforts to envision the whole 21st century, must include some issues slightly beneath the surface as well as the more conventional topics such as technology, the environment, diplomatic alignments, and international economic competition. Forecasts too rarely capture the sweep of real life as they concentrate on one set of trends or one Big Cause. As one result, we see fewer serious forecasts about certain social patterns that don't have the panache of technology or world affairs but that nonetheless involve a fair amount of our future—for example, will Americans keep getting fatter, as they have through most of this century, or will they latch onto French secrets of actually stabilizing weight amid prosperity? Forecasts about culture, save in very specific speculations about how long this or that style will last, are also fairly rare. The forecasting palette, in other words, misses too many colors unless we insist on the same breadth that we employ when we evaluate societies around us.

Some scattered examples: Women's conditions and expectations are changing almost everywhere, although not necessarily in precisely the same fashion; how will this set of developments build into larger patterns in the future? How will the ongoing tension between world "mass culture," much of it exported from the United States, and the attempt to preserve distinctive cultural identities play out over the next several decades? Forecasts that are not sensitive to the numerous dramas currently taking shape, and on an international and not simply a U.S. or advanced-industrial stage, will serve us badly unless we recognize their incompleteness. For example, any forecast of the 21st century must include some further thinking about the spread of nuclear weaponry. Free from Cold War fears, we haven't been paying a lot of attention to this issue of late, save in the case of North Korea. We have, of course, tried to enforce our clearly self-interested policy of denying other governments access to nuclear weapons or, as in the case of Ukraine and Kazahkstan, of removing existing access. But, frankly, this is not likely to work over the 21st century, or even its first half. Technological sophistication and understandable resentment at the obvious power imbalance will push other governments to acquire active nuclear capacity increasingly openly. Will we see the rise of new military tensions, and possibly also the emergence of new regional conquerors based on atomic advantages?

Consider even more sweeping issues for the century to come, not perhaps for its first decades but down the road: Over the past two hundred years, the world has seen mounting emphasis on the primacy of the nation-state as the main unit of political organization. Initially developed in Europe, the nation-state, calling for considerable homogeneity (real or imagined) and very active loyalty, has spread almost everywhere. The collapse of the Soviet Union (following on the heels of the earlier failures of the Ottoman empire in the Middle East and other multiethnic empires in south Asia) is the end of one of the great multinational empires left in the world. But the nation-state is illogical and unusual in several respects. Most societies have more routinely blended diverse peoples, without requiring shared cultures and single dominant loyalties. An increasingly global economy, with multinational corporations, has superseded the utility of the nation-state in many ways. The nation-state is also challenged by the increasing pressures of immigration, which is filling many societies (even Japan) with peoples from diverse backgrounds. Through the evolution of these multinational contacts, through explicit multinational organizations like the European Economic Community, and also possibly through new if currently unpredictable efforts at conquest, will the 21st century see the beginning of the end for the nation-state, a fragile construct, and the reemergence of other, more polyglot forms?

There is the question of religion. This issue did not loom large in the century assessments around 1900 simply because the topic was not at the forefront of definitions of progress. Most Westerners were still nominally religious, but they gave their primary loyalties to secular belief systems like liberalism. A hundred years later, forecasting questions around religion have become more complex. One major secular faith, Marxism, seems largely to have failed. The values of liberalism and a belief in material progress certainly persist, but they depend heavily on a steady economic growth that may be hard to come by, at least worldwide. Furthermore—trend extrapolation again—we already know the power of religious fervor among Christian and Muslim converts in Africa and evangelical converts in Latin America, as well as growing fundamentalist currents in established sectors of Islam and Hinduism. And we can wonder if some kind of religious revival or religious innovation is not essential even in our own midst as a means of disciplining some of the unruliness of our urban society. Where will the 21st century stand in terms of religious developments? Will some of the new complexities visible particularly in the final quarter of the 20th century blossom into a really new spiritual current? Against most modern precedent until very recently, will religion again become a major factor in the world's definition?

What of areas, vital to our daily lives, about which we almost never see forecasts at all because we've suffered so many disappointments and because the factors seem so intractable. What, for example, of race relations in the 21st century? Two decades ago, based on some trends and many hopes, we might have forecast progress. Can we do so today? But can we envision any 21st-century pattern in which race relations—whether improved, deteriorated, or stagnant—do not come in for serious comment? Again, the forecasting net must be cast wide, and we have precious few models of adequacy.

The list of topics to ponder is long. The point is not to cover the whole front but to remind ourselves that some of our standard forecasting modes are much narrower than are our own assessments of what life is all about and of how societies are defined. As we think about the coming century and assimilate the various projections that will vie for our attention, the criterion of breadth and the ability to go beyond conventional focus on equipment and material environment may prove to be vitally important.

Enjoying Forecasts as Art Forms

Forecasts should be enjoyable and thought provoking. Certainly the kinds of forecasts that venture ideas about the 21st century should be entertaining and stimulating, since they can hardly guarantee to be accurate. Reception of forecasts is also a matter of taste; there is no exact science here. As the foregoing suggests, my own taste lies in predictions that are not too heavily technological because I find the role of technology in our future commonly exaggerated and because in my view of history, technology is as much shaped by other factors as it shapes conditions independently. But other people, quite legitimately, may like the mechanical emphasis more than I do. I'm a sucker, at least relatively speaking, for predictions that maintain a complex international focus rather than assuming that whatever drives America drives the world and for forecasts that posit a clear role for the factors of culture and human relationships. Again, this will not be everyone's cup of tea. Forecasts inevitably reflect the criteria we find important in judging the past and evaluating the society around us now, and there is no single correct set of standards. Predicting is fun, and the game must not be spoiled by too much academic nicety.

This said, reception of turn-of-the-century forecasts need not be random. Some predictions are better than others, and forecast recipients should be able to tell the difference. In addition to the probably unnecessary reminders about maintaining skepticism and assessing the underlying optimism or pessimism of a prediction, sorting out forecasts by genre does provide some basis for determining quality and plausibility. The forecast that extrapolates should convey a valid sense of existing trends and some reason, beyond an assumption of momentum, to believe that they will persist, including an explanation of why nothing looming on the horizon is likely to deflect the trend. Analogies can be explained, so there's some reason provided for the choice of historical example and the contention that it suggests legitimate guidelines for understanding a forthcoming change; or analogies can be merely asserted, so we're left with a merely rhetorical device. Breaking out the plausibility of Big Cause approaches is inherently more difficult; there's more simple intuition involved. But the forecast that explains how the dominant new factor connects to the asserted effects is surely more interesting than the random shot that says technology or the environment—for example— will sweep everything before it but offers no probable linkages. Any kind of forecasting lacks full evidence; that's the nature of the beast. Care in construction, awareness of the type of approach being used and some effort to deal with its characteristic vulnerabilities, and factual accuracy at least for the historical base, either in trends or analogies, provide some verisimilitude.

Some forecasters seem to assume a surprising amount of gullibility in their audience. However sincere their own beliefs, they often offer a dramatic assertion— for example, that by the year 2150 life expectancy will be up to 120 years—that can admittedly be grabbed as a passing headline but that has little backing beyond unexamined assumptions. In this example, these assumptions boil down to a faith that medical advance will continue plus a silly extension of one historical datum: Since life expectancy moved up about forty years in the 20th century (thanks, however, mainly to the diminution of infant mortality, which cannot be done again), it should move up another forty before too long. Fully assessing the accuracy of forecasts requires patience and long life—we can only know when we get there. But determining a forecast's logic and thoughtfulness is possible as we sort through the offerings available.

Before we turn out the lights on the final celebrations of the new century's advent, we should cast our imaginations forward to wonder how much will be different, how much basically the same a hundred years hence. Each scenario should be personal, to the extent that any imagined reality must have an individual flavor. But each scenario can be supported by the kinds of forecasts we have experienced as part of our approach to the 21st century and by the ways we have learned to sift through their assumptions and combine their results. We can use reason and historical sense, without depriving ourselves of the ultimately intuitive components. And then, like our counterparts of a hundred years ago, we can live into the new century in part by seeing how many of our projections go awry, and how fast.

twelve

CONCLUSION

THE CATHOLIC CHURCH HAS ALREADY DECLARED 2000 a Holy Year, just as it did for 1900. Some of the planning that will highlight the turn of the century (the church, understandably given the possible apocalyptic confusions, lays less stress on the millennium) has already begun. Pope John Paul II, further, has urged that the year be used to review the church's 2000-year history so that the institution may publicly acknowledge past faults, such as its inadequate response to the Nazi campaign against the Jews.

Catholicism, of course, is a religion intensely conscious of history. It may be unrealistic to expect any such sober look backward from the U.S. public. We're often told that the United States is a distressingly ahistorical society, unwilling to pay serious attention to its past and what it can teach. This blindness to history, the argument continues, is either part of the shallowness of U.S. culture or the charm of a nation still young at heart. Certainly Americans love to complain about learning history. A favored response on airlines, on learning that one's seatmate is a historian, is to note with great pride how much one hated history in high school. (Many historians travel incognito as a result, pretending that they are slaughterhouse workers.) Contemporary Americans certainly love to construct mythical visions of the past to suit their own current wishes without the burdens of serious study. Thus, radicals in the universities may contend that history is just make-believe anyway, with any truth as good as any other, and that therefore one might as well build a past that supports current political agendas. Conservatives, eager to use history to bolster suburbanite values, insist that what is taught in the schools should portray the good qualities of the American and Western experience, largely omitting warts like slaveholding (the main thing to teach about slavery sometimes seems to be that it was abolished) and largely ignoring the pasts of non-Western societies save insofar as they contrast unfavorably with our own.

Whether our tendencies to historical myth building are worse than those of other societies may be open to question, which is not to say that we should not try to be more accurate in our representations of history. We have already discussed the tenaciousness with which the French public holds to long-refuted stories about the medieval millennium. Many Americans do cherish history as part of their national identity, which is a source of some of the problems of distortion that history teachers face when they try to build a balanced curriculum in their subject but also a support for the nation's large crop of professional historians. Attendance at historical museums has been soaring over the past two decades. We may rather enjoy the upcoming opportunity to examine history from some novel vantage points.

In any event, whether we like history or not, the turn of the century and the millennium have to be an occasion to exercise a historical sense, however superficially. There will be no escape. Even if the old myths about the fearful response to Christianity's first millennium maintain their hold, there will be some diligent reporters who ferret out the more balanced historical truth if only to be a bit different. Even if the dominant orientation, at the century's turn, involves looking into the future rather than judging the messy experiences of the past hundred years, history remains inescapable. For forecasts have to refer to the past. They must either establish the nature and strength of current trends in order to argue that these will persist. Or they must cite historical analogies to provide some shape to otherwise amorphous speculations. Or they must talk about why the future is about to break with the recent past, using the latter as a baseline for comparison with the dreadful or remarkable new prospects about to confront us in the 21st century. Any approach involves juxtaposing imagined futures with a judgment of what has already occurred.

Greeting the new millennium or the new century, in sum, calls upon our willingness to explore historical accuracy, to find out whether what we're being told about the last millennium or even the last turn of the century corresponds to the facts. The account that ignores the evidence about the year 1000 or that talks of 1900's optimism while ignoring the complexity of the concomitant fin de siècle mood is irresponsible, and we know enough history to provide the necessary tests. The retrospective that oversimplifies the 20th century to support a latter-day hymn to progress is similarly irresponsible, and again, there is no need to become a historical expert to redress the balance. The forecast that pitches technological determinism without exploring the validity of monocausal explanations or that oversimplifies trend projection based on recent patterns of world demography is also open, if a bit more subtly, to a bad grade in history.

It is impossible yet to know how seriously the Western public will take the imminent symbolic events. The Catholic church's preparations contrast with the surprising lack of references to the end of the century in other arenas, aside from planning parties. The active apocalyptic subculture continues to surprise the mainstream public when it periodically bursts into prominence; there is an unresolved tension about how much the expectation of the millennium will affect us because our culture harbors the basis both for strong reactions and for substantial neglect. So the simplest prediction—about how much it will all matter—still eludes us, just a few years before the event. Will we also, around 2003 or 2005, find ourselves disappointed, perhaps disoriented, because so little has changed? It's possible, at least for some groups, for there may be an analogy between past occasions when fervent anticipations yielded to ongoing realities. The larger result depends on how our sense of the phenomenon develops and on which of the many available interpretations of the calendar symbols, from impassioned to languid, seize our attention. Here, too, is a scenario to monitor, armed with knowledge of real and imagined precedents, as we approach the time when the event will have come and gone.

But we know the event will at least be hailed in passing. We have too many media eager to gain our attention for the rich potential of a new millennium and new century to be downplayed entirely. References to the millennium are already increasing, which makes it easy to predict that they will increase further. For a few years, and possibly longer, we will have to think about centuries and millennia. We may decide that the subject is interesting, allowing some deeper probing into where we stand as a society and where our futures are heading. Whether in passing or more profoundly, we will do a better job in our musings if we're also aware of historical facts and if we can appropriate a larger historical sense. We'll have to assess the past, at least fleetingly, and we'll have to think about the future in relation to the past. A historical guide is inescapable, and a thoughtful guide is preferable to a patchwork woven from scraps and simplifications. Even if we pause from our routines only briefly, as the page of the calendar turns, we can use all the understanding we can get.

POSTSCRIPT:
GETTING EVER CLOSER

Millennial references went into noticeably higher gear after New Year's Day 1997. Various entities realized that there were only three (or four) years to go—three years to plan for the great event or, even more commonly, to milk public interest.

An appropriately named hotel opened in New York (what will it call itself by 2010? what will Twentieth Century Fox do?). *Newsweek* and several other publications launched regular columns, assembling a mixture of forecasts, advice, and news. Public relations firms and even more sober organizations like *National Geographic* planned millennial features of various sorts, to run for the next few years. Party organizing heated up, and new travel groups planned excursions down the Amazon, in India and Nepal, on a ship in Antarctica, for the period from late 1999 to early 2000. Governments got into the act. Saying, "We are present at the future, a moment we must now define for ourselves and for our children," President Clinton pledged government-sponsored lecture series, televised "millennium minutes," and fresh robots planted on Mars. He also urged local initiatives, including campaigns to save historic monuments. Other plans were more ambitious. Iceland scheduled a party to celebrate the New World voyage of Leif Eriksson, which occurred about a thousand years ago; Germany planned an Expo 2000 world's fair, and Britain announced a $1 billion multimedia dome at Greenwich (which elicited massive criticism for aimlessness). Even casual advertisement began to cash in. A new plastic surgery chain was organized under the label Millennium, featuring "cosmetic surgery for the 21st century." Clearly, it was time to get ready, as millennial enthusiasm was getting the wrinkles out.

Public response split in three fairly predictable ways. Fervent millennial activity continued amid some religious groups and New Age adepts, rarely breaking into mainstream notice but displaying increased excitement, particularly in the American West. More casual interest was suggested by periodicals such as *Newsweek*, and presumably many of their readers, but without fully clear focus. Finally, the intensifying hoopla left many others cold, wondering how to make it through another three to four years of nonsense.

One version of the most crucial division was reflected, tragically, in the reception to the Hale-Bopp comet, as it dipped unprecedentedly close to earth in early spring 1997. Most commentary urged attention to the beautiful display with no millennial reference, even tongue-in-cheek. A minority dissented: The Heaven's Gate religious sect, in San Diego, believing that behind the comet a spaceship waited to take them to heaven prior to the world's end, committed mass suicide.

Long-standing religious millennialists like Jack Van Impe polished their argument without major innovation (and without catastrophic results). Thus Van Impe used newsletters and Web sites plus a video entitled "2001 Countdown to Eternity" to supplement television shows. Van Impe continued to argue that major change was imminent: "The world of A.D. 2000 and beyond holds a future that's intriguing, fascinating and challenging. Before us lies the most important decade in the history of the world." All sorts of portents still pointed in this direction, as Van Impe noted that he had spent "weeks" studying "75 volumes covering ancient manuscripts, historical reports, and biblical writings." Six thousand years would have passed since creation, one millennium for each day of creation itself. Rampant immorality in these "last days"—boasting, incontinence, hedonism, disobedience to parents—made it clear that God's hand would not long be stayed. Natural disasters (earthquakes killed over 2 million people in this century), plagues, famines, plus the European Union and the rise of China, which presaged a world dictatorship, all would in turn lead to a seven-year rule of the Antichrist. Van Impe changed emphasis in two respects. While continuing to rain hellfire, he more clearly argued that after this horrible transition a thousand-year reign of God would descend; only after this would chaos return. His message, he insisted, was therefore one of hope, as the saved would enjoy prolonged bliss; hence there was every reason to prepare in joy. Second, he began to loosen the time span a bit. The big change would come "somewhere after A.D. 2000–2007": The latter date was altered from earlier references to 2003, and of course the "somewhere after" introduced possible further hedging.

New Age thinking (excoriated by religious leaders like Van Impe, who saw the movement as one more sign of the imminence of the Antichrist) also moved largely along lines established earlier. Mayan references continued to abound, pointing to 2012 as the end of a cycle, and new emphasis was placed on an alignment in the year 2000 of the planets Mercury, Venus, Mars, Jupiter, and Saturn, which some contended (against all scientific opinion) would lead to massive disruption of the earth's gravity, tidal waves, and other disasters (thus bringing things presumably to a close well before 2012).

For most North Americans (and West Europeans), only vaguely aware of these lines of argument or largely engaged with other interests, there were a few developments of note. Two or three of them deserve comment in light of the arguments put forth in this book, for they had not been fully predictable.

First, there was no question that attention riveted on the year 2000, not 2001. A few people tried seriously to argue that proper chronology pointed to 2000 as the first year; the earlier edition of this book provoked some surprisingly angry (and misinformed) commentary to this effect. More commonly there was no effort at argument, in contrast to the considerable debate that had preceded the 20th century and that, in the English-speaking world, had led to the correct chronological decision. Now, the attraction of 2000 was simply too great. Majority opinion was wrong, but since it was the majority, it was right—we will celebrate when it says. Even efforts to right the record were frequently a bit confused; thus on his "Millennium" show, Seinfeld corrects the bumbling Kramer, who was planning his party for December 31, 1999, but then errs on the sequence between this date and the proper one.

Second, and I confess this has particularly surprised me, millennial attention was displacing any significant discussion of the turn of the century. References to the 21st century do continue to crop up in planning documents and political references. Clinton's 1996 campaign referred so often to "bridges to the 21st century" that the (attention) span risked erosion. But all the media commentary seems to focus on the millennium, using it for many of the purposes to which a more careful approach might put the century. I still expect that in 1999 we will be treated to assessments of the past century and projections about the century to come, and I remain eager to see what tone they take. Right now, however, for those interested in the whole phenomenon at all, the millennium is everything. In combination with New Age and religious agitation, this means that an additional answer to the question posed in a previous chapter, "Where is our fin de siècle?" is quite simply: "It's buried somewhere in the millennium."

There are two further effects. More interest is developing about looking back on the past millennium historically than I would have imagined. Thus the *Economist* named Genghis Khan "man of the millennium," a somewhat surprising ploy for a respected publication. The choice was defendable, but the idea of a top millennial historical figure was somewhat bizarre. Other agencies have swooped in. I have been asked to help identify the "ten most important" cultural developments in the past millennium for one popular, scholarly organization; others were working on comparable lists for technology, politics, and the like. A New York public relations firm asked several historians for a simpler list of the ten most important events. There's nothing wrong with this, so long as it is not taken too seriously and if the disproportionate Western bias is recognized—most lists suggest that the peoples of the world were holding their breaths waiting for Europeans and Americans to sneeze during the past thousand years. As these lists begin to emerge, readers are urged to note that although none is provably "best," some will be a lot better than others.

Above all, the limitations of a millennium as a unit of historical time must be remembered, even if the lists are fun and provocative. Our newfound historical millennialism may encourage us to believe, even if briefly, that the past thousand years have more coherence than they do. Here, even as I participate in some of the list making, I stand by the correctives offered in Chapter 6.

The second result of the intense concentration on millennia, rather than centuries, is simply an intensification of the hyperbole so pervasive in modern commercial culture. Millennial references make sense if one really believes that the calendar shift betokens some massive change in the way the world works, some divine intervention. Otherwise, frankly, they largely serve to sound grandiose about the future. Thus a normally respectable publisher issues a book about the stress caused by American efforts to perform, urging a lifestyle change at the end: On the back cover, the essay is touted as "a timely, cogent, encompassing prospectus for the new millennium." Does this mean that Americans should plan to worry about performance anxiety for the next thousand years?

What does *Newsweek* use its millennial column, introduced with a special thematic fanfare in January 1997, to say? It's actually an interesting effort, both for what it does and for what it doesn't do—though I confess (not being able in fact to predict three years) I'm not quite sure what they'll use as filler until 2000 finally puts the section out of its misery. The column sensibly comments on history, noting the correct view of the year 1000—a delightful result. It skeptically reviews religious and New Age millennialism, featuring, for example, astronomers who note that we do know what the heavens will bring in the next century and that we can be confident that the celestial system is not about to change. But of course, as the millennial title implies, it does turn fairly often to forecasting. The first thematic issue was particularly ambitious, talking about a Chinese military expansion in the year 2005 and so on, but this vulnerable specificity has not been maintained. Forecasts have in fact been of three sorts. First, comments about what's happening now, usually bad, lead to statements that we must hope/expect that things will get better. "Miss Manners" thus notes the rudeness of our age and assumes that we have to move toward greater civility. She admits that after this improvement, which she expects early in the next century, although offering no real evidence, we may oscillate to rudeness again, but then notes (discourteously?) that most of us will be dead anyway, so who cares? Second, a few technology scenarios offer dazzling prospects with no clear time frame. Thus a fashion authority projects programmable clothes, which can be altered daily to promote the desired mood—but no probable date is ventured for this advance, and in fact no probability beyond science fiction is broached. Third, a wide range of specific predictions do dot the column. Thus a new series of antidepression drugs, without the current side effects, may be available by 2007; cremation will increase, to 2010; home care aides will be the fastest-growing job category, to 2005; American families will be smaller, by 2010. What's offered here, clearly, is trend extrapolation, though not usefully identified as such from one column to the next. Nevertheless, the projections are worth thinking about (though the column, eager to be definite, does not ask what might happen to deflect current trends). Moreover, the projections are, sensibly, very short-term, as trend projections should be. This, then, returns us to the obvious question: why millennium?

Clearly, as they must, upcoming calendar events encourage us to think about both past and future. Clearly, to an extent greater than I was able to predict a few years ago (though now, with hindsight, I think I should have been able to), we're being encouraged to use the idea of millennium to organize often very vague, often very limited, forecasts—which are not unlike some of the attempts to look ahead to the 20th century offered in commentary around 1900 (many of which, it will be recalled, turned out to be wrong). For a few years, still, millennium will mean simply the near future, and of course some kind of party, rather than a thousand years. There's a clear risk of triteness, but we've lived through worse.

FOR FURTHER READING

Chapter 3

Several studies allow pursuit of the real or imagined history of the millennium. Along with some facets of Hillel Schwartz's book, see Richard Erdoes, *A.D. 1000: Living on the Brink of Apocalypse* (New York, 1988), which provides the most recent attempt to promote the legend. For the older version, see Jules Michelet, *History of France,* trans. Walter Kelly (London, 1844), vol. 1, pp. 336–340. On revisionism, see George Lincoln Burr, "The Year 1000 and the Antecedents of the Crusades," *American Historical Review* 6 (1901): 429–439; Ferdinand Lot, "Le mythe des terreurs de l'an mille," *Mercure de France* 301 (1947): 639–655; Georges Duby, *L'an mil* (Paris, 1947); Daniel Le Blevec, *L'an mil* (Paris, 1976); Henri Focillon, *L'an mil* (Paris, 1952); A. Vasiliev, "Medieval Ideas About the End of the World: East and West," *Byzantion* 16 (1942/43): 462–502; and Daniel Mil, "L'an mil: Un problème d'historiographie moderne," *History and Theory* 27 (1988): 261–281. Richard Landes presents his approach in "The Year 1000," *The Dictionary of the Middle Ages,* ed. J. Strayer (New York, 1989), vol. 12, pp. 722–723, and "Between Aristocracy and Heresy: Popular Participation in the Limousin Peace of God, 994–1033," in T. Head and R. Landes, eds., *The Peace of God: Social Violence and Religious Response in France Around the Year 1000* (Ithaca, 1992), pp. 184–218. For the history of the use of the myth, see Christian Amalvi, "Du bon usage des terreurs de l'an mil," *L'Histoire* 138 (1978): 10–15.

Chapter 4

To pursue some of the points raised in this chapter, see, in addition to references above for Chapter 3, Hillel Schwartz, *Century's End: A Cultural History of the Fin de Siècle: From the 990s through the 1990s* (New York, 1990), which has fascinating detail but some lapses into gullibility. On earlier traditions, before new years were noted, see Ronald Hutton, *The Rise and Fall of Merry England: The Ritual Year 1400–1700* (New York, 1995). John Hogue, *Nostradamus and the Millennium: Predictions of the Future* (New York, 1987), tries to milk history for sensation, adding ingredients as needed. For treatment of ill-fated prophecies, see Russell Chandler, *Doomsday* (Ann Arbor, 1993). Historians' accounts include James Randi, *The Mask of Nostradamus* (New York, 1990); Marjorie Reeves, *Joachim of Fiore and the Prophetic Future* (New York, 1976); Werner Verbelse, *The Use and Abuse of Eschatology in the Middle Ages,* ed. Daniel Verhelst and Andries Welkenhuysen (Louvain, 1988). Also important is Patrick Geary, *Phantoms of Remembrance: Memory and Oblivion at the End of the First Millennium* (Princeton, 1994); Bernard McGinn, *Visions of the End: Apocalyptic Traditions in the Middle Ages* (New York, 1979); Robert E. Lerner, *The Powers of Prophecy* (Cambridge, 1983). An important study of the U.S. tradition is Paul Boyer, *When Time Shall Be No More: Prophecy Belief in Modern American Culture* (Cambridge, Mass., 1992).

Chapter 6

Not surprisingly, one talented historian has already cashed in on millennial interest, producing an unusual effort to deal with the past millennium historically. It's an elegant job, but in fact it's an example of the familiar overview genre, making no special claims to the millennium as period, except for a venture in forecasting at the end. See Felipe Fernandez-Armesto, *Millennium: A History of the Last Thousand Years* (New York, 1995).

Chapter 8

Two books deal extremely well with the diverse implications of fin de siècle: Carl Schorske, *Fin-de-Siècle Vienna: Politics and Culture* (New York, 1981), and Eugen Weber, *France, Fin de Siècle* (Cambridge, Mass., 1986). See also Robert Jensen, *Marketing Modernism in Fin-de-Siècle Europe* (Princeton, 1994). For some discussion of other kinds of reaction in the United States and Britain, see Asa Briggs, "Toward 1900: The Nineteenth Century Faces the Future," *The Collected Essays of Asa Briggs,* vol. 2 (Urbana, 1985), pp. 42–67.

Chapter 10

Two discussions of the century, focused on international shifts, are particularly challenging: Eric Hobsbawm, *The Age of Extremes: A History of the World, 1914–1991* (New York, 1994), and Geoffrey Barraclough, *An Introduction to Contemporary History* (London, 1964).

Chapter 11

Stimulating, sometimes infuriating efforts at prediction include Alvin Toffler, *Future Shock* (1974), and John Naisbitt, *Megatrends: Ten New Directions Transforming Our Lives* (1982). It's interesting that Toffler soared in the 1970s, Naisbitt in the next decade (with specific reference to replacing Toffler as the most popular futurologist). We don't yet have a 1990s equivalent, although Toffler was trumpeted again by Newt Gingrich, one of his 1970s converts, in 1995. This lack of a new, dominant guru in our own decade may argue either for growing sophistication or for the adequacy of prior efforts, but the resultant void may make the temptation to jump in with another set of forecasts, timed to ring in the next century, all the greater.

On environmental and updated population bomb forecasts, see Donella Meadows, *Beyond the Limits* (1992), which calculates a whole host of variables; Paul R. Ehrlich, *Population Explosion* (1990), and *Healing the Planet* (1991); and James Lovelock, *Gaia Revisited* (1992).

More scholarly efforts are Daniel Bell, *The Coming of Post-Industrial Society: A Venture in Social Forecasting* (1973), and Robert Ayres, *Uncertain Futures* (1979). On the post–Cold War diplomatic scenario, see Samuel Huntington, *The Third Wave: Democratization in the Late Twentieth Century* (1991). See also Paul Kennedy, *The Rise and Fall of the Great Powers: Economic Change and Military Conflicts from 1500 to 2000* (1989). On the perils of analogy, see Richard Neustadt and Ernest May, *Thinking in Time: The Uses of History for Decision-Makers* (1988).

INDEX